Collection of Biblical Imagination & Apologetics:
The Imagination of God & God Against the gods
(Storytelling, Evangelism, Creativity and the Bible)

By Brian Godawa

Collection of Biblical Imagination and Apologetics: The Imagination of God & God Against the gods (Storytelling, Evangelism, Creativity and the Bible)
1st Edition 1.5

Copyright © 2022 Brian Godawa
All rights reserved. No part of this book may be reproduced in any form or by any electronic or mechanical means, including information storage and retrieval systems, without prior written permission, except in the case of brief quotations in critical articles and reviews.

Warrior Poet Publishing
www.warriorpoetpublishing.com

ISBN: 978-1-942858-90-4 (Paperback)

All Scripture quotations, unless otherwise indicated, are taken from the New American Standard Bible®, copyright 1960, 1962, 1963, 1968, 1971, 1972, 1973, 1975, 1977, 1995 by The Lockman Foundation. Used by permission.

Table of Contents

Book 1: The Imagination of God .... *v*
Acknowledgments .... *viii*
Chapter 1 Confessions of a Modern 1
Chapter 2 Literal Versus Literary 10
Chapter 3 Word Versus Image 26
Chapter 4 Iconoclasm 46
Chapter 5 Incarnation 55
Chapter 6 Subversion 67
Chapter 7 Cultural Captivity 85
Chapter 8 What Art Would Jesus Do? 104
Chapter 9: Afterword In Good Company 114
Chapter 10: Appendix Answering Objections 119

Book 2: God Against the gods 133
Preface Of Myth and the Bible 136
Chapter 1 Demonizing the Pagan Gods 143
Chapter 2 Old Testament Storytelling Apologetics 161
Chapter 3 Biblical Creation and Storytelling 176
Chapter 4 The Universe in Ancient Imagination 193
Chapter 5 New Testament Storytelling Apologetics 225
Chapter 6 Imagination in Prophecy and Apocalypse 241
Chapter 7 An Apologetic of Biblical Horror 263
Great Offers By Brian Godawa 275
About the Author 276

Book 1:
The Imagination of God
Art, Creativity and Truth
in the Bible

By Brian Godawa

This book was previously released under the title:
Word Pictures: Knowing God Through Story and Imagination.
Minor changes have been made to the text.

The Imagination of God: Art, Creativity and Truth in the Bible
2nd Edition

Copyright © 2016, 2021 Brian Godawa
All rights reserved. No part of this book may be reproduced in any form or by any electronic or mechanical means, including information storage and retrieval systems, without prior written permission, except in the case of brief quotations in critical articles and reviews.

Warrior Poet Publishing
www.warriorpoetpublishing.com

All Scripture quotations, unless otherwise indicated, are taken from the New American Standard Bible®, copyright 1960, 1962, 1963, 1968, 1971, 1972, 1973, 1975, 1977, 1995 by The Lockman Foundation. Used by permission.

For Kimberly
My godly and sexy wife
who has helped me to live a full life
of spirituality and sensuality.

And for Bishop N. T. Wright
A theologian of story who hasn't
chucked his rationality.

Acknowledgments

I want to thank the following for their help in making this book what it is: First, thanks to Kimberly, for her loving and faithful support, without whom I would not be writing or accomplishing anything in my otherwise pedestrian life. Second, thanks to the *Christian Research Journal* for rejecting the article that eventually became this book. Because they passed, I kept writing—and discovering. (They eventually published what became my chapter on Paul's Areopagus apologetic.) Third, thanks to my editor, David Zimmerman, for his patient editing of my pathetic prose. Special thanks to those who gave input on this manuscript in one form or another: Dave Bahnsen, Ken Gentry, Nancy Pearcey, Joel and Michelle Pelsue, Ken Tamplin, and my fellow post-yadayada *semper reformanda* co-conspirators, Jack Hafer, Neil Uchitel, Andrew Sandlin and Goran Dragolovic.

And as always, special thanks to Joe Potter.

"Imagination does not breed insanity.
Exactly what does breed insanity is reason.
Poets do not go mad; but chess-players do.
Mathematicians go mad, and cashiers,
but creative artists very seldom.
I am not in any sense attacking logic:
I only say that this danger does lie in logic,
not in imagination."
G. K. Chesterton, *Orthodoxy*

"It would surely be much more rational
if conversation rather than dancing made the order of the day."
"Much more rational… I daresay;
but it would not be near so much like a ball."
Jane Austen, *Pride and Prejudice*

Chapter 1
Confessions of a Modern

I love apologetics, philosophy and theology. I've pursued them for many years as a dominant focus in my Christian walk. From my first discovery of worldview thinking in the writings of Francis Schaeffer, through my hungry devouring of every book on defending the faith I could read, my Christianity has developed through the paradigm of apologetics, philosophy and theology.

I've learned a lot of biblical doctrine within the context of how it contradicts unbelieving cults and worldviews. I've come to understand the nature of the "faith once for all delivered to the saints" in terms of rational defense of its propositions. I've defined myself through systematic theology, which includes objections to false doctrines. One might even say I've been obsessed with apologetics and rational inquiry.

When I first sought a reasonable faith, I did the typical Evangelical thing in the 1980s: I read *Evidence That Demands a Verdict* by Josh McDowell and many other books like it. I then embarked on a journey of attempting to memorize every archaeological factoid that supported the Bible, every empirical verification of creation against chance and evolution, every rationalized harmony of every alleged contradiction in the Bible, every historical fulfillment of every prophecy, that I could. I even studied as many unbelieving worldviews as I could in order to prove the rational superiority and truth of Christianity.

Needless to say, this Herculean task was exhausting. Like Atlas bearing the world, I shrugged. I thought that if I could just marshal enough facts, answer enough objections, master the arguments for the existence of God and show how rational Christianity was, then unbelievers would be forced into the position of "accepting" Christianity because it satisfied the modern canons of logic and science. If I met the standards of skepticism, the skeptic would simply *have to* change his mind because he followed logic and science "wherever it led him."

Then I discovered original sin—or more precisely, the noetic (rational) effect of sin. I learned from the Bible that not only has all humankind inherited Adam's curse of disobedience (Rom 5:12-14), but all unbelievers actually know about God and his essential nature but suppress that truth through their wickedness (Rom 1:18-21). As a result, even their reasoning is futile, their logic corrupted, their understanding darkened by willful ignorance (Eph 4:17-18). Every part of man—heart, soul, body *and* mind—is affected by sin.

Biblically, people are not unbelievers because they suffer the lack of reasons, historical verification or scientific proof to believe. They are unbelievers because they know the truth about God and suppress that knowledge sinfully. The problem with unbelievers is not ultimately rational, it is moral. As in the original case with Adam and Eve, sin distorts man's reason as well as his will. The sinner uses sin-tainted reason (Eph 4:18) and empirical observations to rationalize a prejudice against God (Rom. 1:18); he does not use it to discover truth wherever it leads. As Puritan John Owen put it in *The Holy Spirit*,

> That Jesus Christ was crucified, is a proposition that any natural [i.e., unregenerate] man may understand and assent to, and be said to receive: and all the doctrines of the gospel may be taught in propositions and discourses, the sense and meaning of which a natural man may understand; but it is denied that he can receive the things themselves. For there is a wide difference between the mind's receiving doctrines notionally, and receiving the things taught in them really.[1]

The noetic effect of sin chastened my faith in the power of reason, but it did not destroy it.

Logic and Reason

In order to avoid apostasy, heresy and just bad theology, Scripture must be interpreted in context with other Scripture (Mt 4:5-7). The Bible may declare

---

[1] John Owen, quoted by James K. A. Smith in *Christianity and the Postmodern Turn: Six Views*, ed. Myron Penner (Grand Rapids: Brazos, 2005), p. 227.

man's rational faculties as fallen, but that same Bible uses reason and logic all over the place. It's irrefutable.

I studied the Bible with this privileging of reason. I saw how Paul vigorously sought to "persuade" people to repent (Acts 18:4).[2] That means rational argumentation; the Greek word for "repent" literally means "change the mind" (Acts 17:30). I treasured the discovery that God exalts the search for knowledge and wisdom (Prov 1:7; cf. Prov 8:9-10; 9:10; Is 1:18), as well as philosophy rooted in Christ (Col 2:8). I even came to realize that God's own revelation expresses or assumes the primary logical laws of identity, antithesis and non-contradiction (Ex 3:14; 20:3, 16) so often it's not even debatable. The apostle John calls God the *Logos*, a deliberate echo of the Greek notion of the underlying logical structure of the universe (Jn 1:1). Jesus used logic (Mt 21:24-27), and if it's good enough for Jesus...

So the question I struggled over was: How could the Bible be so equally explicit in its affirmation of reason as well as man's sinful corruption of reason? Wouldn't those two cancel each other out? Is the Bible contradicting itself? Or am I misunderstanding the big picture?

Reconciliation of this apparent tension has been attempted by Christians in different ways throughout history, but the bottom line for me is that the Bible teaches both, so we must affirm both or suffer infidelity to God's Word. What follows will show that getting to this bottom line will not be a leap of logic but a dance of imagination.

Propositional Truth

In my pursuit of rational discourse I came to love propositions, especially logical ones. They seemed to be so clarifying, so neat and tidy, in my quest for discovery of truth and reality. A proposition can be defined as a statement that affirms or denies something and is either true or false. In an everyday sense, proposition can simply mean "verbal statement," but in a theological sense it refers to a form of communication of truth that stresses the way things really are—or the factual, objective reality of something. In this sense, a proposition is discerned through the rational mind. A poem or a prayer is not propositional because it conveys subjective emotional expression rather than objective rational description. The phrase "God delivers his people" is a

---

[2] See also Acts 19:26; 26:28; 28:23; 2 Cor 5:11.

propositional statement, but the phrase "God deliver me," is an emotional cry for help.

Scripture contains propositional truth—a lot of it. Contrary to the claims of mysticism, God *can* be known through rational propositions; at least God seems to think so, since he used so many propositions to communicate himself to human beings. God is eternal, immortal and invisible (1 Tim 1:17), God is love (1 Jn 4:8), God knows all things (1 Jn 3:20) and works all things after the counsel of his will (Eph 1:11).

These are just a few of the hundreds of propositional truths about God in the Bible. When King David, the prophet Isaiah and the apostle Paul argue the irrationality of idol worship, they make propositional claims and use logic as a means of proving their argument (Ps 115:1-8; Is 44:12-17; Acts 17:24, 29).

Books

I was persuaded that, unlike some Christian anti-intellectuals, God considers logic to be an important part of understanding him. I was delightfully enraptured to uncover the fact that books are important to God too. In both Old and New Testaments, God's people are shown to be, so to speak, "people of the book." Their spiritual connectedness to God is often linked to reading and obeying the *book* of God's Law (Neh 8; cf. Deut 30:8-10; 2 Chron 34:30). God enshrined his commands in a *book* that Moses placed in a holy location beside the Ark of the Covenant (Deut 31:26). Old and New Testament saints constantly appealed to "the book" of Scripture for verification of their truth claims (Acts 17:11; cf. Ps 40:7; Lk 4:16-21; Heb 10:7). When the apostle Paul defended his faith, he paraphrased Scripture *books* and quoted pagan *books* to point unbelievers to God (Acts 17). Noble-minded Christians compared Paul's teaching against *the book* (Acts 17:11). Indeed, the final form which God encoded his truth to us is in *books*, from Genesis to Revelation (Ex 24:4; Rev 1:11). Being a book-lover myself, I thought, *Me and God, we seem to have a lot in common.*

Words

The more I read, the more I treasured words, since books are full of them. And words are central to the Christian faith as well. The Bible, God's revelation to us, is written in words. God created the universe and all there is using words; he spoke, and it was (Gen 1; Ps 33:6; Heb 11:3). There are literally thousands of examples in Scripture where God uses spoken words to make his point to pagans or his people. In fact, "Thus says the Lord" occurs over four hundred times in Scripture. He chose to use *words* to speak to his prophets and apostles, thus legitimating words as sufficient vehicles for ultimate truth.

The existentialist theory that language is inadequate for true communication or connection between persons is simply not biblical. After creating the universe with words (Gen 1), God created man *in his image* (Gen 1:26-27) then immediately *spoke* to Adam (Gen 1:28-30). He then warned him, *using words,* regarding the danger of disobedience (Gen 2:16-17). Adam's first recorded activity is his verbally *naming* the animals (Gen 2:19), an expression of his authority, reflecting God naming elements of the created order (Gen 1:5, 8, 10).

Children of God grow in their relationship with God through meditation on his *words* (Ps 1), treasuring those *words* in their hearts (Ps 119:11) and reading those *words* (Neh 8). The gospel is typically proclaimed, in the Bible, through verbal preaching of *words* (Rom 10:8-17)[3] and very often defended by *words* (e.g., 1 Pet 3:15; Acts 17).

So part of my responsibility in mirroring God's image, glorifying him and proclaiming and defending the gospel is to be rational, use propositions, read books and use words. So far, so good.

But something went wrong.

Logocentrism

Over the years, as I pursued an emphasis on rational discourse almost exclusively in my spiritual walk. I noticed in myself a tendency toward reducing everything to logical debate. I became argumentative. Encounters with unbelievers and even believers would too often become an endless dispute over minutia that seemed to lead away from the Gospel rather than toward it.

And I became impatient. With such a heavy focus on studying logical and historical argumentation, one becomes acutely aware of just how illogical and historically uneducated so many people are. Most people's beliefs—and their defense of those beliefs—are so riddled with logical fallacies that it boggles the mind. Some of the more astute Christian philosophers I studied taught me to think about the nature of argumentation itself, as well as worldviews. The philosophical presuppositions that everyone operates under are so often

---

[3] See also Is 52:7; Acts 8:12; 13:32; Rom 10:15.

unexamined that when you do bring them to light, they prove devastating to such unreflective viewpoints.

I became impatient with people who parroted received prejudices, actually arguing that Christianity is superstitious while putting their faith in the fictional fantasy of *The Da Vinci Code* and other secular conspiracy theories. So I would engage in rigorous debate with the unenlightened and proceed to destroy unbelieving worldviews like they were going out of style. It was like a genocide of unbelief. "So, you're a naturalist? Well, if you believe everything has a natural cause, then your own thoughts are caused by nature, which means your truth claim of naturalism is self-refuting." WHAM!

"So, you're a relativist? Well, if you believe there are no absolutes, then that is an absolute, and you're relativism is self-refuting." WHAM!

"So, you're a monist? Well, if you believe all is one, and that distinctions between things are illusion, then you cannot disagree with me without making a distinction between your truth claims and my truth claims. Your monism is self-refuting." WHAM!

I felt like the Muhammad Ali of apologetics: Trample like an elephant, sting like a hive of killer bees. But I eventually learned that winning an argument is not always the same as persuasion; you can win the battle of debate but lose the war for a soul.

I started to sense that my approach to apologetics and theology was becoming dehumanizing. I was treating the human being before me as a mere carrier of a set of irrational beliefs that it was my purpose to dismantle into absurdity—all in the cause of "leading every thought captive to Christ." As much as I would claim that the Bible was my ultimate authority, I would be more focused on logical discourse than on truth in its fullness of manifestation in the *person* of Jesus Christ. I lost sight of the fact that Truth is ultimately an *incarnate person*, not solely abstract reasoning (Jn 14:6). Reason, not God, had become my ultimate arbiter.

I was now what I call a "mind-oriented Christian." I tended to reduce other Christians to their doctrinal commitments, judging their status before God based on my creedal scorecard. "Well, you did okay, eight out of ten doctrines correct, but those two wrong ones set you back on the hierarchy of doctrinal knowledge." Through an inordinate emphasis in my faith on logic, rational discourse, words and books, I had transformed my Christian spirituality into a rationalistic philosophy lacking personal relationship and imagination. I thought mere theologically correct belief about reality was the same thing as inhabiting that reality. Emotions were irrational and thus irrelevant, because as all good logicians know, the appeal to pity (emotion) is an informal logical fallacy, and emotions cannot be trusted. Never mind that Jesus appealed to pity to persuade people (see Lk 10:29-37). Never mind that the Bible presents our emotions as a legitimate part of relating to God (see Mt 9:13; 22:37). Never mind that God appeals to pity throughout the Scriptures (Jon 4:10-11),[4] not to mention God's own emotional outbursts of jealousy (Deut 4:24), anger (1 Chron 13:11), bitter weeping and moaning (Jer 48:31-32; Jn 11:35; Lk 19:41), compassion (Lk 15:20), grief (Gen 6:6) and shouts of joy (Zeph 3:17).[5]

I began to discover just what was lopsiding my Christianity and my communication. It was my devaluation of imagination. I had become *logocentric*. I had privileged rational discourse as the ultimate means of discerning truth and neglected the legitimacy of emotion and imagination in understanding God. Reason had become a sort of idol to me. And it was not well with my soul.

It was like a war between word and image in my theology, and I had for all these years considered *word* as the good side and *image* as the bad side—or at least the suspicious side. I needed to relearn a biblical truth: we are not disembodied intellects, we are enfleshed spirit that includes intellect but is not reducible to it. Our faith is not merely an abstract philosophy or mental assent to doctrinal propositions, it is first and foremost a covenanted relationship with the *person* of God.

Word Versus Image

When I refer to *word* and *image,* I do not mean merely literal things, as in the words you are reading versus visual pictures you see. If we think of word and image as categories of discourse, the category of *word* might include words,

---

[4]See also Zech 7:9-10; Prov 22:21-25; Rom 12:20; Mt 9:13.
[5]Modernist Christians argue that such emotional expressions of God are mere anthropomorphisms (human traits applied to God by way of analogy), as if such scientific categorizing negates rather than reinforces their emotional content. This is a non sequitur. Of course God is transcendent and we cannot understand him fully. Of course God does not experience emotions *in the same exact way* that finite, sinful humanity does. But he experiences emotion nonetheless, and he uses those human traits and metaphors, laden with human emotion, as legitimate means of understanding him. If one argues that such anthropomorphisms of emotion are not really emotion, then one would have to be consistent in saying that all anthropomorphisms of God are not really what they claim to be, such as justice, compassion, care or love. All these human metaphors of God involve intense emotion that is intrinsically a part of their image. If God did not want us to understand him as having emotions, he would not have used so many emotional terms and metaphors of himself. If emotions are a part of the *imago Dei* in us, then the appeal to emotion may be logically invalid, but it is biblically valid.

propositions, books, spoken and written prose, preaching and rational discourse, among other things. The category of *image* likewise involves more than mere visual image. The word *image* is a root word for *imagination,* which scholar William Dyrness defines traditionally as "the ability to shape mental images of things not present to the senses."[6] So the category of *image* might include anything that engages the imagination rather than the rational intellect. This would include visual images, music, drama, symbol, story, metaphor, allegory and other forms of creativity.

An example of the difference between these categories of word and image would be systematic doctrines versus theological parables and metaphors; describing God as a rock and fortress may involve the use of words, but it accesses the imagination rather than logical deduction or scientific observation. As Kevin Vanhoozer explains, "The association of ideas in a metaphorical statement is the result neither of induction nor deduction; neither scientific observation nor logical reasoning create metaphors. Indeed, metaphor subverts logic; it has been called an 'intentional category mistake.'"[7]

Traditionally, *word* has been considered more intellectual and *image,* more emotional. *Word* has been linked with abstract communication, *image* with concrete communication. If *word* is more cerebral, *image* is more sensory. The writers of the *Dictionary of Biblical Imagery* define image as

> any word that names a concrete thing (such as *tree* or *house*) or action (such as *running* or *threshing*). Any object or action that we can picture is an image. Images require two activities from us as readers of the Bible. The first is to experience the image as literally and in as fully a sensory way as possible.[8]

Though imagery in the Bible is communicated through words, the usage of words is evocative, not of abstract eternal truths of reason, but of a world of image, symbol, metaphor, simile, and story. As the editors of this dictionary conclude, "the Bible is much more a book of images and motifs than of abstractions and propositions."

---

[6] William A. Dyrness, *Reformed Theology and Visual Culture: The Protestant Imagination from Calvin to Edwards* (Cambridge: Cambridge University Press, 2004), p. 4.
[7] Kevin J. Vanhoozer, *Is There a Meaning in This Text? The Bible, The Reader, and the Morality of Literary Knowledge* (Grand Rapids: Zondervan, 1998), p. 129.
[8] "Introduction: Defining Terms: Image, Symbol, Metaphor, Simile," *Dictionary of Biblical Imagery,* in *The Essential IVP Reference Collection* CD-ROM (Downers Grove, Ill.: InterVarsity Press, 2001).

This traditional dichotomy between word and image is better described as a dialectical tension between *reason and imagination*. I will point out later in the book that images can be just as abstract as words, and words just as emotional as images. The real question regarding the comprehension and communication of truth, then, is not "Are words superior to images?" but "Is reason superior to imagination?"

Or is there a third way?

Over the years this dichotomy between rationality and imagination has been reflected in the broader Christian culture. Some Christians have tended to be so word-oriented that they border on rationalism and distrust the use of imagination, deeming it an idol tool of the devil's workshop. Meanwhile, other Christians have tended to be image-oriented, with a more experiential approach to their faith and a distrust of dogmatic reasoning as close-minded bigotry.

A look at Table 1 charts out how this word-image dichotomy has created a division in the body of Christ.

Table 1		
WORD	**BIASES**	**IMAGE**
Traditional Church	Locale	Contemporary Church
Modernity	Era	Postmodernity
Doctrine	Emphasis	Relationship
Reason	Basis	Experience
Preach the Gospel	Mandate	Live the Gospel
Content of Message	Priority	Style and Form
Proposition	Communication	Story
Truth	Pursuit	Spirit
Rules	Values	Freedom
Rationality	Temperament	Creativity
Books, Speech	Reference	Film, TV, Pop Culture
Dead Orthodoxy	Vulnerability	Anti-Intellectualism
Legalism	Risks	License

Theologically, I located myself on the "word" side of the chart. I sought to understand where this split came from and how it had affected me, and I began to see that my Christianity had been unknowingly affected by the paradigm of *modernity*, whose origin is most often attributed to the eighteenth-century movement called the Enlightenment.

Chapter 2
Literal Versus Literary

In the 1700s, the European Enlightenment introduced a new paradigm of truth and knowledge that demanded a foundation solely on human reason (rationalism) and empirical verification through human sense perceptions (empiricism) to validate truth claims. Science and reason became the only possible "objective" forms of knowledge. Religion was relegated to arbitrary subjective "belief."

The premodern faith paradigm (trusting deity leads to knowledge and truth) had been replaced by a modern scientific paradigm (autonomous human reason and observation lead to knowledge and truth). The rationalist skeptic René Descartes (1596-1650), with his *cogito ergo sum* ("I think, therefore, I am"), became the poster child for a viewpoint that believed human reason could provide certain knowledge of truth, because reason was founded on unchanging laws of reality discoverable by reason.

Isaac Newton (1643-1727), with a paradigm of the universe as a clocklike machine that reduced the knowable universe to mechanistic laws objectively observable by scientists, became the poster child for the scientific side of the Enlightenment story. Eventually every field of knowledge would become a slave to this Enlightenment prejudice of scientific and rational "management" of reality. The "science" of culture became "sociology," the "science" of personality became "psychology." The so-called Age of Faith was replaced by the so-called Age of Reason. As author Stanley Grenz puts it, "This quest led to the modernity characteristic of the twentieth century, which has sought to bring rational management to life in order to improve human existence through technology."[1]

Christians followed suit, seeking to found their faith on "neutral" reason and scientific examination, the ultimate criteria of Enlightenment truth. Grenz and John Franke illustrate this epistemic turn in the theologians of the early twentieth century, like Charles Hodge, who suggested that "just as the natural scientist

---

[1] Stanley Grenz, *A Primer on Postmodernism* (Grand Rapids: Eerdmans, 1996), p. 3.

uncovers the facts pertaining to the natural world, so the theologian brings to light the theological facts found within the Bible."[2] Theologians developed a more scientific study of God, organizing doctrines into systems, much like the periodic table of elements or taxonomic classifications of animal phyla. Conservative Christians reinterpreted theology's chief goal as uncovering theological propositions of universal truths and facts from the Bible.

Even as evangelical Christians fought against liberalism, many of them drifted into the same set of assumptions of modernity: Science and reason are public facts and provable; religion and imagination are subjective faith and private. So, to legitimize Christianity, we must prove it according to the criteria of standards provided by modern science, historiography and philosophy. In the early twentieth century Christian fundamentalism defended biblical literalism with scientific appeals to archaeology and empirical evidence. Proving the historic and scientific reliability of the text of Scripture began to eclipse the narrative of the text. In her book *Total Truth: Liberating Christianity from Its Cultural Captivity*, Nancy Pearcey argues that the outcome was

> what one historian calls "a schizophrenic conception of God." On one hand, "intellectual assurance came from the Divine Engineer," while on the other hand, "personal religious experience assumed the Heavenly Father." Yet the relationship between them was far from equal, for science had been defined as the sole source of genuine knowledge, which meant religion was demoted to subjective feelings.[3]

Philosophical naturalism was unwittingly accepted by Christians as the reigning method of investigating truth.

> First, the very notion that Christians needed a "scientific" exegesis of Scripture represented a degree of cultural accommodation to the age… Moreover, the empiricist insistence that theology was a collection of "facts" led easily to a one-dimensional, flat-footed interpretation of Scripture. Metaphorical, mystical, and symbolic meanings were

---

[2] Stanley J. Grenz and John R. Franke, *Beyond Foundationalism: Shaping Theology in a Postmodern Context* (Louisville, Ky.: Westminster John Knox, 2001), p. 34.

[3] Nancy R. Pearcey, *Total Truth: Liberating Christianity from Its Cultural Captivity* (Wheaton, Ill.: Crossway Books, 2004), p. 307.

downplayed in favor of the "plain" meaning of the text. And by treating Bible verses as isolated, discrete "facts," the method often produced little more than proof-texting... with little regard for literary or historical context, or for the larger organizing themes in Scripture.[4]

Of course, much good has come from Christianity rising to meet the challenge of modernity. Since reason and empirical observation are not intrinsically fallacious, and are indeed created by God, they cannot in and of themselves be against God and can in fact be useful tools. But I would suggest that we have allowed modernity to shape our understanding of Christianity as well. And not in all ways for the better.

Hans Frei, in his classic *Eclipse of Biblical Narrative,* explains that before the eighteenth and nineteenth centuries, the study of the Bible was predominantly narratively driven. That is, while believers have always had to defend their claims to biblical miracles and doctrines, they nevertheless studied their Scriptures in the form in which they were written: not as textbook dissertations of timeless universal truths but as stories and letters written to the people of God at a certain time and place in history. But in response to the Enlightenment attempt to demythologize Christianity, apologists have spent millions of pages and man-hours seeking to prove the accuracy of biblical texts down to the jot and tittle. Does flat earth terminology make the Bible unscientific (Rev 7:1)? Was the creation account an ancient attempt to describe modern Big Bang cosmology (Gen 1)? Was Jesus mistaken in claiming the end of the world within his generation (Mt 23:36)?

Rather than embracing the imaginative language used in so many biblical texts, theologians and apologists began to distrust it. Frei accuses Bishop Butler, a major influence in this tradition, of increasingly modeling biblical studies after "precision and sobriety, if not always the economy, of scientific discourse divorced from immediate appeal to sensibility."[5] The study of theology and apologetics turned from the narrative text to the factual event *behind the text.* It's almost as if the biblical narrative became eclipsed by the pursuit of factual empirical verification of the text; a modern scientific obsession.

---

[4]Ibid., p. 301.

[5]Hans Frei, *The Eclipse of Biblical Narrative: A Study in Eighteenth and Nineteenth Century Hermeneutics* (New Haven, Conn.: Yale University Press, 1974), p. 52.

> Religious apologetics of all hues presented one obstacle, and historical criticism another. Both worked to good effect in preventing the exploration of a narrative interpretation of the biblical stories. Both were of course deeply enmeshed in the question of the factual status of the narrated events.... It has remained an obsessive preoccupation of theologians and many biblical scholars ever since.[6]

In my well-intentioned pursuit of defending the Bible, I voraciously consumed these obsessively "factual" volumes. Many of them would often apply the rules of evidence in a court of law in order to prove the Bible.[7] I began to see the text of the Bible less in terms of its narratives, poetry and images, and more in terms of a legal and scientific deposition intended to withstand modern analytic scrutiny. Rather than seeing the text through *literary* conventions of ancient Jewish culture, I would tend to see it through *literal* conventions of my modern scientific culture. I became suspicious of poetic metaphors and hyperbole, because after all, those are subjective and enigmatic and eventually lead to liberal discrediting of the Bible as mythology. No, the Bible must be primarily literal propositional truth, a textbook of doctrine more than anything else. Literary genre and convention in the Bible was an annoying distraction from the clarity of rational precision.

I thought that if the Bible says the stars will fall from the sky, then stars must literally fall from the sky or else I'm a liberal who doesn't believe the Bible. If the Bible says that the whole world will hear the gospel before Jesus returns, then by Jove, Jesus will not set foot on terra firma until every single person in every remote corner of the world has heard the gospel. Otherwise I am a liberal who doesn't believe the Bible.

The way in which I began to realize that my "literalism" was really unbiblical "hyper-literalism," was through my study of eschatology, the "end

---

[6] Ibid., pp. 137-38.

[7] What I mean by this is that our rules of legal proof do not validate the Bible because they are derived from the Bible. You can't "prove" the source of a notion from the results of the source of that notion. It is the source (the Bible) that proves the derivation (legal concepts). For example, the belief in a God who orders nature according to his orderliness is what drove many early modern scientists like Galileo, Isaac Newton and Lord Kelvin and other Christian scientists to pursue finding the "laws of nature, and of nature's God." Our commonly accepted legal principle that the punishment should fit the crime is based on the Old Testament notion of "lex talionis," eye for an eye. So, if our scientific and legal procedures are based upon the foundation of a biblical worldview, then logically, one cannot deny that foundation without denying the edifice built upon it. Of course, this does not make our interpretations of science or law absolute, like the Bible, because our building can be flawed even if the foundation is not.

times."[8] Through studying the culture of ancient Israel I began to see that Jewish culture is poetic and laden with imaginative expressions, not analytic and laden with scientific factoids, like we in the West now read things. I began to appreciate what theologian Abraham Kuyper explained as the literary nature of biblical revelation as opposed to "barren proposition":

> The rationale for the diverse literary forms in Scripture is that revelation strikes all the chords of the soul, and not just one, e.g., the rational one. This makes it clear that the historical doctrine of revelation is not the barren propositional one it is often charged with being.[9]

Take for example the collapsing universe imagery of Jesus' Olivet Discourse:

> But immediately after the tribulation of those days the sun will be darkened, and the moon will not give its light, and the stars will fall from the sky, and the powers of the heavens will be shaken. (Mt 24:29)

I had been indoctrinated to believe that this event, heralding the coming of Christ, must be hyperliteral or a "barren proposition," that is, stars will literally fall from the sky and the heavens will literally shake. Well, God may do miracles but he doesn't do absurdities. Stars are suns and are a whole lot bigger than earth. One "star" alone would burn up the earth long before it even arrived here.

Rather than try to reconcile current scientific understanding of stars with biblical apocalyptic, it is more biblical to seek to read the text through the eyes of that first century Jew who wrote it. And that Jewish writer was steeped in Old Testament imagery. So when I looked into the Old Testament to find where that imagery is used, I discovered that sun, moon and stars are often used symbolically to represent rulers and governing powers. In Judges 5 stars are explained as representing ruling kings:

---

[8] One of the most helpful books for exploring the end times through the eyes of first century Jews is Gary DeMar's *Last Days Madness: Obsession of the Modern Church* (Powder Springs, Ga.: American Vision, 1999).

[9] Kevin J. Vanhoozer, "The Semantics of Biblical Literature," in *Hermeneutics, Authority and Canon*, ed. D.A. Carson and John D. Woodbridge (Grand Rapids: Zondervan, 1986), p. 78.

> The kings came and fought; then fought the kings of Canaan.... "The stars fought from heaven, from their courses they fought against Sisera." (Judg 5:19-20)[10]

Another example of this obvious symbolic description of the fall of ruling powers as the "shaking of heavens and earth" comes from the prophet Haggai:

> Then the word of the LORD came a second time to Haggai...saying, "Speak to Zerubbabel governor of Judah, saying, 'I am going to shake the heavens and the earth.' I will overthrow the thrones of kingdoms and destroy the power of the kingdoms of the nations." (Hag 2:20-22)

The text itself makes the analogous comparison that God's shaking of the heavens and the earth is a poetic reference to his overthrow of thrones, kingdoms and nations, not geographical earthquakes.

What's more, this same kind of terminology of stars and darkened sun and moon was used in several biblical prophecies to describe the fall of governments and political authorities. Isaiah describes God's judgment and destruction of Babylon and her rulers the same way:

> For the stars of heaven and their constellations will not flash forth their light; The sun will be dark when it rises, and the moon will not shed its light. (Is 13:10)

As a matter of fact, when this prophecy was fulfilled and Babylon was overrun by the Medes in 539 B.C., the sun, moon and stars did not darken. But this is only a contradiction if one demands a modern scientific literalistic reading of an ancient Jewish passage that is obviously cryptic and figurative of falling leaders. Isaiah describes the fall of Edom's rulers under God's judgment with the same kind of language, but he paints an even more dramatic picture:

> And all the host of heaven will wear away, And the sky will be rolled up like a scroll.... For My sword is satiated in heaven,

---

[10] Other places where sun, moon and stars are symbolic of ruling authorities or spiritual heads: Gen 37:9-10; Rev 12:1-6.

Behold it shall descend for judgment upon Edom, And upon the people whom I have devoted to destruction. (Is 34:4-5)

When the Maccabees destroyed Edom in 100 B.C. in fulfillment of this prophecy, the sky did not literally roll up like a scroll, and the starry hosts of heaven did not wear away, but the rules and nation of Edom sure did.

Both the Old and New Testament prophets did not misdescribe literal objects they could not understand like meteorites or atomic explosions. They were not describing literal astronomical events defying the laws of physics. In short, they were not writing scientifically or literally. They were writing *figuratively*. They were deliberately using images they were already familiar with to depict the serious nature of God's wrath about to fall upon a nation or people.[11]

The biblical description of the "earth-shattering" power of the New Covenant begins to mean something when we read in Hebrews that we have received an "unshakable kingdom." It is not a physical description of the universe shaking, but a figurative one of the permanence and victory of the New Covenant over all human authority in heaven and on earth.

> "Yet once more I will shake not only the earth, but also the heavens." This expression, "Yet once more," denotes the removing of those things which can be shaken, as of created things, so that those things which cannot be shaken may remain. Therefore, since we receive a kingdom which cannot be shaken. (Heb 12:26-28)

The replacement of the Old Covenant with the New Covenant is here described as God "shaking the earth and heaven," because to the ancient Jew, the covenants of God with his people are the most important thing in the universe. In fact, the Covenant was described in terms of creating the "heavens and earth" when God gave it to Moses after parting the Red Sea:

> For I am the LORD your God, who stirs up the sea and its waves roar (the LORD of hosts is His name). I have put My words in your mouth and have covered you with the shadow

---

[11] For more biblical examples of this collapsing universe and earth shattering hyperbole used of the fall of worldly powers see Jeremiah 4:23-30; Amos 8:9; Isaiah 24:1-23; 40:3-5; Nahum 1:4-6. For an excellent book about the nature of apocalyptic imagery and symbolism in the Bible, a must-buy book is *Last Days Madness*, by Gary DeMar (Powder Springs, Ga.: American Vision, 1999).

of My hand, to establish the heavens, to found the earth, and to say to Zion, "You are My people." (Is 51:15-16)

The Old Covenant was an "establishment of heavens and earth," so when the writer of Hebrews speaks of shaking the "heavens and the earth" he is referring to the elimination and replacement of covenants. In fact, when the first Temple, the center of that "heaven and earth" covenant, was destroyed in 587 B.C., the prophet Jeremiah not only used earth-shattering images again, but described the event as if the entire universe was in need of being recreated:

> I looked on the earth, and behold, it was formless and void; And to the heavens, and they had no light. I looked on the mountains, and behold, they were quaking, And all the hills moved to and fro. I looked, and behold, there was no man, And all the birds of the heavens had fled. I looked, and behold, the fruitful land was a wilderness, And all its cities were pulled down Before the LORD, before His fierce anger. For thus says the LORD, "The whole land shall be a desolation, Yet I will not execute a complete destruction. For this the earth shall mourn And the heavens above be dark." (Jer 4:23-28)

With all this understanding of the Covenants being described in terms of "heavens and earth," and the destruction of the emblem of the covenant, the Temple, being the collapse of the universe, then the Hebrews 12 reference to God shaking the heavens and earth once more becomes an obvious prophecy of the destruction of the second Temple that actually did occur in A.D. 70. When the second Temple was destroyed, this was God shaking the heavens and the earth of the Old Covenant and replacing it with a new permanent unshakable kingdom covenant that will remain forever.

So we see that all this biblical talk of quaking mountains, darkening skies, new heavens and a new earth is simply powerful figurative imagery used to depict the spiritual importance of the Covenants, both Old and New, not some literal physical phenomena of which we have no historical recording. That is the power of imagery. As New Testament scholar N. T. Wright explains,

> We do this all the time ourselves. I have often pointed out to students that to describe the fall of the Berlin Wall, as one well might, as an "earth-shattering event" might perhaps lead

some future historian, writing in the *Martian Journal of Early European Studies* to hypothesize that an earthquake caused the collapse of the Wall, leading to both sides realizing they could live together after all. A good many of apocalyptic literature in our own century operate on about that level of misunderstanding.[12]

There are of course many straightforward descriptions in the Bible of historical events, but they are often interwoven with these imaginative images that help us understand the spiritual reality or meaning behind the event, because imagery has a way of picturing truth that abstract rational language does not.

A Whole Lot More Bunch of Hyperbole

Another example of the role of imagination in Scripture can be illustrated in the "Great Tribulation" that Jesus predicted in his Olivet Discourse. "For then there will be a great tribulation, such as has not occurred since the beginning of the world until now, nor ever will" (Mt 24:21). Prophecy pundits focus on the extremity of this pronouncement as proof of its future fulfillment. Surely we have not seen the kind of tribulation in history that is without equal. Yet in the Old Testament, the prophet Joel describes judgment upon Israel during his lifetime:

> Surely it is near, A day of darkness and gloom, A day of clouds and thick darkness. As the dawn is spread over the mountains, So there is a great and mighty people; *There has never been anything like it, Nor will there be again after it To the years of many generations.* (Joel 2:2, emphasis added)

Elsewhere in the Old Testament, when Nebuchadnezzar besieged Jerusalem during the prophet Ezekiel's era, God describes a tribulation that is very similar to the one described in the Olivet Discourse:

> I will do among you what I have not done, and the like of which I will never do again. Therefore, fathers will eat their sons among you, and sons will eat their fathers; for I will execute

---

[12]N. T. Wright, *The New Testament and the People of God* (Minneapolis: Fortress, 1992), p. 282.

judgments on you and scatter all your remnant to every wind.
(Ezek 5:9-10, emphasis added)

This destruction, which included cannibalism and a Diaspora of Jews, Scripture says God "will never do again." That makes at least three different times in the Bible (Ezekiel, Joel, Matthew) where Israel is described as being surrounded by pagan armies, and suffering great tribulation and desolations including a Diaspora. And each time is spoken of *as if it has never happened like this and would never happen again like this.*

But in A.D. 70, when Jerusalem was surrounded by Roman armies, Israel suffered a very similar fate as they did in Ezekiel's time: the people were starved and forced into cannibalism, and scattered to every wind in a Diaspora. Of this event the Jewish historian Flavius Josephus, reflecting good Jewish hyperbole, says,

> The war which the Jews made with the Romans hath been the greatest of all those, not only that have been in our times, but, in a manner, of those that were ever heard of.[13] Accordingly, the multitude of those that therein perished exceeded all the destructions that either men or God ever brought upon the world.[14]

Josephus' writings are not Scripture, but they certainly illustrate the kind of hyperbolic language ancient Jews tended to use, which mirrors the language used in the Bible

Biblical apologists run verbal circles around themselves trying to justify these statements as literal claims rather than literary exaggerations. Why? Because literalism requires exact scientific precision. But the ancient Jews were not applying these modern constraints to their premodern literature. They weren't contradicting themselves. They were speaking hyperbolically to stress the seriousness of the issue. The Scriptures are full of imaginative hyperbole that defies modernist reason. For example, two kings are spoken of as men of unique trust in God.

> [Hezekiah] trusted in the LORD, the God of Israel; so that after him there was *none like him* among all the kings of Judah, *nor*

---

[13] Josephus *Wars of the Jews* Preface, Section 1.
[14] Josephus *Wars* 6:9:4.

among those who were before him. (2 Kings 18:5, emphasis added)

Before [Josiah] there was no king like him who turned to the LORD with all his heart... nor did any like him arise after him. (2 Kings 23:25, emphasis added)

These two men of God are very much like each other in their unique trust in God. If you take the Bible *literally* in all its writing, you must conclude that the Bible contradicts itself. But not if you understand it *literarily*. In fact, Solomon is described in a similar way:

Behold, I have given you a wise and discerning heart, so that there has been *no one like you before you, nor shall one like you arise after you.* (1 Kings 3:12, emphasis added)

And this Scripture is "literally" contradicted by Jesus in reference to himself: "Something greater than Solomon is here" (Mt 12:42).

Well, was Jesus greater than Solomon or was he not? Which is right, the Old Testament or the New? Who is more trusting of God—Hezekiah or Josiah? Which of the similar Tribulations are the greatest? All these alleged contradictions become irrelevant when one sees the literary exaggeration that is going on here.

Exaggeration is not lying when it takes the form of a colloquial saying that expresses the emotional intent of the author. The biblical writers are ancient Jews expressing strong emotional images of destruction, faith and greatness, not geological, astronomical, empirical measurements. Those statements are not *literally* true because they were not *intended* to be literally true. And their readers knew it.

The Bible is simply full of this kind of hyperbole, especially in the apocalyptic writings of the prophets. *The Dictionary of Biblical Imagery* clarifies again:

The events described in apocalyptic literature are often presented with literary techniques found more commonly in poetry: metaphor, hyperbole, personification, irony, numerical patterns and so forth. These special effects allowed apocalyptic to describe heaven and the future with captivating imagery... more like an impressionistic painting than like a photograph in high resolution. Individual details remained a puzzle, but the big picture was clear.[15]

Hyperbole does not reduce the Scriptures to fairy tales or unhistorical documents. Rather, it is an understanding of how God interweaves image with word to paint a picture of truth that retains an element of mystery beyond human rational reductionism.

> While the Bible is a very realistic book, rooted in actual, everyday events set in space-time history, there is also much about it that is fantastic…. The Bible seems to flaunt the element of fantasy by tending toward a rhetoric of hyperbole—the exaggerated statement that conveys heightened feeling in an obviously nonliteral form. "A thousand may fall at your side, ten thousand at your right hand," says the poet (Ps 91:7 RSV) in a heightened picture of battlefield deliverance. Again, "You will tread on the lion and the adder" (Ps 91:13 RSV). Similarly, the exultant confidence of David is so strong that he boasts that in God he "can crush a troop" and "leap over a wall" (Ps 18:29 RSV). The truth this hyperbolic rhetoric conveys is not literal or factual truth but emotional truth. The resulting spirit is exultant and buoyant, but it is not literal.[16]

Literary critic Northrop Frye correctly points out the irony that the meaning behind our colloquialism "gospel truth" implies historical factuality, and yet the very last "gospel truth" uttered in the closing of the Gospel of John is a "dazzling hyperbole" of "intentional exaggeration":

> And there are also many other things which Jesus did, which if they were written in detail, I suppose that even the world itself would not contain the books that would be written. (Jn 21:25)[17]

---

[15] "Genre of Apocalypse: Understanding Apocalyptic," in *Dictionary of Biblical Imagery*, AGES Software.

[16] "Rhetorical Patterns: Rhetoric of Make-Believe," in *Dictionary of Biblical Imagery*, AGES Software.

[17] Northrop Frye, *The Great Code: The Bible and Literature* (New York: Harcourt Brace Jovanovitch, 1981), p. 54.

The reader can only smile at the humorous irony of imagining modern apologists calculating the number of seconds and minutes in Jesus' life from birth to death and resurrection, then translating those segments of time into page counts, all in order to prove that Jesus' thirty three years of actions in fact could not be contained in all the books in the world at that time. Or perhaps they would try to make the ridiculous argument that since Jesus exists eternally, his history would require an infinite amount of books. The fact is that this gospel claim is not scientifically or historically true because hyperbole *is not intended to be a scientific or historical claim in the first place!*

Role Reversal

Because of the Bible's mixture of the literal with the figurative, the Bible student must be careful to consider the possible "literalness" of what may appear to be figurative language. The very success and growth of the discipline of archaeology derives from the pursuit of men who refused to believe that the Bible was unhistorical myth or fanciful folktales. The history of science is filled with Christians like Matthew Maurey, the founder of modern oceanography, who interpreted apparently poetic Bible passages literally in a way that led to such scientific discoveries as ocean currents (Ps 8:8; Is 43:16), the hydrologic cycle (Eccles 1:7; Job 36:27-28), the jet stream (Eccles 1:6) and air pressure (Job 28:25), to name a few.[18]

The Bible is so rich with integrated poetic *and* literal imagery that we should all be cautious about "eisegeting" our own bias into the text. If "exegesis" means drawing information out of the text of Scripture, then "eisegesis" means importing information into the text. There is simply no wooden or absolute hermeneutic of "literalness" or "figurativeness" that can do justice to the text. Context helps determine usage, but even context can be difficult to decipher. Literary interpretation of the Bible is not so much a science as an art.

One of the reasons why the Jews of the first century did not recognize the visitation of their own Messiah was because even *they* took the Bible too literally. Indeed, they were expecting a military or political king who would crush Rome (Dan 2:44-45), restore the nation of Israel back from exile into their land (Zeph 3:14-20), build a new kingdom on earth (Dan 7:14) from

---

[18] Inspired by an email discussion with Nancy Pearcey. For an interesting documentation on Matthew Maurey, see <www.bible.ca/tracks/matthew-fontaine-maury-pathfinder-of-sea-ps8.htm>.

Mount Zion in Jerusalem (Is 52), rebuild the Temple (Ezek 40—48), reinstate the Davidic monarchy (Ps 89:38-51) in a new "age to come" (Is 61)—all based on Old Testament prophecy. Even Jesus' own disciples misunderstood the literary nature of these promises as literal earthly political power (Mt 20:20-28; Acts 1:6). Jesus' kingdom *did* crush Rome, though not through military revolution, Jesus *did* restore Israel, *did* rebuild the Temple (Acts 15:14-16), *did* reinstate the Davidic monarchy (Lk 1:32), and he *is* the King of kings who came to Mount Zion (Mt 21:5) and rules over all things at the right hand of his father (1 Pet. 3:22).[19] He just didn't do those things in the literal way that they had envisioned, but in a *literary* way. We see how the *literary* meaning of Israel and the Temple was first fulfilled in Christ and is now fulfilled in the church as his "body" (Rom 2:28-29; Eph 2:19-22). Christ's rule in his kingdom may be current and real, but certainly not an earthly reign of outward political power (Lk 17:20-21).

New Testament scholar Mark Allan Powell explains that the Gospel narratives deliberately lampoon believers who are literal-minded. The Gospel of John alone illustrates many examples of literalizing and "missings of the boat": Nicodemus misunderstanding spiritual rebirth as *literally* re-entering a mother's womb (Jn 3:4); disciples thinking that Lazarus is *literally* taking a nap, when Jesus uses sleep as a metaphor for death (Jn 11:12); the disciples thinking Jesus has someone *literally* sneaking him provisions when he says, "I have food that you know not of" (Jn 4:33); and even grossly misconstruing Christ's Eucharistic reference to *literal* cannibalism (Jn 6:51-52)! Powell affirms the conclusion that these frequent misunderstandings are intended to teach the reader how to read the Gospel correctly; not a wooden literalism but a literary narrative of symbolism, metaphor, image *and* history all rolled up into one.[20] This literary complexity may not satisfy the strict literalist who demands precise categories and simple answers, but it's the God's-honest truth.

Even though they consider God's Word to be absolute and eternal in its authority, New Testament authors, *writing with God's authority,* often do not quote Old Testament Scriptures verbatim but rather paraphrase them (Rom 11:8-10), allegorize them (Gal 4:21-31), typologize them (Rom 5:14), quote from a Greek translation (the Septuagint) rather than the Hebrew originals, quote using a mixture of Hebrew original and Greek translation (Jn 10:34) and

---

[19] N. T. Wright, *Jesus and the Victory of God* (Minneapolis: Fortress, 1996), pp. 205, 219, 223, 477-539.
[20] Mark Allan Powell, *What Is Narrative Criticism?* (Minneapolis: Fortress, 1990), p. 28.

from unknown translations that vary from both Greek and Hebrew (Mt 4:7).[21] Biblical authors did not believe that a scientific, word-for-word exactitude was necessary for an understanding of Scripture as God's authoritative word. *Literary* is not necessarily *literal*.

Biblically, the impact of imagery on the human audience is exaggerated, fantastic, nonliteral, dramatic, visual, experiential, emotional—and just as true as any of the historical, literal, abstract or rational propositions and words contained in those same pages. In its poetry, prophecy and proclamation, this mixture of word and image, rationality and imagination is so intertwined that even those in the first century had difficulty interpreting it! You simply cannot scientifically exegete the Scriptures as if it is a textbook of scientific facts or culturally transcendent doctrines or "objective" historical reporting. Biblical interpretation requires an aesthetic exegesis that takes into account the literary genre and artistic nature of the text.

Many Christians tend to impose a modern scientific standard upon their understanding of the Bible, an ancient Middle Eastern sacred text. They seem to be preoccupied with "the Bible as a true picture of the facts in all spheres of knowledge, secular, as well as religious."[22] Interestingly, this understanding began with Princeton theologians, such as Charles Hodge and B. B. Warfield, who sought to defend the Bible against "modernist" attacks in the nineteenth century. In seeking to meet the standards developed by atheistic scientific discourse, they unwittingly subordinated the Scriptures to those standards. Since then, the Bible has been reinterpreted to be in agreement with every fashionable scientific theory from evolution to the Big Bang and every fleeting literary theory from form criticism to deconstruction.

But scientific theories have changed so many times and with such drastic difference that a scientific approach to Scripture has actually proven to be historically fallacious. Those Christians desperately seeking to make the Bible "reveal" the Big Bang, for example, may eventually discover themselves as discredited in their faith as the Christians before Galileo who wed their biblical interpretation to Aristotelian science. "Whoever marries the spirit of the age in one generation," the saying goes, "becomes a widow in the next." Our understanding of a "scientifically accurate" description of reality is a historically new construct that could not have been in the minds of the biblical writers.

---

[21] Walter C. Kaiser Jr., *The Uses of the Old Testament in the New* (Chicago: Moody Press, 1985), pp. 4-5.

[22] Carl Raschke, *The Next Reformation: Why Evangelicals Must Embrace Postmodernity* (Grand Rapids: Baker Academic, 2004), p. 125.

They were not intending a scientific physical description of reality *in our modern sense of the words*. They were speaking within their cultural literary conventions of something beyond words. Neither did the biblical writers use these cultural conventions while secretly knowing the general theory of relativity. That too is an unfair projection of our modern viewpoint back onto their culture.

As Kevin Vanhoozer concludes "'Error' is... a context-dependent notion. If I do not claim scientific exactitude or technical precision, it would be unjust to accuse me of having erred."[23] The Bible is without scientific error because it intends to describe reality not in scientifically precise terms *but in cultural or literary terms*.

Does this kind of imaginative interpretation start a person on the slippery slope of liberal mythologizing of everything in the Bible, including miracles? Hardly. If that were the case, then the biblical writers themselves would have to be called liberals; they were the ones who used imaginative hyperbole and exaggeration so liberally. But allowing for imaginative interpretation does make things a little harder to compartmentalize into evangelical boxes of settled answers and rational certainties. The fact that some things in Scripture are figurative and some literal are functions of literary genres and techniques, not scientific and rationalistic analysis. It may make the process of interpretation more difficult, but difficulty is not an argument against the truth of a belief.

In my fear of becoming "liberal," and in my overemphasis on the rational, I discovered that I had been interpreting the Bible in a way that it was not intended to be interpreted. *Literalism* has become a code word for reducing Biblical language to raw physical description or rational timeless truths, rather than allowing for the imaginative poetic language of a Jew situated within the ancient Middle East. Yes, there is much in the Bible that is historical realism, much that is *literally* true, but it is mixed in with so much imagery, hyperbole and symbol that I simply can no longer claim to read the Bible *literally*. Instead, I've come to read the Book "literarily."

---

[23]Kevin Vanhoozer, *The Inerrancy of Scripture*, accessed February 5, 2008, at <www.episcopalian.org/efac/articles/inerrancy.htm>.

Chapter 3
Word Versus Image

In addition to being a lover of the mind, I am also a visual and dramatic artist. I love imagination and creativity. But in my pursuit of spirituality, knowledge, reality, truth and persuasion—because of my unbalanced word-orientation—my imagination was relegated to second-class status.

Here I was, an artist by inclination, training and profession, and yet the very concept of "image" was suspicious to me because of the propositional orientation of my faith. I didn't think the art that came from my intuition, my emotions or my imagination was necessarily *sinful*, it was just *inferior*. Images weren't intrinsically evil, but they *were* dangerous, like playing with matches, or better yet, like playing with a loaded gun. And why? Because they depended too much on emotion. And emotions were "irrational." And irrationality was the enemy of rationality.

Like a good evangelical Christian, I lamented our visual media-saturated society. I grieved with Neil Postman that we were "amusing ourselves to death"; media like television had replaced the reliability of words and rational discourse with the unreliable manipulation of visual images and emotional expression. I assumed that my emphasis on reason, propositional truth, words and books was simply an objective biblical paradigm.

But as I looked closer at the Bible, I began to discover the modernist bias that blinded me. I began to discover a different picture than the one I had painted myself into.

Bezalel the Artist

Philosophy and theology have traditionally been constructed from three components: metaphysics (reality), epistemology (knowledge) and ethics (morality). But I think another ancient formula (from Plato) gets it more right: the Good, the True and the Beautiful. Aesthetics (the study of beauty) is as necessary to our theology as truth and goodness. Yet all too often, it is relegated to a supplemental or optional elective in the curriculum of our faith.

God considers beauty to be an integral part of our relationship with him. The artist is no mere hobbyist but rather a tool in the hand of God for accomplishing that purpose. A closer look at Scripture about the making of the first tabernacle for the worship of God helped to illuminate this importance for me:

> Then Moses said to the sons of Israel, "See, the LORD has called by name Bezalel the son of Uri, the son of Hur, of the tribe of Judah. And He has filled him with the Spirit of God, in wisdom, in understanding and in knowledge and in all craftsmanship; to make designs for working in gold and in silver and in bronze, and in the cutting of stones for settings and in the carving of wood, so as to perform in every inventive work. He also has put in his heart to teach, both he and Oholiab, the son of Ahisamach, of the tribe of Dan. He has filled them with skill to perform every work of an engraver and of a designer and of an embroiderer, in blue and in purple and in scarlet material, and in fine linen, and of a weaver, as performers of every work and makers of designs."
>
> "Now Bezalel and Oholiab, and every skillful person in whom the LORD has put skill and understanding to know how to perform all the work in the construction of the sanctuary, shall perform in accordance with all that the LORD has commanded." Then Moses called Bezalel and Oholiab and every skillful person in whom the LORD had put skill, everyone whose heart stirred him, to come to the work to perform it. (Ex 35:30—36:2)

It is not insignificant that this is the very first passage in the Bible in which God fills a person with his Spirit; *and that person was an artist.* It was not mere skill that was required to build this beautiful edifice. It would take an artist to fulfill that blueprint from God. We're also told God filled Bezalel with wisdom, understanding, knowledge and artistic craftsmanship. The exact same traits God grants to prophets (Num 24:16), priests (1 Sam 2:35), and kings (1 Kings 5:12), yet here he puts it all into an artist. And this wasn't an isolated incident. Later, another artist by the name of Hiram is described as being filled with "wisdom, understanding and skill" (1 Kings 7:14), and Huram-abi is yet another artisan called a "skilled man, endowed with understanding" (2 Chron 2:13). Artists have a high calling from God.

The tabernacle (and by extension, later, the temple) was the heart of the Jewish religion, the very place of God's presence in their midst (2 Chron 5:13-6:2). It was the means through which they received atonement for sins. It was the symbolic center of the universe.[1] So God did not take art lightly. But it is important to note here that God did not give every detail of the design, weaving, embroidery and engraving. God left many of the details to the artisans themselves. And he used an internal calling to draw the artists. Art was a holy calling to God, but it was a subjectively experienced one ("everyone whose heart stirred him").

Lastly, art is not merely a calling, but creativity is shown in Scripture to be a gift from God. The Lord is described as "putting skill" into the artisans and "filling them with skill." To God, art is not a mere personal fancy, or a side hobby to the real calling in life, like "preaching the Gospel" or some other "spiritualized" sacred thing. No, art is a spiritual calling just as much as prophet, priest or king.

So by way of summary, this passage points up several important aspects of the value of art and artists to God:

God fills artists with his Spirit.
God values art highly.
God values artists highly.
Art is a calling from God.
Creativity is a gift of God.

Signs and Wonders

Roughly 30 percent of the Bible is rational propositional truth and laws, while 70 percent of the Bible is story, vision, symbol and narrative—that is, *image*.[2] The thousands of miracles that God performed for his people were not abstract propositions, but sensate visual signs (images) intended to elicit faith and trust in their Creator.

---

[1] As explained later in this book, when God establishes his covenant, he calls it "establishing the heavens and the earth" (Is 51:15-16), and when the temple, as emblem of that covenant, is destroyed in Jeremiah's time, it is described in terms of the universe returning to the original "darkness and void" of Genesis 1:2 (Jer 4:23 -27).

[2] My actual research uncovered 20 percent propositional truth, 80 percent story, vision, symbol and narrative. But I added a handicap of 10 percent to the propositional side so I could not be accused of blinded prejudice. Of course, most of the propositional content and imagery is integrated with each other, so a strictly "scientific" separation is not possible. Both are necessary to God's revelation, but the sheer comparison of volume is illuminating.

It is no coincidence that the phrase "signs and wonders" is used by biblical writers. A "sign" is a visual experiential symbol pointing to truth or proving a proposition (Heb 2:4).[3] So one of God's most dramatic means of persuasion recorded in the Bible is through the signs or *images* of miraculous wonders.[4]

Dreams and Visions

And then there are dreams and visions—God's form of television and movies: Joseph's dreams of fat and skinny cows (Gen 41), Ezekiel's spinning wheels (Ezek 1) and valley of dry bones (Ezek 37), Nebuchadnezzar's nightmare statue (Dan 2), as well as other visions given to key figures throughout the Old Testament.

It doesn't end there. God uses visual images in dreams and visions to New Testament believers such as Ananias (Acts 9:10), Joseph (Mt 1:20), Peter (Acts 10:10-11) and Paul (2 Cor 12:1-4). The apostle Peter reiterates the significance of visions and dreams on the Day of Pentecost:

> This is what was spoken of through the prophet Joel: "And it shall be in the last days," God says, "That I will pour forth of My Spirit upon all mankind... And your young men shall see visions, And your old men shall dream dreams." (Acts 2:16-17)

No matter how one defines "last days" in this passage, the point remains: images are still an important means to God for communicating truth under the New Covenant.

The Visual Word of God

God does not consider imagery to be an inadequate or inferior means of communicating as compared with words. In fact, he often considers image to be equally important with words, or he wouldn't have used so much visual imagery described *as his word*. Which raises the question: Are dreams and visions, signs and wonders really all that different from words?

---

[3] See also Deut 6:22; Dan 4:1-3; Acts 14:3; 2 Cor 12:12.

[4] It is important to note that while God used miracles as signs or verification, he did not intend them to be absolute or ultimate in terms of proof. Faith is the biblical ultimate: Jn 4:48; Lk 16:31; 2 Cor 5:7.

In Isaiah 2:1 we read about Isaiah's vision: "the *word* which Isaiah the son of Amoz *saw.*"[5] In Micah 1:1: "the word of the Lord which came to Micah… which he *saw.*" In Isaiah 13:1 and Habakkuk 1:1 the expression, "the oracle which the prophet *saw*" is used synonymously with God's "Word."[6] In Ezekiel 1:1-3, we read Ezekiel telling us that his visions of God are "the Word of the Lord." The prophet Zechariah says that the "Word of the Lord" came to him "as follows," and then he recounts the vision he *saw* (Zech 1:7-8). Amos says of God's revelation to him in several places, "the Lord God *showed* me" (Amos 7:1, 4; 7, 8:1). When God pictures his "Word" to Amos, Zechariah and Jeremiah, he asks them, "What do you *see*?" (Amos 7:8; 8:2; Zech 4:2; 5:2; Jer 1:11, 13; 24:3). God did not float Hebrew words in the air like ancient skywriting. He is defining image-based *visions* as his *Word.*[7]

Speaking of God's visual Word, the last book in the Bible—God's final word to us—is an epic vision, a feast of visual imagery and theater. Regardless of one's interpretation of this mysterious book, the images of apocalyptic horsemen, multiple-headed beasts and monsters running around killing people in Revelation are more akin to a modern horror film or fantasy epic than a systematic theology or sermon.

As these passages illustrate, according to God's prophets, the very concept of "God's Word" is not an exclusively word-oriented concept. The visual imagery that God paints and dramatizes, just as much as anything he has verbalized through words, is God's *Word*. As theologian Kevin Vanhoozer points out, Scripture "is not merely the disclosure of information about God (revelation) but a collection of diverse kinds of divine communicative acts"[8]— images and actions as well as literal *words* that are spoken or written. In fact, God's most important *word* is not a spoken or written word at all but an incarnate human being. Hebrews 1:1-2 proclaims that God, after speaking long ago through the prophets in many ways, has ultimately "spoken to us in His Son." We know about his Son through reading the words of Scripture, but what we know is not so much philosophical speculation about truth but dramatic incarnation of truth.

---

[5] See also Isaiah 1:1 and 13:1 to the same effect.

[6] See also Nahum 1:1. The Hebrew for "oracle" means "utterance."

[7] One exception to this rule is Dan 5:5, where God's hand *does* in fact engage in writing judgment on a wall in Aramaic.

[8] Kevin J. Vanhoozer, *The Drama of Doctrine: A Canonical-Linguistic Approach to Christian Theology* (Louisville, Ky.: Westminster John Knox, 2005), p. 47.

A common assumption among modernist Christians is that "preaching the Word of God" refers almost exclusively to a man standing on a podium elevated above an audience who are seated in pews all facing the speaker. This man lectures them for an hour or so as the climax of the "church service." Theatrical drama in such contexts is sometimes considered to be sacreligious. Many would not even begin to fathom the notion that art outside this church context could be a legitimate form of "preaching God's Word." Too bad for them, because God does.[9]

Images of God

God does not merely use images to reveal his *message*. He often uses images to reveal *himself*. A burning bush (Ex 3:2), a pillar of cloud and a pillar of fire (Ex 13:21-22), a "glory cloud" that covered the tabernacle (Ex 40:34-35), and an angelic messenger (Josh 6:12) are just a few choice examples. Consider the dozens of metaphors used of God, such as a lion (Hos 5:14), a lamb (Rev 21:22), a shepherd (Ps 78:71), a farmer (Ps 80:8), a vinegrower (Is 15), a potter (Rom 9:20-23), a drunken soldier (Ps 78:65), a father (2 Cor 6:18), a lover (Jer 3:20), a bridegroom (Is 62:5), a king (Ps 10:16), a consuming fire (Heb 12:29), a shield (Gen 15:1), a rock (Ps 18:46), a fortress (Ps 31:3), a cornerstone (Is 28:16), a morning star (Rev 22:16), a hen (Mt 23:37) and an eagle (Jer 49:22). Some of God's favorite images to use for his presence are thunder, lightning, clouds, smoke, and fire (Ex 19:16-18; Rev 11:19). Ezekiel's famous vision of God's glory included many-faced, many-winged, genetically spliced creatures around a throne with wild whirling wheels and a man of glowing metal and radiant fire in the center (Ezek 1)—one of the most interesting visuals in all the Bible, a stunning high-definition, Dolby sensurround feast.

The fact that God uses anthropomorphisms—human traits attributed to a nonhuman subject—to talk about himself is a powerful indicator of the value of imagination and human imagery in communicating and understanding truth. In the pages of the Bible, God is described dozens upon dozens of times as having eyes (Prov 15:3), ears (1 Pet 3:12), a nose (Gen 8:21), a face (Ps

---

[9]It is important to note, of course, that God's visions, dreams, signs and wonders are almost always accompanied by (if not explained through) words. This should be a cautionary note to postmoderns who attempt to elevate image above word. But this mutual embeddedness of word and image does not suggest the superiority of either word or image, but rather their mutual dependency and equality of ultimacy in God's usage of language.

114:7), arms (Ezek 20:33), and hands (Mk 12:36) with fingers (Deut 9:10), feet (Ex 24:10), a heart (Gen 6:6), a mouth (Is 1:20) with lips (Job 11:5) that even vomits (Rev 3:16). These are not physical descriptions; God is a spirit, not a physical body (Jn 4:24). These images, then, are obviously used as metaphors for us to understand God as personal, rather than abstract. Even though God uses reason and is referred to as the Logos (Jn 1:1), that Logos is biblically understood not as abstract rationality but as the *personal sustainer* of the universe, a spirit that became flesh (Jn 1:14), incarnate in the story of man. Word become image. But more on that a little later.

In addition to these cloaked images of God, the Scriptures also speak in dozens of places of God appearing without a description of how he appeared. Among these appearances God makes are to Abram (Gen 12:7), Isaac (Gen 26:2), Jacob (Gen 35:9), Amos (Amos 7:7), and Solomon (2 Chron 1:7). Speculation would be fruitless, but the point remains that appearances are visual or sensate experiences. In one instance, God is described as appearing through his spoken words alone (1 Sam 3:21), which once again illustrates the interconnectedness of words and imagery, but is certainly not the hermeneutical key to all the other appearances, since they involve the language of visual sight.

Drama, Theater and Parable

Rather than merely give sermons, God often had his prophets give plays. Isaiah's shocking performance art was to walk around naked as a *visual* "sign and token" of the shame Israel was about to experience at the hands of Egypt (Is 20:2-4). Ezekiel could be considered a thespian prophet. God told him to perform a war epic as a prophecy, complete with a miniature city besieged by battering rams (Ezek 4:1-3). Then God has Ezekiel engage in the longest performance art prophecy ever recorded by laying on his sides for 430 days, tied up in ropes, eating food cooked over burning excrement, with an emblem of the sins of Israel on top of him (Ezek 4:4-8). He concludes this performance by cutting his hair and beard, and dispersing it in various ways to dramatically depict God's concluding judgment (Ezek 5:1-4). God then had Ezekiel perform a theatrical prophecy of exile by covering his face, dragging his baggage around day and night, and digging a hole in a wall to store it, all while saying "I am a sign to you" (Ezek 12:1-11). Ezekiel then had to tremble and shudder while eating as another dramatic sign of the anxiety that Israel will feel in their exile (Ezek 17—20). And later, God had him perform a sign of two sticks, symbolizing Judah and Israel, becoming one, not unlike a magician before his audience (Ezek 37:15-23). Mere words were not enough for God. He wanted spectacle; he wanted lights, camera, action!

Jeremiah is called "the weeping prophet." But he should have been called "the acting prophet," because so many of his prophecies were theatrical performances: hiding his girdle by the Euphrates (Jer 13:1-11), breaking a potter's bottle in the valley of Hinnom (Jer 19:1), walking through all the gates of Jerusalem (Jer 17:19-27), wearing a yoke on his neck (Jer 27:1-14), purchasing the deed to a field (Jer 32:6-15), burying stones in some pavement (Jer 43:8-13), and casting a scroll into the Euphrates (Jer 51:59-64).

The prophet Nathan tells a parable to King David in order to bypass his intellectual rationalization (2 Sam 12:1-7). Another prophet physically wounds himself to embody God's word to Ahab (1 Kings 20:35-43). God commands Hosea to marry the prostitute Gomer in order to dramatically and existentially personify Israel's spiritual adultery and God's grace (Hos 1:2; 3:1). And the children of Hosea become incarnational images of the New Covenant promise.[10] Even more dramatic and existential, God takes the life of the prophet Ezekiel's wife as a sign for how he will treat rebellious Israel during the captivity under Babylon (Ezek 24:15-27). In the New Testament, God uses the visual spectacle of a picnic blanket filled with unclean animals to persuade Peter of the New Covenant inclusion of Gentiles (Acts 10). Agabus binds his hands as a prophetic enactment of Paul's future in Rome (Acts 21:11).

Several books of the Bible are deliberately structured according to theatrical conventions. The books of Job and Jonah are depicted in dialogues reminiscent of ancient plays, including prologues, epilogues and several acts. Job's friends function as the chorus of ancient theatrical performances. God's theological discourse with Job is not so much a rational lecture of truth as it is a dramatic exhibition of sarcastic rebuke—all from within a sensational tornado as God's microphone. The book of Mark resembles a Greek tragedy following Aristotelian structure, involving a prologue (Mk 1:1-15), complications (Mk 1:16—8:26), a recognition scene (Mk 8:27-30) and a

---

[10] Hosea's first child is named Jezreel, which means "scattered by God," predicting the Diaspora of the Jews. The second child's name, Lo-Ruhamah, means "without mercy," and the third, Lo-Ammi, means "not my people." God then summarizes this incarnational prophecy of images in Hosea 1:10, which is quoted by Paul in Romans 9:25-26 as a prophecy of the New Covenant.

reversal of the fortunes of the leading character followed by the denouement (Mk 8:31—16:8).[11]

That Scripture follows conventional, even pagan art forms does not imply that Scripture is fictional. God considers theatrical expression to be a highly valuable means of communicating truth even if modern Christians do not. In fact, the use of narrative and drama to communicate God's Word and covenant is so prevalent in Scripture that some theologians suggest we approach our theology in dramatic terms rather than the usual modernist metaphysical terms of facts, ideas and propositions. Kevin Vanhoozer suggests we see the Bible not as "a handbook of revealed information, the systematization of which leads to a set of doctrinal truths," but as a dramatic script written by God for the stage of the world, with humans as the actors, God as the author, the Holy Spirit as director, and the church as playing out the final act. "To become a Christian is to be taken up into the drama of God's plan for creation."[12] Theology is not an intellectual exercise of mentally constructing an accurate picture of reality in our ideas—and of "being right." It is a theatrical performance, where Christians participate in God's story of redemption. In this sense, our understanding of God is not so much *theology* (the study of God's Word), but *theo-drama* (the performance of God's Word).[13]

Story Conventions in the Bible

Modernists tend to be suspicious of claims that Scripture follows conventional art forms because they assume this places an artificial constraint on the Word of God. "Straightforward" historical accounts or "eyewitness testimony" is considered to be the unadulterated presentation of God's truth. But all telling of history follows cultural norms and structures, oftentimes even pagan ones. There is simply no such thing as a stripped-down "account of history" without human convention or interpretation.

For example, the covenantal structure that many scholars have discovered in biblical covenants as well as the literary structure of the entire Pentateuch reflects the structure of Ancient near Eastern pagan Suzerain treaties between conquering kings and their vassal subjects.[14] Those scholars do not consider

---

[11]"Theater," *Dictionary of Biblical Imagery*, OakTree Software.

[12]Vanhoozer, *Drama of Doctrine*, p. 71.

[13]Ibid.

[14]Meredith G. Kline, *The Structure of Biblical Authority* (Eugene, Ore.: Wipf and Stock, 1997).

such accommodation to be syncretism (compromise with the world) but rather an adaptation of cultural norms of communication. In the same way, dramatic structure applied to biblical events does not necessarily mean history or truth is being abandoned or altered but rather that all human understanding of truth is organized and structured according to some paradigm of interpretation. There are no brute facts. All literature is an author's interpretation.

The legal structure employed in some Old Testament literature does not consist of actual legal documents, but legal communication *embodied through narrative*. In the same way, New Testament theology in such letters as Romans follows a linear and rational structure, but as scholar James D. G. Dunn points out, "is still far removed from a dogmatic or systematic treatise on theology."[15] Romans, like all New Testament epistles, is written to a specific church addressing specific historical problems with practical application of doctrinal truth. This is not to deny the value of systematics or legal protocol but merely to dethrone these approaches from their modernist exaltation as highest priorities in understanding God.

It would be most appropriate to describe Scripture as eclectic in its approach to communication and persuasion. In his Gospel, Luke sets about to corroborate eyewitness testimony and settle some factual disputes, written toward a mostly Gentile audience. Matthew seems to focus on Jewish readers, stressing Old Testament symbolism. John's Gospel reads like a hybrid of Qumran apocalyptic and Hellenistic wisdom.[16] Leviticus may stress legal liturgical details, but Job is an epic sweeping play. Both major and minor prophets are often written as lawsuits to a judge, but unlike modern legal procedure, they are written poetically and allusively. In fact, many biblical prophecies are virtual film festivals of shocking images, metaphors and similes.

The modern Cartesian emphasis on clear and distinct ideas (systematic theology and rational propositions) has a difficult time pinning down the prophets' ubiquitous use of ambiguous metaphors, parables and symbols. To this day, theologians cannot agree on their interpretations of several prophetic visions with absolute certainty. From Daniel's puzzling monsters to Revelation's mysterious

---

[15] James D. G. Dunn, *The Theology of Paul the Apostle*, (Grand Rapids: Eerdmans, 1998), p. 25.

[16] I am not suggesting that the Gospel of John is Hellenistic or that it evolved from Hellenism—as the history of religions school wrongly argues. There is simply a stylistic identification with, or reflection of, the surrounding Greek culture. We use the cultural genres that we are embedded within to communicate our unique perspective. The Gospel of John is more basically Jewish, indicating that it is a Hebrew subversion of Hellenistic genre rather than a synthesis of it. See James H. Charlesworth, ed., *John and the Dead Sea Scrolls* (New York: Crossroad, 1991). More on subversion in chapters four and five.

beasts, God's images may be doorways into truth, but they are not always analytically precise or understandably clear (2 Pet 3:16).

Sometimes revelatory images are explained clearly (Gen 41:25-32), sometimes they are not (see Ezek 1; Mt 13:10-11; and Revelation). And sometimes they are explained and yet remain obscure (Dan 7). Christians have battled without final resolution for centuries over the meaning of Gog and Magog in Ezekiel 38—39. Commentators agree that the Millennium passage (Rev 20) is one of the most difficult in Scripture to interpret. Is the book of Revelation a symbolic allegory of the cyclical history of the church, as in amillennialism; an ancient description of a literal future, as in premillennialism; or historical symbolism of past history, as in postmillennialism? Yet all of these interpretations are considered legitimate orthodox Christian alternatives. One of them may be right, but all of them could be wrong. Why wasn't God more clear? If only God would have given us a systematic theological index!

Ezekiel's famous epic vision of measuring the temple takes a full four chapters of description (Ezek 40—43). Even though God tells Ezekiel to describe this temple to the people of Israel (43:10-11), scholars have pointed out that this cannot be a literal rebuilt temple because its measurements exceed the capacity of Jerusalem to house it.[17] The measurements, though apparently precise, do not match Solomon's temple nor the actual Temple built by the Jews afterward. We might speculate from the New Testament that this is a spiritual symbol of the rebuilt temple that the body of Christ has become (Eph 2:19-21; 1 Cor 3:16; 6:19; 2 Cor 6:16), but this is still speculation, because God did not give a clear word of explanation.

This is not to say that truth or Scripture is relative or that allusiveness of meaning is a sign of unimportance, but only that our reasoning should be humbled. So-called rational certainty is simply not applicable to the many puzzling mysteries of Scripture. Maybe, just maybe, God didn't want the "precision" of systematic theology or "certainty" of scientific analysis, since he often avoided those ways of communicating in favor of narrative, aesthetic or poetic imagination.

The fear of ambiguity and allusive meaning causes modernist Christians to interpret biblical parables as containing one theological meaning. They want the parables and stories to be mere illustrations of a doctrinal idea. But this

---

[17]Patrick Fairbairn, *The Visions of Ezekiel* (London: Wakeman Trust, 1851, reprint 2000) p. 433.

misses the heart and intent of ancient storytelling. Scholar Kenneth E. Bailey, an expert on Middle Eastern New Testament studies, explains that

> a biblical story is not simply a "delivery system" for an idea. Rather, the story first creates a world and then invites the listener to live in that world, to take it on as part of who he or she is.... In reading and studying the Bible, ancient tales are not examined merely in order to extract a theological principle or ethical model.[18]

Theologian Kevin Vanhoozer agrees that doctrinal propositions are not "more basic" than the narrative and in fact fail to communicate what narrative can. He writes in his book *The Drama of Doctrine*, "Narratives make story-shaped points that cannot always be paraphrased in propositional statements without losing something in translation."[19] If you try to scientifically dissect the parable you will kill it, and if you discard the carcass once you have your doctrine, you have discarded the heart of God.

Bailey concludes that such stories and parables are means of understanding truth through existential inhabitation of the story. As we enter into the stories and see ourselves in them, we see truth in a way that mere logical or doctrinal discourse simply cannot evoke. But such imaginative inhabitation of stories becomes messy for the Christian who wants to have rational certainty. It makes God's truth a bit too ambiguous and subjective.

Rather than ignoring portions of God's word which do not meet the scientific analytic precision of modernity, we should chasten our rationality. Analytic precision and systematic reasoning are not God's preferred means of communication. Imagination through word pictures and story, with their existential embodiment and their rational imprecision and ambiguity, is God-ordained language after all.

Metaphor

Jesus taught about the kingdom of God mostly through parables. And those parables communicated invisible reality in terms of visible, sensate and dramatic images and metaphors. To him, the kingdom of God was far too deep and rich a

---

[18] Kenneth E. Bailey, *Jacob and the Prodigal: How Jesus Retold Israel's Story* (Downers Grove, Ill.: InterVarsity Press, 2003), p. 51.

[19] Vanhoozer, *Drama of Doctrine*, p. 50.

truth to entrust to rational abstract propositions. He chose pearls, dragnets, leaven, mustard seeds, virgins, children, slaves, hired workers, vineyards, and buried treasure over syllogisms, abstraction, systematics or dissertations. And his usage of such metaphors and images was not a primitive form of discourse, as if ancient Jews were not sophisticated enough to understand abstraction. In fact, at the time of the writing of the New Testament, Israel was educationally immersed in the Hellenistic culture that dominated the Middle East with its heavily abstract thinking. Jesus could do abstraction. He chose not to.

It would be more accurate to say that stories and parables were the dominant means used by Jesus to convey theological truth as opposed to propositional logic or theological abstraction. As scholar N. T. Wright suggests, "It would be clearly quite wrong to see these stories as mere illustrations of truths that could in principle have been articulated in a purer, more abstract form."[20] He reminds us that theological terms like *monotheism* "are late constructs, convenient shorthands for sentences with verbs in them [narrative], and that sentences with verbs in them are the real stuff of theology, not mere childish expressions of a 'purer' abstract truth."[21] Wright concludes that storytelling is in fact the way theology was done in both Testaments:

> If Jesus or the evangelists tell stories, this does not mean that they are leaving history or theology out of the equation and doing something else, instead.... [If] this is how Israel's theology... found characteristic expression, we should not be surprised if Christian theology, at least in its early forms, turns out to be similar.[22]

Brad Young, who has written in depth on the Jewishness of Jesus' theology, reminds us that the Western view of theology as a discipline is more philosophical than Jesus' own Eastern culture within which he taught.

As Christians, we study God and systematize belief. The Eastern mind tends to view God through the emotions of human personality and individual experience. God is viewed through the lens of metaphors and parables of real life, which make the abstract concepts more concrete.[23]

---

[20] N. T. Wright, *The New Testament and the People of God* (Minneapolis: Fortress, 1992), p. 77.
[21] Ibid., p. 78.
[22] Ibid.
[23] Brad H. Young, *Jesus the Jewish Theologian* (Peabody, Mass.: Hendrickson, 1995), p. 272.

Our Western bias toward rational discourse can too easily blind us to the biblical power of story and word pictures to embody truth. Bailey writes about the tendency of Western culture with its stress on reason and logic to reduce biblical metaphors and parables to mere illustrations of concepts, as if word pictures or images were not essential but rather mere window dressing to the teaching of theological truth. "This," he says, "is a time honored way to 'do theology.'" But then he enlightens us,

> There is, however, another way to create and communicate meaning. It involves the use of word pictures, dramatic actions, metaphors and stories. This latter method of "doing theology" shines through the pages of Scripture. Dale Allison has written, "Meaning is like water: it is shaped by the container it fills." The biblical writers and reciters make extensive use of metaphors, parables and dramatic actions. Jesus does not say, "God's love is boundless," Instead, he tells the story of the prodigal son. He does not say, "Your benevolence must reach beyond your own kith and kin." Rather, he tells the story of the Good Samaritan.[24]

Bailey sees Jesus as "clearly a 'metaphorical theologian' whose primary style of creating meaning was the skillful use of metaphor, parable and dramatic action."[25] And this "word picture" theology means that stories are not mere carriers of doctrine, as if they can be discarded once the doctrine or "truth" is figured out. A parable does not contain a single truth or doctrine. It is a complex web of relationships and ambiguity interacting with the audience and their understanding and misunderstanding of God. Stories must be inhabited by the audience for the truth to be understood properly. They cannot be separated from the truth they embody.[26]

The parable of the prodigal son, for instance, is a complex network of metaphors for Jesus (the father), Gentiles and outcasts (the younger son), self-righteous Jews (the older son) and their relationships. Bailey contends that the parable is not even intended to express salvation of an individual as much as it is intended to be a retelling of the story of Jacob (and therefore, the

---

[24] Bailey, *Jacob and the Prodigal*, pp. 21-22.

[25] Ibid., p. 22.

[26] Ibid., pp. 51-52.

story of Israel) with Jesus as the replacement of Israel, along with other challenges to people's view of God.[27]

It was certainly an enlightening moment in my own life when I came to realize my modernist prejudice in considering modern theological terms superior to biblical imagery and stories. Table 2 is an example of the kind of comparisons I had to make to reflect on my modernizing tendency.

C. S. Lewis pointed out that the technical term for God, "The transcendent Ground of Being," is simply not as rich or full of meaning as the scriptural metaphor "Our Father who art in heaven."[28] Of course, the creation of theological terms is not inherently wrong, and metaphors are not the only way in which Scripture communicates God's attributes. But we have to be careful that our theological shorthand will not overshadow or replace biblical longhand. The very theological words themselves reflect the modernist tendency to reduce truth to scientific terminology (every word having the suffix of "ology" or "ence"), which may ultimately depersonalize faith and cast theology as a "scientific" study rather than a holistic biblical relationship with God.

Table 2. Modern Theological Terms and Corresponding Biblical Images	
Modern Theological Term	**Biblical Image**
Omnipotence	God has a strong right arm (Ps 89:13)
Omnipresence	If I make my bed in Sheol, you are there (Ps 139:8)
Omniscience	God counts the hairs on your head (Ps 139:9)
Transcendence	People are grasshoppers to God (Is 40:2)
Immanence	You have enclosed me behind and before (Ps 139:4)
Immutability	God will not wear out like clothes (Ps 102:26)
Aseity	I am the Alpha and Omega (Rev 22:13)
Providence	We are the clay, God is our potter (Is 64:8)

Scholar Peter J. Leithart goes so far as to say that theology as modern Christians understand it is *against* the biblical approach to truth, precisely because theology uses a professional language that is academic and obscure, "whereas the Bible talks about trees and stars, about donkeys and barren women, about kings and queens and carpenters."

---

[27]Ibid.

[28]Kevin Vanhoozer, "The Semantics of Biblical Literature," in *Hermeneutics, Authority and Canon*, ed. D. A. Carson and John D. Woodbridge (Grand Rapids: Zondervan, 1986), p. 78.

> Theology tells us that God is eternal and unchangeable in His being, wisdom, power, holiness, justice, goodness and truth. The Bible tells us that God relents because He is God (Joel 2:13-14), that God is "shrewd with the shrewd" (Psa. 18:25-29), that he rejoices over us with shouting (Zeph. 3:14-20), and that He is an eternal whirlwind of triune communion and love. Theology is a "Victorian" enterprise, neoclassically bright and neat and clean, nothing out of place. Whereas the Bible talks about hair, blood, sweat, entrails, menstruation and genital emissions.[29]

Israel's theology was *told as stories*. The organizing principles of Jewish theology are characteristically expressed through narratives of creation, election, exodus, monarchy, exile and return.[30] So it was most appropriate when Jesus and the apostles proclaimed the New Covenant as the fulfillment of those stories—in stories and parables as well. Wright, a Pauline scholar, points out that even the apostle Paul's most "emphatically 'theological' statements and arguments are in fact expressions of the essentially Jewish story now redrawn around Jesus."[31] He points out that for the early Christians, disputes "were carried on not so much by appeal to fixed principles, or to Jewish scripture conceived as a rag-bag of proof-texts, but precisely by fresh retellings of the story which highlighted the points at issue... not a theory or a new ethic, not an abstract dogma or rote-learned teaching, but a particular story told and lived."[32]

It would not be an exaggeration to suppose that Jesus would probably be scolded by conservative evangelical theologues for not taking the kingdom of God more seriously, because he seemed to spend most of his time telling confusing stories rather than tightly organized three-point sermons. And even worse, Jesus would often avoid explaining those stories, preferring the "dangerous" ambiguity that modern evangelicals complain leads to an unclear "gospel presentation" or subjective interpretation (Mt 13:10-15). Jesus just wasn't precise enough by modern theological standards. Jesus just wasn't a modern evangelical.

---

[29] Peter Leithart, *Against Christianity* (Moscow, Id.: Canon Press, 2003), pp. 46-47.
[30] Wright, *New Testament*, p. 215.
[31] Ibid., p. 79.
[32] Ibid., p. 456.

The Tabernacle and Temple

Even a cursory look at the visual detail that God dictated to Moses for the tabernacle illustrates that imagery is valuable to God; he commands it as part of the holiest of activities—worship.

Part of the traditionalist Christian suspicion of imagery in worship comes from a misinterpretation of the Second Commandment prohibiting the worship of images.

> You shall not make for yourself an idol, or any likeness of what is in heaven above or on the earth beneath or in the water under the earth. You shall not worship them or serve them; for I, the LORD your God, am a jealous God. (Ex 20:4-5)

Some Christians expand the command against worshiping images into a broader suspicion of *all* images, as if God himself is telling us to avoid imagery *in* worship because images are manipulative and dangerous, and lead to idolatry.

This is a shameful distortion of Scripture that creates an unbiblical Christian culture. "To use in worship" is not the same thing as "to worship." Five chapters after God tells the Israelites not to make likenesses of things in heaven or on earth to worship them, he commands the Israelites to make likenesses of things in heaven and on earth *to use in their worship of God!* God directs artists to make images of angels on the Ark of the Covenant (Ex 25:18). He has them craft almond trees and blossoms on the Holy Place instruments (Ex 25:31). He tells them to make pomegranates on the hems of the high priest (Ex 28:33), along with stones on his breastplate that function as symbolic references to the twelve tribes (Ex 28:25). Later, when God has Solomon build the temple, he adds even more visual images of things in heaven and on earth: huge statues of angels in the Most Holy Place, *the location of the very presence of God* (1 Kings 6:23-27); an altar imaged as a molten sea on the back of a dozen oxen with a rim like a lily flower (2 Chron 3—4); angels, palm trees and flowers carved and engraved all over the place (1 Kings 6:35); and multitudes of beautiful materials, precious metals, precious stones, rare woods, exotic colorful linens and other architectural visuals (2 Chron 3—4). At the very heart of the covenant worship of God was *beautiful sensate imagery.*

To all this visual imagery, add loud music (1 Chron 23:5), hundreds of singers singing their theology through psalms (1 Chron 25:6-7) and myriads of dancers (Ps 150), and you have an image-rich experience of God. It now makes more sense what the psalmist meant when he wrote:

> One thing I have asked from the LORD, that I shall seek: That I may dwell in the house of the LORD all the days of my life, *To behold the beauty* of the LORD And to meditate in His temple. (Ps 27:4, emphasis added)

God's truth and beauty were reflected in the beautiful *imagery* of the temple. And the use of such manifold images in worshiping God was not inherently suspicious or idolatrous. Only the use of images as objects themselves of veneration would fit that category.

Sacrament

Most Protestants agree that there are at least two sacraments in the Christian faith, Baptism and the Lord's Supper. Some theologians consider sacraments to be a "means" of grace. At the very least, they are visual *images* of our belief, or as Augustine put it, "the visible sign[s] of an invisible grace."[33]

Baptism is an experiential image of death to sin and resurrection in Christ (Rom 6:1-7), a cleansing of sin (1 Pet 3:18-21). The Lord's Supper is a memorial image of uniting with God through symbolically consuming him (Jn 6:48-58). This imagery of eating the flesh and drinking the blood of Christ was so prevalent in the early church that Christians were accused by pagans of cannibalism.[34] You can't get any more image-focused than that.

Such eating of the flesh of deity was also used by pagans (Jer 7:18), which leads some theologians to conclude that one evolved out of the other. But this evolutionary theory of the sacrament is a silly non-sequitur. Different religions use similar images because we all create from the same human pool of imagination and thought.[35]

---

[33] Allan D. Fitzgerald et al., ed., *Augustine Through the Ages* (Grand Rapids: Eerdmans, 1999), p. 707.

[34] From Minucius Felix, "Octavius," *The Ante-Nicene Fathers,* vol. 4, trans. R. E. Wallis, AGES Software (Albany, Ore.: AGES Software 2.0, 1997), pp. 348-49.

[35] The Aztecs, who ate sacramental bread as the flesh of a deity, had no cultural connection to the Middle East. From Sir James George Frazer, "Eating the God Among the Aztecs," in *The Golden Bough: A Study in Magic and Religion,* accessed February 5, 2008, at <http://www.bartleby.com/196/121.html>.

Most modern evangelicals experience the Lord's Supper as a purely symbolic act in their church service. They eat a piece of bread or cracker and take a sip of grape juice or wine. But the first Christians had a fuller experience of the Lord's Supper as an embedded element of a total meal eaten together (1 Cor 11:20-23). The Lord's Supper was, after all, an adaptation of the Passover meal, also an entire meal eaten in its fullness as a sacramental experience, not a solitary symbolic gesture (Lk 22:7-20). In a way, evangelicals have wrested the symbolic act of communion from its more incarnate image of a full meal. *We have turned a meal that is symbolic into a symbol that is meal-like.* Why? Because word is more important to us than image. We tend to think that what's most important is the abstract idea, not the concrete experience, so why not reduce the idea of communion to its simplest symbolic act? And thus we build a version of Christianity that is more modernist than biblical.

Atonement through Christ's death on the cross was prefigured in Numbers 21, when God had Moses craft a bronze sculpture of a serpent on a pole to use as a sacrament of deliverance (healing) for those bitten by fiery serpents (Jn 3:14-15). We see from the episode that *visual art was used as a means of grace by God.* Later in 2 Kings 18:3-4, we learn that that image became an idol. But once again, we must note the difference between an image being used "in worship" as a sacramental means of grace and an image being an object of veneration or worship itself.

Those who argue for the priority of word over image will sometimes say that the images of sacraments are dependent on words for their meaning. Without textual context, for example, baptism remains mere splashing of water. Without verbalization of the meaning, the Lord's Supper is a mere meal. True enough. But this does not prove the *superiority* of words over images but rather the *interdependency* of words and images. For without the incarnate experiences of splashing water and consuming the bread and wine, the words remain mere abstractions. In sacrament, word and image are beautifully intertwined with equal ultimacy. You cannot have one without the other. The *Dictionary of Biblical Imagery* explains that

> the Bible is much more a book of images and motifs than of abstractions and propositions.... The stories, the parables, the sermons of the prophets, the reflections of the wise men, the pictures of the age to come, the interpretations of past

events all tend to be expressed in images which arise out of experience. They do not often arise out of abstract technical language... The Bible is a book that images the truth as well as stating it in abstract propositions.[36]

The Bible is rich with images in its theological method and worship of God. It is filled with imagination and word pictures, overflowing with poetic language and sensate imagery, dominated by narrative or story. In contrast, modern theology's emphasis on systematic and scientific discourse places it in danger of inadequacy and a serious misunderstanding of God, for the structure and method of theology affects the content of theology. If the Bible communicates God and truth (theology) primarily through story, image, symbol and metaphor, then a theology that neglects those methods is not being strictly biblical in its method. A scientific approach to God will ultimately depersonalize God through analysis and redefine Christianity through philosophical abstraction rather than embodying God's personal presence through lived-out stories.

So the question naturally arises, how did we get here? Where did this scientific and systematic suspicion and rejection of imagination start? That is for the next chapter.

---

[36] "Introduction," *Dictionary of Biblical Imagery*, OakTree Software.

Chapter 4
Iconoclasm

With all this imagery saturating the Scriptures, why is there such a lack of aesthetic understanding and development in the evangelical tradition? We find a partial answer in the iconoclasm of the sixteenth-century Reformation, which freed art from its captivity to the religious dogma of immanence but simultaneously recaptivated it to a new dogma of transcendence.

By the late Middle Ages (1300-1500), the Roman Catholic Church was the dominant religious force of the Western world. Its worship culture emphasized immanence—spiritual relationship with God was mediated through physical objects and the senses of the worshiper. This immanence stressed God's involvement with the created order, imparting grace or redemption through visible objects. Relics of alleged pieces of saints' bodies or fragments of Christ's cross were housed in shrines with altars, which the faithful would make pilgrimages to see. William Dyrness notes that these objects "not only reminded worshipers of supernatural reality but actually became a detached fragment of God's power."[1] Images of Christ and the saints, called "icons," became important theological tools for teaching the illiterate as well as objects of veneration.[2]

Liturgical drama—mystery plays, passion plays and miracle plays—was commonly used during this period to instruct peasants and celebrate feasts, festivals, and holy days. Churches were huge, glorious edifices full of wood and stone statues of the Virgin Mary, saints, prophets and martyrs; paintings of everything from the birth of Christ to his resurrection, and stained glass windows depicting the "stations of the cross." Medieval Christians of the era, Dyrness concludes, "took it for granted that the human relationship to God and

---

[1] William A. Dyrness, *Visual Faith: Art, Theology and Worship in Dialogue* (Grand Rapids: Baker, 2001), p. 34.

[2] William A. Dyrness, *Reformed Theology and Visual Culture: The Protestant Imagination from Calvin to Edwards* (Cambridge: Cambridge University Press, 2004), p. 21.

the supernatural world was visually reflected and mediated through this visible order of things."[3] Scholar Margaret Miles explains that in an image-rich church,

> the worshipper was placed bodily in relation to a visually articulated spiritual universe. The present earthbound gravity of the individual worshipper was emphasized by his or her physical location beneath whirling scenes of heavenly bliss in which saintly human beings, angels, scriptural figures, and putti [winged cherubs] achieved a weightlessness that translated the ultimate goal of the spiritual life into visual terms.[4]

The Reformers saw such mediatorial art as distracting at best and idolatrous at worst. Ulrich Zwingli described the slavish devotion that parishioners would engage in before these images:

> Men kneel, bow, and remove their hats before them; candles and incense are burned before them; men name them after the saints whom they represent; men kiss them; men adorn them with gold and jewels; men designate them with the appellation merciful or gracious; men seek consolation merely from touching them, or even hope to acquire remission of their sins thereby.[5]

The cult of relics and images was vehemently preached against by the Reformers, and the people repented by vandalizing and destroying such images in churches throughout the land. Leaders of the Reformation condemned this vigilante iconoclasm as illegal and immoral, but they could not control the monster of vigilante iconoclasm they had birthed.[6]

The Elevation of the Word and the Liberation of the Arts

Rather than being an elimination of visual culture, however, the iconoclasm replaced the visual culture of immanence with a visual culture of

---

[3] Ibid., p. 26.
[4] Margaret R. Miles, *Image as Insight: Visual Understanding in Western Christianity and Secular Culture* (Boston: Beacon Press, 1985), p. 110.
[5] Ulrich Zwingli, quoted in ibid., p. 99.
[6] Sergiusz Michalski, *The Reformation and the Visual Arts: The Protestant Image Question in Western and Eastern Europe* (New York: Routledge, 2005), p. 74.

transcendence.[7] If immanence stressed God within the created order, transcendence stressed God's separation from the created order. Necessarily more abstract, transcendence became the new focus of Reformers such as John Calvin, who "privileged the ear over the eye" by elevating the written and preached word over the visual image as God's superior means of communication.[8] Margaret Miles describes it as a new "elitism of the word."[9]

The removal of images from churches gave visual expression to the belief that worshiping God was an internal spiritual matter, not an external one. Bare, stark white churches were not a rejection of imagery per se, but rather an attempt to refocus believers on the transcendent nature of God. Zwingli gleefully described churches in Zurich, Switzerland, "which are positively luminous; the walls are beautifully white."[10] This plainness of design lent a new voice to the role of minimalism and elegant simplicity in artistry, not to be confused necessarily with ugliness or lack of aesthetic.

Sola Scriptura, a key doctrine of the Reformation that Scripture alone was the final authority over the church, did not merely dismantle the hierarchy of power that the priesthood wielded over the masses. It also became an influence on the church architecture and worship as well.[11] As word became privileged over image, and the ear privileged over the eye, Protestant churches recentered the church service around the preached word.[12] All instruction, prayers and singing were organized around the preached word. Images on display were often typographic displays of Scripture; illuminated manuscripts, because their artistry supported the text of Scripture, continued to be created.

---

[7] Dyrness, Reformed Theology, p. 6. See also, Margaret Miles, *Image as Insight*, pp. 122-23.

[8] Dyrness, *Reformed Theology*, p. 6.

[9] Miles, *Image as Insight*, p. 104.

[10] Paul Corby Finney, ed., *Seeing Beyond the Word: Visual Arts and the Calvinist Tradition* (Grand Rapids: Eerdmans, 1999), p. 13.

[11] A corollary to this internalization of the truth from public concrete visual expression to personal inner abstract piety is the spectre of individualism. Author Daniel Hardy explains that Medieval churches "enacted communal society by extended liturgical performances," while Protestant meetinghouses, the replacement of Roman cathedrals, "housed the inner transformation of individuals by the preached Word of God" (quoted in ibid., p. 9.) The turn from externalized religion to internalized religion was not merely an exchange of outward idolatry with "true" spirituality as the Reformers claimed. It also tended toward an elevation of the individual conscience as supreme arbiter. Luther's famous stand of conviction, "my conscience is captive to the Word of God," is a profound break with the authoritarianism of the Roman Church and an expression of the Bible as supreme authority, but it also carried with it the seeds of individualism and sectarian dogmatism that led to intolerant splintering of Protestant creeds and churches, and in some ways, fueled the bloody Thirty Years' War (Kevin Vanhoozer, *Is There a Meaning in This Text?* [Grand Rapids: Zondervan, 1998], p. 171).

[12] Finney, *Seeing Beyond the Word*, pp. 8-9.

Because of the Reformed belief in the priesthood of believers rather than a priesthood of elite religious authorities, all of life—not merely church life—became sacred. And that included the arts. Zwingli and Calvin never disparaged visual art used for "secular" purposes. Their focus was on images used in worship.[13] Consequently, the arts were liberated from a religious stranglehold of "grand ideological and religious systems."[14] In the words of William Tyndale,

> There is no work better than another to please God; to pour water, to wash dishes, to be a cobbler, or an apostle, all are one; to wash dishes and to preach are all one, as touching the deed, to please God.[15]

Martin Luther was even stronger in his denunciation of the secular-sacred dichotomy:

> The idea that the service to God should have only to do with a church altar, singing, reading, sacrifice, and the like is without doubt but the worst trick of the devil.... The whole world could abound with the services to the Lord, not only in churches but also in the home, kitchen, workshop, field.[16]

One would not have to paint a scene from the Bible in order to honor God with their art. Simple ornamentation could do so. Still lifes took on a whole new sacred meaning, along with paintings of everyday life. Before this time, portrait painting was dominated by aristocracy and wealthy merchants. The Protestant Reformation brought a populist effect on aesthetics with an increase in art depicting the "common man."

The Calvinist concept of nature being God's "second book of truth" led to the origin and development of the famous seventeenth-century landscape art of the Dutch Netherlands.[17] Reformed artists like Albrecht Dürer are credited with being major influences on the origin of landscape painting, something that

---

[13] John Calvin, *Commentary on Genesis, vol. 1, Genesis 4:20* (Albany, Ore.: Ages Software 1.0, 1998); Michalski, *Reformation and the Visual Arts*, p. 71.

[14] Michalski, *Reformation and the Visual Arts*, p. 194.

[15] William Tyndale, *A Parable of the Wicked Mammon* (1527), accessed February 5, 2008, at <www.xristos.com/Pages/Quotes_page.htm>.

[16] Martin Luther, accessed February 5, 2008, at <www.xristos.com/Pages/Quotes_page.htm>.

[17] Reindert L. Falkenburg, "Calvinism and the Emergence of Dutch Seventeenth-Century Landscape Art," in Finney, *Seeing Beyond the Word*, pp. 343-51.

was considered without much merit until this paradigm change.[18] After all, if creation glorifies God as his handiwork of beauty, why wouldn't a simple landscape do so as well as an altar piece of the Last Supper?

The Enlightenment caricature of the Reformers as having a "horror of art" was a misrepresentation.[19] At the same time that Zwingli was removing pipe organs and images from the churches of Zurich, he was playing regularly in an instrumental group and illustrating his tracts on the Lord's Supper with wood engravings.[20] In a sense, Protestant iconoclasm made the whole of life religious, not merely church life, and it was the theological foundation of the liberation of the arts from exclusively ecclesiastical use. The Reformers were not opposed in principle to the arts, but rather to the adoration and sanctification of works of art in religious liturgy.

Suspicion of Image and Devaluation of Aesthetics

Yet, in spite of this artistic liberation that came through Reformation theology, evident in the music and art of the era (including Reformed masters such as Rembrandt and Dürer), there is nevertheless a lack of visual and dramatic tradition in Protestantism.[21] The Reformation suspicion of images soon bled into the prevailing secular culture to include many forms of imagination and creativity. As Dyrness notes, "all attempts at using imagery, drama, even cultural festivities, in the service of the communication of Christian truth appeared to be given up by around 1580."[22] It was a pendulum swing that would impact Protestant involvement in the arts for centuries to come.[23]

This extreme reaction is not entirely without justification, when one considers the tendency of human nature to be, as Calvin put it, a "factory of idols." In the same way an alcoholic must abstain from drinking in order to get well, so a populace infected with widespread idolatrous worship of images opted for a radical response. Martin Luther attempted a call to moderation, but such titans of the Word as Calvin, Zwingli, Knox, Bucer and others wrote extensively about the

---

[18]Gene Edward Veith, *Painters of Faith: The Spiritual Landscape in Nineteenth-Century America* (Washington, D.C.: Regnery, 2001), p. 21.

[19]Philip Benedict, "Calvinism as a Culture?" in Finney, *Seeing Beyond the Word*, p. 21.

[20]James R. Tanis, "Netherlandish Reformed Traditions in the Graphic Arts, 1550-1630," in Finney, *Seeing Beyond the Word*, p. 372.

[21]Michalski, *The Reformation and the Visual Arts*, p. 40. See Veith's Painters of Faith for an excellent exploration of the Dutch tradition and its profound impact on landscape painting.

[22]Dyrness, *Reformed Theology*, p. 124. Also Benedict, "Calvinism as a Culture?" p. 31.

[23]Finney, *Seeing Beyond the Word*, p. 8.

wrong use of images but comparatively little on the right use of the arts—occasional and scattered sidebars or tangents pertaining to a particular Scripture, but almost nothing of significant theological development.[24] The net effect of this virtual ignoring of the theological value of art is the implicit devaluing of it. As the saying goes, actions speak louder than words, and a systematic theology without a developed aesthetic is an implicit sign of an underlying belief that beauty is not an essential part of theology.

Calvin's prejudice was clearly didacticism, an elevation of utility and doctrinal teaching as the supreme form of communication. Thus, his tendency was to favor representational art of historical events used to "admonish" or "teach" over other imagery that was more decorative or abstract because they had "no value for teaching." In one of the only places where he writes more than a passing comment about art, Calvin refers to musical instruments, and by extension the other arts as well, as being able to "minister to our pleasure, rather than to our necessity, still it is not to be thought altogether superfluous; much less does it deserve, in itself, to be condemned."[25] Hey, at least it's not altogether superfluous; only partially superfluous.

In their appeal to divert the money for church decoration to the poor, Calvin and others unwittingly devalued art further.[26] But both beauty and charity are important to God and both are necessary. God gave commands to love the poor (Deut 15) *and* collected massive amounts of money to build the splendorous Tabernacle (Ex 36), a model reflected in cathedrals and their ornamentation. Excess can be waste, but splendor and beauty are not intrinsically excess.

In Matthew 26, a woman pours expensive perfume on Jesus' feet. The disciples complain with a similar refrain to that of Luther and Calvin: "Why this waste? For this perfume might have been sold for a high price and the money given to the poor" (Mt 26:8-9). Jesus puts them in their place by saying that she has done a good thing, not a wasteful thing, in symbolic preparation for his burial.

---

[24]Ibid., p. 79.

[25]"And yet I am not gripped by the superstition of thinking absolutely no images permissible. But because sculpture and painting are gifts of God, I seek a pure and legitimate use of each. Therefore it remains that only those things are to be sculptured or painted which the eyes are capable of seeing. . . . Within this class some are histories and events, some are images and forms of bodies without any depicting of past events. The former have some use in teaching or admonition; as for the latter, I do not see what they can afford other than pleasure. And yet it is clear that almost all the images that until now have stood in churches were of this sort. . . . I only say that even if the use of images contained nothing evil, it still has no value for teaching." John Calvin, *Institutes of the Christian Religion* 1:11:12 (Albany, Ore.: AGES Software 1.0, 1998).

[26]Michalski, Reformation and the Visual Arts, p. 69; and Benedict, "Calvinism as a Culture?" p. 28.

Perfume was used to mask the smell of death with an attractive aroma—a symbol of eternal life (Lk 23:56). Beauty is not waste. Christians, in their zeal for theology, often neglect the necessity for aesthetic beauty in their worldview.[27]

It could be said that the various Reformed strains of art that did survive the iconoclasm controversy did so in spite of the dominant voices of iconoclasts. Calvinists like Rembrandt would paint pictures of Christ despite the accusation by many that this was a violation of the Second Commandment. Calvinist Claes Jansz Visscher published Bibles heavily illustrated with engravings in an attempt to help people understand the stories better. (He also published political tracts against the iconoclasts.)[28] Albrecht Dürer, a Lutheran engraver, was praised by many Calvinists, despite his view that both eye and ear are necessary to our reality and relationship with God.

> The art of painting is made for the eyes, for sight is the noblest sense.... A thing you behold is easier of belief than [one] that you hear; but whatever is both heard and seen we grasp more firmly and lay hold on more securely. I will therefore continue the word with the work and thus I may be the better understood.[29]

Dürer had it right. Both word and image were necessary. Perhaps what Calvin missed in his logocentrism was that the ear is no more transcendent than the eye.[30] Both ear and eye are a God-ordained sensate part of how we interact with him.[31]

Dualism and Dichotomy

The false separation of the senses leads to a matter-spirit dualism in some Reformed theology that reflects the very secular-sacred dichotomy that Reformers debunked.[32] Reformers claimed, for example, that the immanent

---

[27] See Calvin Seerveld, *Bearing Fresh Olive Leaves: Alternative Steps in Understanding Art* (Carlisle, U.K.: Piquant, 2000), pp. 1-5.

[28] Ilja M. Veldman, "Protestantism and the Arts: Sixteenth- and Seventeenth-Century Netherlands," in Finney, *Seeing Beyond the Word*, p. 417.

[29] Albrecht Dürer, as quoted in Margaret R. Miles, *Image as Insight*, p. 116.

[30] Dyrness, *Reformed Theology*, p. 69.

[31] Ibid., p. 121.

[32] While Luther was just as emphatic of God's transcendence, he did not embrace the matter-spirit dualism of the others, seemingly maintaining an equal emphasis on God's immanence in his theology. Consequently, Luther displayed "greater attention to buildings, liturgy and music as allies in Christian

sensate worship of the Old Covenant was surpassed by a transcendent "spirit" (read: "abstract") worship of the New Testament. Hebrews 9, for example, describes the visual elements in the temple as but shadows of the true Tabernacle in heaven. The "spiritual" New Covenant is the fulfillment of the symbolic imagery of the Old Covenant temple (considered childish or immature); therefore, images are no longer important to God in worship.[33]

But this is surely a confusion of categories. It is not that the visual imagery of the temple is being superseded by an invisible abstraction. It is rather a temporary incarnation being replaced with an eternal incarnation. Hebrews 10:1 says the Old Covenant law and temple are only shadows of the heavenly temple. But that heavenly temple is no less sensate. When we are resurrected, we will be so in our physical bodies, not abstract ones (1 Cor 15:12-56)—imperishable and transformed bodies, but physical ones with senses, just like Jesus (1 Jn 3:2). So the "heavenly/shadow" comparison in this passage is not one of sensate versus abstract but perishable versus imperishable, temporary versus eternal.

When Jesus told the Samaritan woman that people would no longer worship in this mountain or that, but that "true worshippers would worship the Father in spirit and in truth" (Jn 4:24), he was not discrediting Old Testament imagery in worship, he was discrediting localized cultural exclusion of other nationalities. Elsewhere in Scripture, we are told that the church is the body of Christ, which is the rebuilt temple that God promised (Acts 15:13-18; Eph 2:19-22).[34] This is not the replacement of a physical image with an abstract spiritual idea but the expansion of the visible incarnation (image) of God's dwelling place from a specific geographical location to a worldwide universal location.

Both brick and mortar temple (Old Testament) and flesh and blood church (New Testament) are physical tabernacles of God (2 Cor 6:16). Neither is an abstract thought or spirit. In fact, the very atonement of Christ, since it is expressed in terms of Old Testament temple worship, cannot be understood in propositional abstractions apart from that imagery. The imagery has not been negated but fulfilled and extended in its meaning. Old Testament imagery is the foundation for understanding the New Covenant, and as such, is still necessary to it.

---

faith." Finney, *Seeing Beyond the Word*, pp. 16, 28.

[33] "It is absurd to drag [temple imagery] in as an example to serve our own age. For that childish age, so to speak, for which rudiments of this sort were intended is gone by." Calvin, *Institutes of the Christian Religion* 1:11:3.

[34] See also 1 Cor 3:16; 6:19; Heb 12:18-22; 2 Cor 6:16.

In the mind of the Reformers, with their emphasis on transcendence over immanence, "the finite cannot contain the infinite."[35] While this slogan may be true of the works of human hands, what is the incarnation of Christ but finite humanity containing the infinite God? In the incarnation, the ontological and theological reality of transcendence and immanence coexist in harmony. More will be said on the incarnation in the next chapter, but suffice it to say that its balance of two opposites, as with any mystery doctrine (see table 3), is degraded by an emphasis of one extreme against the other.

The Bible affirms both the transcendence and immanence of God as equally ultimate, many times in the very same passage. For instance, Paul, when preaching to the pagans on Mars Hill, at the same time affirms God's transcendence ("God does not dwell in temples made with hands") and immanence ("in Him we live and move and exist," Acts 17:24, 28). Jeremiah 23:23 asks rhetorically, "Am I a God who is near [immanence], declares the LORD, and not a God far off [transcendence]?" Colossians 1:16-17 says that all things were created "by him, through him, for him" (transcendence) "and in him all things hold together" (immanence). So a theology that fails to affirm God's transcendence and immanence with equal ultimacy is not true to the Scriptures, even if it is true to the Institutes of the Christian Faith.

Table 3. Mystery Doctrines of the Bible and the Distortions That Accompany Dualistic Separations		
One *Unitarianism*	TRINITY (John 1:1)	Many *Tritheism*
God *Docetism*	CHRIST (John 1:14)	Man *Arianism*
God's Sovereignty *Fatalism*	PROVIDENCE (Isaiah 10:12-15)	Human Responsibility *Pelagianism*
Word *Modernism*	TRUTH (John 1:14)	Image *Postmodernism*
Law *Legalism*	GOSPEL (Romans 3:20-24)	Grace *Antinomianism*
Transcendent *Existentialism* *Deism*	God (Acts 17:24, 28)	Immanent *Pantheism*

---

[35]Carlos M. Eire, *War Against the Idols: The Reformation of Worship from Erasmus to Calvin* (Cambridge: Cambridge University Press, 1986, 1998), p. 2. Also Finney, *Seeing Beyond the Word*, p. 4.

Chapter 5
Incarnation

In 2004, the movie *The Passion of the Christ* was released to an American box office bonanza of over $400 million. Evangelicals and unbelievers alike filled the theaters for this image-rich, experiential interpretation of the Gospel narratives, connecting to it in more numbers than any other filmic presentation of Christ.

Evangelicals could never have made this movie. Roman Catholic Mel Gibson was barraged with "suggestions" by well-meaning evangelical screeners of the movie to place Bible verses such as John 3:16 ("For God so loved the world that He gave His only Son") at the end because they felt that it wasn't a clear enough presentation of the gospel. If it does not have words, then it is not a reliable or trustworthy communication to moderns.

The movie *did* have words, plenty of them, and even a Bible verse to set the stage for the meaning of the violent experience the viewer was to be immersed within. It just wasn't John 3:16. It was instead Isaiah 53:5: "He was wounded for our transgressions, crushed for our iniquities; by his wounds we are healed."

Ironically, given that evangelicals have regularly boycotted R-rated movies because of sex and violence, *The Passion* is arguably one of the most violent mainstream films ever made.[1] It took a Tridentine Roman Catholic to translate the Gospels to a postmodern, image-oriented culture, because Roman Catholics maintain a theology of immanence that Protestants have overshadowed with a theology of transcendence.[2]

---

[1] The claim that it is appropriate violence because it is in the context of redemption and faith simply points up the double standard that evangelicals hold in their rejection of other violent or profane movies that are equally redemptive in their context. I write more about this in *Hollywood Worldviews: Watching Films with Wisdom and Discernment,* updated ed. (Downers Grove, Ill.: InterVarsity Press, 2009).

[2] It is no coincidence that Gibson's production company is called Icon Entertainment. Icons are images of veneration dating back to medieval Christianity.

Immanence & Idolatry

Some Evangelicals and Reformed believers read the Second Commandment—which forbids graven images of God—and conclude that pictures or movies of Jesus Christ are inherently idolatrous. This kind of reasoning led to the exclusion of the *Jesus Film Project* from a recent convention of a major Reformed denomination. *The Jesus Film* is a movie of Jesus' life and ministry strictly adapted from the Gospel of Luke. According to Project statistics, six billion people in twenty-nine years—more people than any ministry in the entire history of Christianity—have been exposed to the gospel through the narrative and moving images of this film.[3] Yet it wasn't acknowledged as a legitimate ministry of the gospel by at least one Christian denomination.

Theologian Ken Gentry writes of the danger of confusing categories when addressing the prohibitions of images as a prohibition of Jesus Christ's human form:

> A picture of Christ is a picture of his humanity, for he does, in fact, possess a truly human body (as well as a truly human soul). A picture of Christ is not a picture of his inner, divine essence, nor even of his soul. Rather it is a picture of his external bodily form. Thus, a picture of Christ's human form is a picture of his humanity, not his deity; it is a picture of man (the God-man), not a picture of God.[4]

Of course, how one pictures Jesus also reflects one's theology, and that theology could itself be unbiblical. For instance portraying Jesus as a spiritual being whose speaking is always underlined by angels singing could reflect a Gnostic interpretation of Jesus as lacking in flesh and blood humanity. But likewise, the desire to stress Jesus' human side can become equally aberrant in separating him from his deity.

The superiority of Christ over previous revelation lies in his *incarnation*— his becoming flesh, a physical manifestation in time and space, beyond mere abstraction. Notice the opening words of the book of Hebrews:

---

[3] Accessed February 5, 2008, at <http://www.jesusfilm.org/progress/statistics.html>.

[4] Ken Gentry, "Christ, Art, and the Second Commandment," position paper by the author. Available at www.kennethgentry.com.

> God, after He spoke long ago to the fathers in the prophets in many portions and in many ways, in these last days has spoken to us in His Son... And He is the radiance of His glory and the exact representation of His nature. (Heb 1:1-3)

The incarnation is here intentionally spoken of in terms of a *visualization* of God's glory. The Greek word used for "exact representation" is *charakter*, which was a tool for engraving.[5] Remember the Second Commandment? "Thou shalt not make unto thee any graven image" (KJV). Jesus is referred to in terms of the very thing God prohibited to us: graven imagery.

This theme is reiterated in Colossians 1:15 where Jesus is referred to as "the image of the invisible God." The word for image there is *eikon*, from which we get the English word, "icon," a statue or likeness.[6] In the ancient world, a king would represent his dominion in provinces where he could not personally appear with the erection of images *(eikons)* of himself.[7] Jesus Christ is God's personal *eikon*, the visible representation of God's presence in time/space history.

This is not to say that God the Father or God the Spirit are physical and have a beard and look like the man Jesus. And it does not mean that God can be worshiped through pictures, sculptures or other visual images. But it also cannot mean merely that Christ reflects God's character in his behavior alone. Paul is using a visual metaphor for a reason. The theological concept of incarnation involves living embodiment, the visible expression within time and space of what is otherwise unseen. As the apostle John writes, "The Word became flesh, and dwelt among us, and we saw His glory, glory as of the only begotten from the Father, full of grace and truth" (Jn 1:14).

John emphasizes the image aspect of the incarnation not merely in "beholding his glory," but also in the phrase "dwelt among us," which is a translation of the Greek word for "tabernacle," or "pitching his tent."[8] Jesus is the New Testament *image* of the tabernacle of God's presence. Even if this were merely a reference to Christ's behavior, it would be experiential reality in concrete history, not philosophical speculation of abstract virtues.

---

[5] *Strong's Greek Dictionary of the New Testament* 2.2 (Oaktree Software).

[6] Ibid.

[7] Gerhard von Rad, "ei0kw&n," in *Theological Dictionary of the New Testament*, ed. Gerhard Kittel, trans. Geoffrey W. Bromiley, 4 vols. (Grand Rapids: Eerdmans, 1964), 2:392.

[8] *Strong's Greek Dictionary of the New Testament*.

Jesus as the incarnate Word is not a self-evident axiom or timeless principle of reason. He is not reducible to propositional syllogisms. At the heart of Christianity is not merely a philosophy or worldview but an incarnate person. Christian theology should maintain an equal ultimacy of both word *and* image because at the core of our faith is this equal ultimacy in the incarnation: Word made flesh.

Incarnation, Story and Persuasion

Images are concrete expressions of abstract ideas, the existential embodiment of the rational word. Images, whether they are stories, pictures or music, are *incarnations* of ideas—words made flesh. Image is the personification of logic, the enfleshment of proposition. C. S. Lewis valued myth because in it "we come nearest to experiencing as a concrete what can otherwise be understood only as an abstraction.... It is only while receiving the myth as a story that you experience the principle concretely."[9] Theologians Gordon Fee and Douglas Stuart admit that the narrative nature of biblical revelation allows us "vicariously to live through events and experiences rather than simply learning *about* the issues involved in those events and experiences," because "the Bible is not a series of propositions and imperatives; it is not simply a collection of 'Sayings from Chairman God' as though he looked down at us from heaven and said, 'Hey you down there, learn these truths.'"[10] Narrative imagery incarnates truth.

Incarnation is one of the most powerful means of communication. Whether we relate to a character in a story, enter the world of a painting, feel the heart of a song or embrace the joy of a dance, we are making a connection with truth or ideas through existential experience of what is otherwise an abstract proposition. People are rational beings, but more so, we are *personal* beings. We are incarnate.

Movies are one of the modern world's strongest examples of storytelling. When you watch a movie, you are watching a story that is an incarnation of a worldview. The hero embodies the superior worldview; the villain, the inferior worldview. The drama of the story comes from the conflict of their opposing

---

[9]C. S. Lewis, *God in the Dock: Essays on Theology and Ethics*, ed. Walter Hooper (Grand Rapids: Eerdmans, 1970), p. 66.

[10]Gordon Fee and Douglas Stuart, quoted in Kevin J. Vanhoozer, "The Semantics of Biblical Literature," in *Hermeneutics, Authority and Canon*, ed. D. A. Carson and John D. Woodbridge (Grand Rapids: Zondervan, 1986), pp. 80-81.

worldviews, which drive their actions to conflict with each other. By the end of the story, the hero's worldview is proven superior to the villain's in his victory over the villain. Robert McKee sees story as

> humanity's prime source of inspiration, as it seeks to order chaos and gain insight into life. Our appetite for story is a reflection of the profound human need to grasp the patterns of living, not merely as an intellectual exercise, but within a very personal, emotional experience. In the words of playwright Jean Anouilh, "fiction gives life its form."[11]

Story incarnates the abstract concept of dialectical argumentation: thesis, antithesis, synthesis. And it is through incarnation, through the embodiment of worldviews and their resultant human behavior that story connects so deeply with the human psyche. As we identify or sympathize with the hero, we enter into his worldview, and experience the dialectic with him.

A good example of the power of image to embody otherwise rational argumentation is the movie *The Exorcism of Emily Rose*. Writer and director Scott Derrickson tells the story of a Roman Catholic priest on trial for criminal negligence in the death of a college girl named Emily Rose. Emily had come to the priest because she believed she was demon-possessed. In the midst of a laborious exorcism ritual, she died from self-inflicted wounds.

The protagonist of the story is Erin Bruner, a spiritual agnostic who serves as the priest's defense attorney. Throughout the trial the prosecutor mocks her attempt to prove the *possibility* of demon possession. Such superstitious arguments, he argues, are unbecoming of legal procedure in a modern scientific world. Emily had epilepsy, he attempts to prove, which required medication, not "voodoo."

The movie presents both sides of the argument so equally that the story leaves Bruner still an agnostic. But the viewer is left with a strong openness toward the legitimacy of a spiritual world, having been shown the raw experience of demon possession in contrast to the rationalizing tendency of scientism. Derrickson uses the story as a metaphor for the stranglehold of modernity on the western mind, and the inadequacy of rationalism and the scientific method in discovering all truth.

---

[11] Robert McKee, *Story: Substance, Structure, Style and the Principles of Screenwriting* (New York: HarperCollins, 1997), p. 12.

Story is persuasive because it embodies worldview in a narrative. In the same way that logic may follow a rhetorical structure, so story—and really all art forms—follows a structure that leads the audience to a conclusion. Most traditional stories as well as mainstream movies trace the redemption of the protagonist (or "hero"), a process used similarly by the apostle Paul in his testimony before King Agrippa (Acts 26). Here is the summary of this outline:[12]

1. *Goal:* What the hero wants
2. *Plan:* How the hero will get what he wants
3. *Adversary:* Keeps the hero from getting what he wants (external)
4. *Flaw:* Keeps the hero from getting what he wants (internal)
5. *Apparent Defeat:* Circumstance that suggests the hero will not get what he wants
6. *Self-revelation:* Realization of the hero's flaw (internal)
7. *Final Confrontation:* Face-off between the hero and the adversary
8. *Resolution:* The change to the hero reflected in his life
9. *Theme:* What the hero learns through his story

A story's hero seeks out his goal. An adversary seeks to stop the hero, but the hero is also confronted by an internal flaw. The obstacles in the story build to the point where it appears that the hero will never get what he wants. At the end of his rope, the hero has some kind of revelation about himself and his internal flaw—what he really wants is not what he really needs. By confronting that internal flaw, the hero finds what he needs to overcome his adversary and achieve what he really needs, and oftentimes also achieves what he originally wanted as well. That structure is the very same structure of conversion or persuasion.

The drama of a story is the clash of worldviews, with one worldview—which the storyteller wants us to consider superior—arising as victor. Some protagonists, of course, don't change; these become the catalyst for others around him to change. In *Braveheart*, William Wallace is resolute in his determination to fight the king of England to the death for Scotland's freedom. Despite his death, his unyielding conviction becomes an inspiration to Robert the Bruce, who rises up to take Wallace's place.

---

[12] For a detailed explanation see Brian Godawa, *Hollywood Worldviews* (Downers Grove, Ill.: InterVarsity Press, 2009), pp. 79-86.

But most protagonists emerge from their story changed. The character arc—the hero's journey from beginning through middle and on to the end—reflects the change in the hero's worldview. At the beginning of the story, there is a flaw in the hero's perception of the way things should be. As a result of his journey through the story, and because of the obstacles he faces, the hero learns something about the world that he did not know. That change of mind is the redemption of the hero.

Adversaries are not always evil villains in the traditional sense. Rather they serve to confront the hero's worldview and sometimes reveal the change necessary to the hero. In *Bruce Almighty,* Bruce is not satisfied with his life's circumstances. He thinks he can do better than God, so God gives Bruce his powers to teach him a lesson. Bruce discovers that he is not capable of "playing God," and he relinquishes his will back to God. Bruce's character arc goes from selfish and arrogant to selfless and humble before God. In this story, God is the adversary, but he turns out not to be a villain. Rather, God is the source of Bruce's learned wisdom.

Identification

Rather than making strictly logical arguments about truth or reality, a story carries us along existentially in a universe where arguments are incarnate, where worldviews are lived out and lead to positive or negative results. If the audience likes the protagonist, if they identify with him in some way, then they follow him on his journey and learn the lesson he learns along with him. This is why it is so important for the audience to be discerning about who they are rooting for. They are not merely being entertained when watching a movie or television show; they are being exposed to an incarnate argument about the way life ought or ought not be lived, about the nature of truth in human experience.

There are many ways that stories create a connection between the audience and the protagonist in order to persuade through identification. One is through sympathy; many people love to root for the underdog or the hero who has suffered great injustice. Humor is another basic way to draw the audience into the protagonist's viewpoint; audiences love to laugh at and with a humorous personality. Likeability is also a means of identification. People will like a protagonist even if he is a criminal, if that protagonist is perceived as cool.

Yet another means of identification with the audience is universal desire. If the hero is seeking something that we all seek in one way or another, then we relate to him and sympathize with him. Freedom, significance, protection of family, success, justice and love are all examples of universal desires that most of us can relate to.

Love Interest

The love interest in a story usually embodies what is lacking in the protagonist, the perfect complement to the hero. In order to discover his flaw, the hero has to lose his love interest. This is why the standard formula for love stories is (1) boy meets girl, (2) boy loses girl, (3) boy gets girl. Only by confronting his flaw and becoming a better person is the hero worthy of his lover. That is redemption.

Reflection

Another aspect of storytelling rhetoric is the reflection character, the person in the story who is going through the same problems but who seeks resolution in a different way. This is the dramatic way of discrediting counterarguments (antithesis) against the theme (thesis) of the story. In *Braveheart*, Robert the Bruce wants the same thing as William Wallace: a free Scotland. But he pursues this goal through negotiations and compromise with the king of England, rather than the uncompromising fight that Wallace engages in. Bruce is the man of self-preservation and Wallace is the man of self-sacrifice. By seeing Bruce's negotiation with the tyrannical king leading only to more slavery, the argument against compromise is sealed.

Incarnation

Just as logical argumentation contains rhetorical rules of argumentation, so storytelling contains persuasive rhetoric. Let's take a look at just a few of the many other ways in which storytelling in movies uses the language of image and drama to effectively persuade the audience.

It is no surprise that stories that incarnate an idea can often have as much if not more impact than the labyrinthine meanderings of logical debate. Human beings are not reducible to disembodied intellects. We are also emotional beings whose reality is historically experienced within space and time. Truth is not merely mathematically measured against abstract doctrinal propositions; it is existentially experienced.

This goes for our approach to understanding the Bible as well. As Curtis Freeman puts it, we must read the Bible "not as disembodied minds seeking knowledge, but as embodied selves with histories searching for the story of our lives."[13]

God used incarnation to communicate the seriousness of Israel's apostasy by commanding Hosea to marry the prostitute Gomer. The parable of the Good Samaritan is an incarnation of the argument defining the responsibility of loving one's neighbor as universally applicable to everyone, as opposed to the logical and legal technicalities used by the Pharisees to justify their lack of compassion.

Subversion

Subversion—the retelling of one mythology in terms of another—is another rhetorical strategy of storytelling. The film *Underworld* uses the accepted mythologies of *Romeo and Juliet* and the horror genre of vampires and werewolves to address the controversial idea of interracial romance. The tribal families of vampires and werewolves have been feuding for centuries, killing each other in the dark of night. Along comes a hybrid vampire/werewolf that threatens the werewolves' sense of identity and the vampire's power over the werewolves. The hybridization of these two cultures threatens the power of the majority and the survival of the minority. Utilizing these other mythologies bypasses the deep-seated prejudices of viewers to address the thorny issue of racism.

The Scriptures are themselves acts of subversion. The apostle John subverts the Hellenistic doctrine of *Logos* in John 1:1, taking a term loaded with pantheistic worship of abstract Reason as the underlying order of the universe, and subverting it by redefining it as "becoming flesh" in the person of Jesus Christ.

Analogy

An analogy is an inference that if two things are similar in some ways, they are similar in other ways as well. Some Christian philosophers argue that all

---

[13] Curtis Freeman, "Toward a *Sensus Fidelium* for an Evangelical Church," in *The Nature of Confession: Evangelicals and Postliberals in Conversation*, ed. Timothy R. Phillips and Dennis L. Okholm (Downers Grove, Ill.: InterVarsity Press, 1996), pp. 164-65.

truth is analogous. That is, nothing can be known apart from comparing it to something already known or assumed.

In movies, images that embody a similarity between ideas connects those ideas in identity. For example, the movie *The Island* is a futuristic sci-fi story about a corporation that creates clones to harvest body parts for clients as needed. The clones are kept in isolation and in ignorance of their true identity. The corporation uses euphemisms of the clones—"products"—to dehumanize them. The corporation tries to kill the clones before they are discovered. Henchmen make their way through a series of clones suspended in large plastic bags; they look like fetuses in amniotic sacks. These clones are injected with drugs and the plastic sacks are slashed open. Others are put into a chamber to be gassed. A black man challenges the owner of the corporation, suggesting that this is how slaves were treated in early American history. Through all these analogous images, viewers are reminded of abortion, euthanasia, the Jewish holocaust and black slavery. This connective analogy shows the dehumanization involved in cloning to be similar to that engaged in by other atrocities.

The evil of the Beast in the biblical book of Revelation is analogized in his many-headed, blaspheming and animalistic, flesh-eating nature, while the sacrificial and peaceful nature of the Lamb depicts Christ's purity and goodness. Nathan's parable to King David analogizes his murder of Uriah to a man stealing another man's only ewe lamb (2 Sam 12:1-7).

Generalization

In debate, generalization is usually considered a logical fallacy because it takes a particular example of something and generalizes to a universal, when in fact, this is not always true. This is also the problem of most prejudice in our culture. However, as the old adage goes, stereotypes exist because they are to some degree true. There is a sociological preponderance of certain character traits or behaviors in certain cultures.

The fact that not everyone of a cultural community is exactly the same does not disprove that there are in fact many who are. We are sociological creatures and as such display common traits in our communities. Many Christians in the evangelical culture use similar language that others do not, such as "born again," "saved," "the blood of Jesus." And so they also behave in similar ways such as "witnessing" or quoting the Bible. Animal rights activists, Wall Street financiers, Democrats, Republicans, soccer moms and Hollywood celebrities all have similar behaviors within their cultural communities.

In a story, placing common phrases into a character's mouth or common behaviors in their actions identifies them with a certain cultural community. The character becomes a symbol for that community. The more common phrases and behaviors displayed in the character, the more easily universalized they are. And when the storytellers make those linguistic and behavioral connections, and then show the consequences on that character, they are incarnating the argument against that worldview.

The villain in *The Island* is the head of the corporation. He explains his motivations using the familiar language of modern scientists: the clones have no souls; they are a means to good ends for society, such as the curing of diseases like Leukemia. Modern scientists make similar arguments to justify public funding or approval of controversial schemes, such as embryonic stem cell research. By placing that familiar language in the villain's mouth, the storyteller makes a general connection of those ideas with villainy. This may not seem fair or logical to those who disagree, but it is the nature of storytelling to embody a worldview or paradigm in its characters.

Jesus' parables contain many examples of generalizations of different kinds of people. The snooty self-righteous religious hypocrite was one of his favorites (Lk 10:25-37; 18:10-14; Mt 23).

Symbolism

In a story, a character may become a symbol for a particular worldview; the consequences of that character's experience become a symbol for what that worldview leads to. In *A Beautiful Mind*, the schizophrenic John Nash is a symbol for modernity: reducing truth to mental reasoning cripples our humanity, just as Nash was crippled by his "disease." As a doctor tells Nash, his mind is his problem. He can't reason his way out. And by the end of the film, Nash explains to the Nobel Prize audience that he discovered real truth in the heart, not the head. So elevating the mind to the absolute determiner of truth leads to self-destruction. But redemption and real truth is found in human connection through love.

In *Charlie and the Chocolate Factory*, the five different kids who win tickets to tour Willy Wonka's factory become symbols of the negative results that different types of parenting bring. A suburban overachiever shows the perils of hypercompetition. A fat German boy serves as a symbol of conspicuous consumption. A spoiled little rich girl gets everything she asks for by whining. A video-game enthusiast embodies antisocial behavior. And of course, there is Charlie, whose poor but loving family sacrifices their needs for his happiness. The storyteller communicates his view of what parenting should really be like through children as symbols of different approaches.

In his letter to the Galatians, the apostle Paul allegorizes Hagar and Sarah as symbols for Jews in bondage to law and Christians as true children of Abraham (Gal 4:21-31). Jerusalem and Mount Zion itself are frequently used as symbols for the church or the people of God (Heb 12:18-24). Tax collectors are used as symbols of greed and distance from God (Mt 5:46; 11:19).

Conclusion

Though many of these examples of story rhetoric would be criticized as being logical fallacies, they are nevertheless used and given legitimacy in the Bible as effective means of communication and persuasion. They cannot be written off with the wave of a modernist hand as "emotional manipulation." An argument can be logically invalid, but its conclusion still true, and its effect powerful.

Chapter 6
Subversion

The Bible is often image-oriented in its communication of truth. And rather than rejecting all non-Christian imagery as useless in the area of truth or persuasion, the Bible redefines such imagery in a new context of the Judeo-Christian worldview. It redeems culture through subversion, which is radical reinterpretation or undermining of commonly understood images, words, concepts or narratives.

The Old Testament, a covenantal text of ancient Israel, reflects what scholar John Walton calls the "cognitive environment" of the ancient Near Eastern culture.[1] That is, God providentially breathed (inspired) his Word through human authors, who reflected thought forms and images of their surrounding culture, redefined or interpreted through their religion. This does not mean that Israel borrowed pagan notions or that their faith evolved out of other religions, but rather that all cultures within a common time and location use common imagery, symbols and motifs to linguistically express their unique interpretation of reality. The writers of the Law and the Prophets of the Old Covenant are no different.

The Law given to Moses on Mount Sinai, as well as the structure of the entire Pentateuch, reflects the same structure as the pagan suzerain-vassal treaties of the ancient Near East. The creation account in Genesis 1 contains the same motifs of separation, naming and function that pervades Egyptian and Mesopotamian creation stories.[2] In the Bible, God's power and authority, as well as his creative act of bringing order out of chaos, are expressed through his battle with and domination over the large sea serpent called "Leviathan" or "Rahab" (Job 26:12-14; 41; Ps 74:12-15; Is 27:1; 51:9-10). This same motif of creation versus serpentine chaos was prevalent in Israel's surrounding pagan cultures. For example, in the Babylonian creation myth

---

[1] John H. Walton, *Ancient Near Eastern Thought and the Old Testament: Introducing the Conceptual World of the Hebrew Bible* (Grand Rapids: Baker, 2006), p. 21.

[2] Ibid., p. 88.

Enuma Elish, Marduk has a victorious battle with the dragon Tiamat. In Canaanite texts the storm god Baal battles his enemies Sea and River to establish his rule over the gods. In these cases, as well as in the Bible, a deity battles a sea monster that embodies the powers of chaos in order to establish that deity's kingly rule.[3] In Egyptian and Mesopotamian religion, the temple was considered the center of the cosmos. Its architecture and design was a microcosm that reflected the macrocosm of the universe. The temple was described as being situated on a "cosmic mountain," a holy hill where creation first began, along with a river that flowed out of the mountain as the source of eternal life.[4] So too in the Bible God's temple was a designed microcosm of the universe (Ps 78:68-69) on the holy hill, the cosmic Mount Zion (Ps 43:3-4; Is 2), where an Edenic river of eternal life is symbolically described as flowing out of its gates (Ezek 47:1-12).

Though these examples only scratch the surface of the common cognitive environment that Israel shared with its pagan neighbors, they also reflect Israel's subversive reinterpretation of those images, motifs and symbols through their own narrative to express a monotheistic God who condemned other gods as worthless idols and who chose Israel to be his royal priesthood to bring redemption to the lost pagan world.

The New Testament likewise engages in such reinterpretation of pagan images and symbols. The apostle Paul quotes from Jewish legends as well as from pagan poets in his argumentation to both believers and unbelievers. In 2 Timothy 3:8 Paul refers to Moses' opponents "Jannes and Jambres," a reference to Pharoah's magicians in Exodus 7—9, who attempted to reproduce God's miracles and plagues. But there is no mention of the names Jannes and Jambres in the entire Old Testament. So how did Paul know the names of the two magicians? The ancient church fathers Origen[5] and Ambrose claimed these names were drawn by Paul from the Jewish pseudepigraphal work entitled Jannes and Jambres, which describes the Exodus episode from the perspective of these two magicians—one repentant, the other unrepentant.[6] There is also a long Jewish tradition recorded in the

---

[3]Bernhard W. Anderson, *Creation Versus Chaos: The Reinterpretation of Mythical Symbolism in the Bible* (Philadelphia: Fortress, 1987), pp. 15-26.

[4]Walton, *Ancient Near Eastern Thought*, pp. 113-34.

[5]Origen, Commentary on Matthew 27:8. "Jannes and Jambres," *The International Standard Bible Encyclopedia*, ed. James Orr (1915; OakTree Software 1.0).

[6]James H. Charlesworth, ed., *The Old Testament Pseudepigrapha*, vol. 2 (New York: Doubleday, 1983), pp. 427-42.

targum of these two names.[7] In either case, the sources are unorthodox at best, heretical at worst.

Jude 9 describes Michael the Archangel disputing with the devil over the body of Moses, an incident that is spoken of nowhere else in Scripture but which appears, according to some ancient church fathers, in a lost Jewish book called The Assumption of Moses.[8] Jude also quotes an extant nonbiblical Jewish apocalyptic called 1 Enoch when he writes,

> Enoch, in the seventh generation from Adam, prophesied, saying, "Behold, the Lord came with many thousands of His holy ones, to execute judgment upon all, and to convict all the ungodly of all their ungodly deeds which they have done in an ungodly way, and of all the harsh things which ungodly sinners have spoken against Him." (Jude 14-15)

> Behold, he will arrive with ten [thousand times a thousand] of the holy ones in order to execute judgment upon all. He will destroy the wicked ones and censure all flesh on account of everything that they have done, that which the sinners and the wicked ones committed against him. (1 Enoch 1:9)[9]

Biblical scholars agree that 1 Enoch's imagery and mythological fantasy are not scriptural and in many places fanciful fiction. But Jude quotes a particular prophecy nonetheless as a true one.

Such biblical references to non-scriptural mythology and imagery does not validate those source references as completely true in all aspects, no more than quoting a newspaper means that paper gets all the facts right. And it doesn't invalidate biblical authority any more than acknowledging that not everything a liar says is false. But what it does validate is circumspect usage of cultural images and mythologies as connecting points with the Gospel.

---

[7] "Jewish tradition makes them sons of Balaam (Targum of Jonathan on Num. xxii. 22), and places their rise at the time the Pharaoh gave command to kill the first-born of Israel (Sanhedrin, f. 106a; Sotah 11a), and supposes them to have been teachers of Moses, the makers of the golden calf (Midrash Tanhuma, f. 115b)." "Jannes and Jambres," in Philip Schaff, *The New Schaff-Herzog Encyclopedia of Religious Knowledge*, 6:95, accessed February 4, 2008, at <www.ccel.org/ccel/schaff/encyc06/Page_95.html>.

[8] Richard J. Bauckham, *2 Peter, Jude, Word Biblical Commentary 50* (Waco, Tex.: Word, 1983), pp. 73-74.

[9] James H. Charlesworth, ed., *The Old Testament Pseudepigrapha* (New York: Doubleday, 1983), 1:13-14.

But the Bible doesn't merely quote Jewish unbiblical mythology and imagery; it also quotes Hellenistic cultural imagery. In 1 Corinthians 15:33 Paul quotes a common phrase of the day: "Bad company corrupts good morals." The phrase has its origin in the Greek comedic dramatist Menander's play, *Thais*. Menander was known for his bawdy portrayals of private life in raunchy comedies, like the Farrelly Brothers (*There's Something About Mary*) or Sacha Baron Cohen (*Borat*).[10] Evidently, the apostle had exposed himself to the sitcoms and R-rated movies of his day. Elsewhere, Paul depicts the persecution sufferings of the faithful as a "theatrical spectacle" to the audience of the world—original reality show programming (1 Cor 4:9; Heb 10:33).[11]

And speaking of spectacles, in Philippians 3:13-14 and 1 Corinthians 9:24-27, the publicly familiar Roman or Isthmian athletic games are used as another incarnate picture of the race and fight of Christian faith. The triumphal procession of Roman emperors dragging their defeated foes through the city streets is reimagined as a visual metaphor for Christ's own victory in 2 Corinthians 2:14-16 and Colossians 2:15.[12]

Acts 17: Paul at the Areopagus

Athens was the Los Angeles or New York of its time, the place where new ideas were explored with great passion by the Greek and Roman poets, the cultural leaders of the ancient world. The poets would espouse philosophy not merely through didactical tracts and oration but also through poems and plays for the populace, just as the popular artists of today propagate pagan worldviews through music, television and feature films.

Paul's Areopagus discourse has been used to justify opposing theories of apologetics by Christian crosscultural evangelists, theologians and apologists alike. It has been used to justify such divergent theories of apologetics as evidentialism and presuppositionalism.[13] It has been

---

[10] Raymond F Collins and Donald P. Senior, *First Corinthians* (Collegeville, Minn.: Liturgical Press, 1999), pp. 560-61; Victor Davis Hanson and John Heath, *Who Killed Homer? The Demise of Classical Education and the Recovery of Greek Wisdom* (New York: Encounter Books, 2001), pp. 124, 148-49.

[11] "Theater," *Dictionary of Biblical Imagery*, AGES Software.

[12] "Classifying Convergence Between Pagan and Early Christian Texts: 2.8 Adaptation," *The Dictionary of New Testament Background*, Ages Software.

[13] Evidentialism is the belief that sinners can be persuaded to faith through evidence of the historical reliability of the Bible, the miracles and the resurrection of Jesus. Presuppositionalism is the belief that evidence does not persuade sinners because all evidence is interpreted through the presuppositions (assumptions) of their worldview. Unbelievers therefore should be persuaded through addressing their worldviews and presuppositions.

interpreted as being a Hellenistic (i.e., culturally Greek) sermon as well as being entirely antithetical to Hellenism. Martin Dibelius concludes,

> The point at issue is whether it is the Old Testament view of history or the philosophical—Stoic—view of the world that prevails in the speech on the Areopagus. The difference of opinion that we find among the commentators seems to offer little prospect of a definite solution.[14]

One thing that most all of these divergent viewpoints have in common is their modernist emphasis on Paul's discourse as rational debate or empirical proof. What they tend to miss is the narrative structure of his presentation. And perhaps it is the narrative structure that contains the solution to Dibelius' dilemma. An examination of that structure reveals that Paul does not so much engage in philosophical debate as he does retell the pagan story within a Christian worldview framework.

First, our examination must put Paul's presentation in context. He is brought to the Areopagus, which was not merely the name of a location but also the name of the administrative and judicial body that met there, the highest court in Athens. The Areopagus formally examined and charged violators of the Roman law against "illicit" new religions.[15] Though the context suggests an open public interaction and not a formal trial, Luke, the narrator, attempts to cast Paul in Athenian narrative simile to Socrates, someone with whom the Athenians would be both familiar and uncomfortable. Luke describes the reaction of some of the philosophers on hand to Paul in verse 18: "He seems to be a proclaimer of strange deities," a phrase that resembles Xenophon's description of Socrates' crime: "rejecting the gods acknowledged by the state and… bringing in new divinities."[16] Luke depicts Paul from the start as a heroically defiant Socrates, a philosopher of truth against the mob.

Paul's sermon clearly contains biblical truths that are found in both Old and New Testaments: God as transcendent Creator and Sustainer, his providential control of reality, Christ's resurrection and the final judgment. It is highly significant to note, however, that throughout the entire discourse Paul did not quote a single

---

[14] Martin Dibelius and K. C. Hanson, *The Book of Acts: Form, Style, and Theology* (1956; reprint, Minneapolis: Augsburg Fortress, 2004), p. 98.

[15] Robert L. Gallagher and Paul Hertig, *Mission in Acts: Ancient Narratives in Contemporary Context* (Maryknoll, N.Y.: Orbis, 2004), pp. 224-25.

[16] Xenophon, *Memorabilia* chap. 1. See also Plato, *Apology* 24B-C; *Euthyphro* 1C; 2B; 3B.

Scripture to these unbelievers. Paul certainly was not ashamed of the gospel and regularly quoted Scriptural references to the Jewish people (Acts 26:22-23; 28:23-28); therefore, his avoidance of Scripture in this instance is instructive of how to preach and defend the gospel to pagans. Quoting chapter and verse may work with those who are already disposed toward God or the Bible, but Paul appears to consider it inappropriate to do so with those who are hostile or opposed to the faith. Ben Witherington adds, "Arguments are only persuasive if they work within the plausibility structure existing in the minds of the hearers."[17] Paul, rather than Bible-thumping these heathens, addresses them using the narrative structure of Stoic philosophy.[18]

Missions scholars Robert Gallagher and Paul Hertig explain that the facts of Paul's speech mimic the major points of Stoic beliefs. They quote the ancient Roman academic Cicero who outlines these Stoic beliefs:

> First, they prove that gods exist; next they explain their nature; then they show that the world is governed by them; and lastly that they care for the fortunes of mankind.[19]

Paul enters into the discourse of his listeners. He plays according to the rules of the community he is trying to reach. An examination of each point he makes in his oration will reveal that this identification he is making with their culture is not merely with their structural procedures of argument, but with the content of the Stoic worldview. He is retelling the Stoic story through a Christian metanarrative.[20]

Paul begins his address with a rhetorical convention among Athenians, noted by such luminary Greeks as Aristotle and Demosthenes:[21]

---

[17] Ben Witherington III, *The Acts of the Apostles: A Socio-Rhetorical Commentary* (Grand Rapids: Eerdmans, 1998), p. 530.

[18] This raises the spectre of the centuries-long debate over natural theology. Can sinners be persuaded by the natural revelation of unaided reason or must they hear the special revelation of God's Scriptures to be saved? Paul certainly here speaks of special revelation when he mentions the resurrection of Christ and the final judgment. But he does so without Scriptural reference. So the real question is: Must one quote Bible chapter and verse to speak special revelation? Evidently not, according to Paul.

[19] Cicero *On the Nature of the Gods* 2.4, cited in Gallagher and Hertig, *Mission in Acts*, p. 230.

[20] Although the text reveals that both Epicureans and Stoics were there (Acts 17:17-18), it appears that Paul chooses Stoicism to identify with, perhaps because of its closer affinity with the elements of his intended message.

[21] Aristotle, *Pan. Or.* 1, Demosthenes, *Exordia* 54, cited in Witherington, *Acts of the Apostles*, p. 520.

> Men of Athens, I observe that you are very religious in all respects. (Acts 17:22)

He affirms their religiosity, which also had been acknowledged by the famous Athenian dramatist Sophocles: "Athens is held of states, the most devout"; as well as the Greek geographer Pausanias: "Athenians more than others venerate the gods."[22]

Paul goes on:

> While I was passing through and examining the objects of your worship, I also found an altar with this inscription, "TO AN UNKNOWN GOD." Therefore what you worship in ignorance, this I proclaim to you. (Acts 17:23)

The "Unknown God" inscription may have been the Athenian attempt to hedge their bets against any god they may have missed paying homage to out of ignorance.[23] Paul quoted the ambiguous text as a point of departure for reflections on true worship, which was the same conventional technique used by Pseudo-Heraclitus in his Fourth Epistle.[24]

Paul continues:

> The God who made the world and all things in it, since He is Lord of heaven and earth, does not dwell in temples made with hands; nor is He served by human hands, as though He needed anything, since He Himself gives to all people life and breath and all things. (Acts 17:24-25)

The Greeks had many sacred temples throughout the ancient world as houses for their gods. The Stoics and other cultural critics, however, considered such attempts at housing the transcendent incorporeal nature of deity to be laughable. Zeno, the founder of Stoicism, was known to have taught that "temples are not to be built to the gods."[25] Euripides, the celebrated Athenian tragedian,

---

[22] Sophocles Oedipus Tyrannus 260, Pausanias Description of Greece 1.17.1, cited in Charles H. Talbert, Reading Acts: A literary and Theological Commentary on the Acts of the Apostles (Macon, Ga.: Smyth & Helwys, 2001), p. 53.

[23] Dibelius and Hanson, Book of Acts, p. 103.

[24] Talbert, Reading Acts, p. 153.

[25] Explained of Zeno by Plutarch in his Moralia 1034B, as cited in Juhana Torkki, The Dramatic Account of Paul's Encounter with Philosophy: An Analysis of Acts 17:16-34 with Regard to Contemporary Philosophical Debates (Academic diss., Helsinki University Printing House, 2004), p. 105.

foreshadowed Paul's own words with the rhetorical question, "What house fashioned by builders could contain the divine form within enclosed walls?"[26] Paul's contemporary, the Stoic philosopher Seneca, was known to have said, "Temples are not to be built to Him with stones piled up on high."[27]

The Hebrew tradition also carried such repudiation of a physical dwelling place for God (1 Kings 8:27; Is 66:1-2), but the context of Paul's speech rings particularly sympathetic to the Stoics residing in the midst of the sacred hill of the Athenian Acropolis, populated by a multitude of temples such as the Parthenon, the Erechtheion, the Temple of Nike and the Athenia Polias.

The idea that God does not need humankind, but that humankind needs God as his creator and sustainer (Acts 17:25) is common enough in Hebrew thought (Ps 50:9-12), but as Dibelius points out,

> The use of the word "serve" is, however, almost unknown in the Greek translation of the Bible, but quite familiar in original Greek (pagan) texts, and in the context with which we are acquainted. The deity is too great to need my "service," we read in the famous chapter of Xenophon's Memorabilia, which contains the teleological proof of God.... From the Eleatic School onwards, the idea that God is not in need of anything is repeated in all the schools of Greek philosophy till the Neo-Pythagoreans and the Neo-Platonists.[28]

Seneca wrote, "God seeks no servants; He himself serves mankind," which is also reflected in Euripides' claim that "God has need of nothing," and Plutarch's "God is self-sufficient."[29] Paul is striking a familiar chord with the Athenian and Stoic narratives.

> He made from one man every nation of mankind to live on all the face of the earth. (Acts 17:26)

---

[26] Euripedes, fragment 968, cited in F. F. Bruce, *Paul Apostle of the Heart Set Free* (1977; reprint, Cumbria, U.K.: Paternoster, 2000), p. 240.

[27] According to Lactantius, *Institutes* 6.25, cited in Talbert, *Reading Acts*, p. 155.

[28] Dibelius and Hanson, *Book of Acts*, pp. 105-6.

[29] Seneca, *Epistle* 95.47; Euripides, *Hercules* 1345-46; Plutarch, *Moralia* 1052D, as cited in Talbert, *Reading Acts*, p. 155.

Subversion

Cicero noted that the "universal brotherhood of mankind"[30] was a common theme in Stoicism—although when Stoics spoke of "man" they tended to exclude the barbarians surrounding them.[31] Nevertheless, as Seneca observed, "Nature produced us related to one another, since she created us from the same source and to the same end."[32] The Athenians would certainly not be thinking of the Hebrew Adam when they heard that reference to "one." The "one" they would be thinking of would be the gods themselves. Seneca wrote, "All persons, if they are traced back to their origins, are descendants of the gods," and Dio Chrysostom affirmed, "It is from the gods that the race of men is sprung."[33] What is also striking in Paul's dialogue is that he neglects to mention Adam as the "one" from which we are created, something he readily did when writing to the Roman Christians (Rom 5:12-21). Paul may have been deliberately ambiguous at this point by not distinguishing his definition of "one" from the Greeks', in order to maintain consistency with the Stoic Greek narrative. He is undermining Stoicism through the Christian worldview, which will not be defined until the climactic plot twist at the end of his narrative.

> ...having determined their appointed times and the boundaries of their habitation. (Acts 17:26)

Christians may read Acts 17:26 and immediately consider it an expression of God's providential sovereignty over history, as in Genesis 1, where God determines the times and seasons, or in Deuteronomy 32:8, where he separates the sons of men and establishes their "boundaries." But Paul's Athenian audience would refer to their own intellectual heritage on hearing these words. As Juhana Torkki points out, "The idea of God's kinship to humans is unique in the New Testament writings but common in Stoicism. The Stoic [philosopher] Epictetus devoted a whole essay to the subject."[34] In that essay, Epictetus writes:

---

[30] Cicero, *On Duties* 3.6.28, quoted in Michelle V. Lee, *Paul, the Stoics, and the Body of Christ* (Cambridge: Cambridge University Press, 2006), p. 88.

[31] Bruce, *Paul*, p. 241.

[32] Quoted in Lee, *Paul, the Stoics, and the Body of Christ*, p. 84.

[33] Seneca, *Epistle* 44.1; Dio Chrysostom, *Oration* 30.26, as cited in Talbert, *Reading Acts*, p. 156.

[34] Torkki, *Dramatic Account of Paul's Encounter with Philosophy*, p. 87.

When he tells plants to bloom, they bloom, when he tells them to bear fruit, they bear it, when he tells them to ripen, they ripen.... Is God [Zeus] then, not capable of overseeing everything and being present with everything and maintaining a certain distribution with everything?[35]

Cicero, in one of his *Tusculan Disputations*, writes that seasons and zones of habitation are evidence of God's existence.[36] Paul continues, with every sentence Luke narrates, to engage Stoic thought by retelling its narrative.

That they would seek God, if perhaps they might grope for Him and find Him, though He is not far from each one of us. (Acts 17:27)

The image in Acts 17:27, as one commentator explains, "carries the sense of 'a blind person or the fumbling of a person in the darkness of night,'" as can be found in the writings of Aristophanes and Plato.[37] Christian apologist Greg Bahnsen suggests that it may even be an Homeric literary allusion to the Cyclops blindly groping for Odysseus and his men.[38] In any case, the image is not a positive one. F. F. Bruce affirms the Hellenistic affinities of this section by quoting the Stoic Dio Chrysostom. "Primaeval men are described as 'not settled separately by themselves far away from the divine being or outside him, but . . . sharing his nature.'"[39] Seneca, true to Stoic form, wrote, "God is near you, He is with you, He is within you."[40]

This idea of humanity, blindly groping around for what is, in fact, very near is also a part of scriptural themes (Is 59:10; Deut 28:29), but with a distinct difference. To the Stoic, God's nearness was a pantheistic nearness. They believed everything was a part of God and God was a part of everything, something Paul would vehemently deny (Rom 1) but, interestingly enough, does

---

[35] Epictetus, *Discourse* 1.14, quoted in A. A. Long, *Epictetus: A Stoic and Socratic Guide to Life* (Oxford: Oxford University Press, 2002), pp. 25-26.

[36] Cicero, *Tusculan Disputations* 1.28.68-69, as cited in Talbert, *Reading Acts*, p. 156.

[37] Aristophanes, *Ec.* 315; *Pax* 691; Plato, *Phaedo* 99b, cited in Witherington, *Acts of the Apostles*, pp. 528-29.

[38] Greg Bahnsen, *Always Ready: Directions for Defending the Faith*, ed. Robert Booth (Atlanta: American Vision, 1996), pp. 260-61.

[39] Dio Chrysostom, *Olympic Oration* 12:28, cited in F. F. Bruce, *The Book of the Acts, New International Commentary on the New Testament*, rev. ed. (Grand Rapids: Eerdmans, 1988), p. 339.

[40] Seneca, *Epistle* 41.1-2, cited in Talbert, *Reading Acts*, p. 156.

not do so at this point. He continues to maintain a surface connection with the Stoics by affirming the immanence of God without explicitly qualifying it.

Paul thus far has implicitly followed the Stoic narrative without qualifying the differences between it and his full narrative. He now, however, becomes more explicit in identifying with these pagans, favorably quoting some of their own poets to affirm even more identity with them.

> For in Him we live and move and exist, as even some of your own poets have said, "For we also are His children." (Acts 17:28)

"In him we live and move and exist" is a line from Epimenides' well-known *Cretica*:

> They fashioned a tomb for thee, / O holy and high one– /
> But thou art not dead; / thou livest and abidest for ever / for,
> in thee we live and move and have our being.[41]

"We are his offspring," is from Epimenides' fellow-countryman Aratus in his *Phaenomena*:

> Let us begin with Zeus, Never, O men, let us leave him
> Unmentioned. All the ways are full of Zeus,
> And all the market-places of human beings. The sea is full
> Of him; so are the harbors. In every way we have all to do
> with Zeus, For we are truly his offspring.[42]

Aratus was most likely rephrasing Cleanthes' poem *Hymn to Zeus*, which not only refers to men as God's children, but to Zeus as the sovereign controller of all—in whom men live and move:

> Almighty Zeus, nature's first Cause,
>   governing all things by law.
> It is the right of mortals to address thee,

---

[41] Bruce, *Book of the Acts*, pp. 338-39.
[42] Ibid.

> For we who live and creep upon the earth are
> all thy children.[43]

These are the same elements of Paul's discourse in Acts 17:24-29.

The Stoics themselves had redefined Zeus to be the impersonal pantheistic force, also called the "Logos," as opposed to a personal deity in the pantheon of Greek gods.[44] This Logos was still not anything like the personal God of the Hebrew Scriptures. What is disturbing about this section is that Paul does not qualify the pagan quotations that originally were directed to Zeus. He doesn't clarify by explaining that Zeus is not the God he is talking about. He simply quotes these hymns of praise to Zeus as if they are in agreement with the Christian Gospel. The question arises, why does he not distinguish his gospel narrative from theirs?

The answer is found in the idea of subversion. Paul is subverting their concept of God by using common terms with a different definition that eventually undermines their entire narrative. He begins with their conventional understanding of God but steers them eventually to his own. The imago dei (image of God) in pagans reflects distorted truth, but a kind of truth nonetheless.

Now Paul turns his attention to idolatry.

> We ought not to think that the Divine Nature is like gold or silver or stone, an image formed by the art and thought of man. (Acts 17:29)

The Stoics believed that the divine nature could not be reducible to mere artifacts of humanity's creation. Epictetus called humans a "fragment of God."

> You have within you a part of Him.... Do you suppose that I am speaking of some external God, made of silver or gold? It is within yourself that you bear Him.[45]

Zeno taught that "men shall neither build temples nor make idols"; Dio Chrysostom wrote, "The living can only be represented by something that is

---

[43] C. Loring Brace, *Unknown God, Or Inspiration Among Pre-Christian Races 1890* (Whitefish, Mt.: Kessinger, 2003), p. 123.

[44] Joseph Lienhard, *The Bible, the Church, and Authority: The Canon of the Christian Bible in History and Theology* (Collegeville, Minn: Liturgical Press, 1995), p. 11.

[45] Epictetus, *Discourses* 2.8.11-12, cited in Gallagher, *Mission in Acts*, p. 232.

living."[46] Paul is addressing the biblical mocking of "idols of silver and gold" (Ps 115:4) in language his hearers would understand: the language of the Stoic narrative.

Paul goes on.

> Therefore having overlooked the times of ignorance, God is now declaring to men that all people everywhere should repent, because He has fixed a day in which He will judge the world in righteousness through a Man whom He has appointed, having furnished proof to all men by raising Him from the dead. (Acts 17:30-31)

For the Stoics, ignorance was an important doctrine. It represented the loss of knowledge that man formerly possessed, knowledge of their pantheistic unity with the logos. Dio Chrysostom asks in his *Discourses*, "How, then, could they have remained ignorant and conceived no inkling... [that] they were filled with the divine nature?"[47] Epictetus echoes the same sentiment: "Why then are you ignorant of your own kinship?... You are bearing God about with you, you poor wretch, and know it not!"[48] Pauline "ignorance" was a willing responsible ignorance, a hardness of heart that came from sinful violation of God's commands (Eph 4:17-19)—but yet again, Paul does not articulate this distinction. He instead makes an ambiguous reference to a generic "ignorance" that the Stoics would most naturally interpret in their own terms. As Talbert describes, "In all of this, he has sought the common ground. There is nothing he has said yet that would appear ridiculous to his philosophic audience."[49]

Here is where the subversion of Paul's storytelling rears its head, like the mind-blowing twist of a movie thriller. Everything is not as it seems. Paul the storyteller got his pagan audience to nod their heads in agreement, only to be thrown for a loop at the end. Repentance, judgment and the resurrection, all antithetical to Stoic beliefs, form the conclusion of Paul's narrative. Witherington concludes of this Areopagus speech surprise ending,

---

[46]Clement of Alexandria, *Miscellanies* 5.76; Dio Chrysostom, *Oration* 12.83, cited in Talbert, *Reading Acts*, p. 156.

[47]Dio Chrysostom, *Discourses* 12.27; cf. 12.12, 16, 21, cited in Gallagher, *Mission in Acts*, p. 229.

[48]Epictetus, *Discourses* 2.8.11-14, cited in Gallagher, *Mission in Acts*, p. 229.

[49]Talbert, *Reading Acts*, p. 156.

Greek notions have been taken up and given new meaning by placing them in a Jewish-Christian monotheistic context. Apologetics by means of defense and attack is being done, using Greek thought to make monotheistic points. The call for repentance at the end shows where the argument has been going all along—it is not an exercise in diplomacy or compromise but ultimately a call for conversion.[50]

The Stoics believed in a "great conflagration" of fire where the universe would end in the same kind of fire out of which it was created.[51] This was not the fire of damnation, as in Christian doctrine. It was rather the cyclical recurrence of what scientists today would call the "oscillating universe." Everything would collapse into fire, and then be recreated again out of that fire and relive the same process and development of history all over again: The same Socrates would be reborn and would suffer again the betrayal of his city-state and drink the hemlock yet again. And this would occur over and over again from fire into fire and back again.

Paul's call of final, noncyclical, once-for-all judgment by a man was certainly one of the factors that caused some of these interested philosophers to scorn him (Acts 17:32). Yet note again that even here, Paul does not give the name of Jesus. He alludes to him and implies his identity, which seems to maintain a sense of mystery about the narrative (something modern evangelists would surely criticize Paul for). At times, silence can be louder than words, and implication can be more alluring than explication.

The other factor sure to provoke the ire of the cosmopolitan Athenian culture-shapers was the proclamation of the resurrection of Jesus. The poet/dramatist Aeschylus wrote what became a prominent Stoic slogan, "When the dust has soaked up a man's blood, once he is dead there is no resurrection."[52] So Paul's explicit reference to the resurrection was certainly a part of the twist that he used in his subversive storytelling to get the Athenians to listen to what they might otherwise ignore.

A couple of important observations are in line regarding Paul's reference to pagan poetry and non-Christian mythology. First, it points out that, as an orthodox Pharisee who stressed separation of holiness, he nevertheless did

---

[50]Witherington, *Acts of the Apostles*, p. 524.

[51]Ibid., p. 526.

[52]Cited in Bruce, *Paul: Apostle of the Heart Set Free*, p. 247.

not consider it unholy to expose himself to the godless media and art forms of his day (books, plays and poetry). He did not merely familiarize himself with them, he studied them—well enough to be able to quote them and even utilize their narrative. Yes, Paul primarily quoted Scripture in his writings, but he also quoted sinners favorably when appropriate.

Second, this appropriation of pagan cultural images and thought forms by biblical writers reflects more than mere quoting of popular sayings or shallow cultural reference. It illustrates a redemptive interaction with those thought forms, a certain amount of involvement in and affirmation of the prevailing culture, in service to the gospel. A comparison of Paul's sermon in Acts 17 with Cleanthes' *Hymn to Zeus*, a well-known summary of Stoic doctrine, reveals an almost point-by-point correspondence of ideas, which certainly suggests a deliberate identification by Paul with the narrative of the Stoics, while not ultimately compromising the Gospel.[53] The list of convergences between the Mars Hill discourse and Stoic ideas are summarized in figure 6.1.[54]

Figure 6.1. Stoic ideas converge in Acts 17	
STOIC IDEA	ACTS 17
Incorporeal nature of God	v. 24-25
God's self-sufficiency	v. 25
Brotherhood of man "oneness"	v. 26
Providence over seasons and habitations	v. 26
Man's blind groping	v. 27
Immanence/Pantheism	v. 27-28
Zeus/Logos	v. 28
Man as God's offspring	v. 28
Divine nature not gold or silver	v. 29
Wisdom versus ignorance	v. 23, 30
Justice	v. 30-31

The *Dictionary of New Testament Background* cites over a hundred New Testament passages that reflect convergence between pagan and early

---

[53] See M. A. C. Ellery, trans., *Hymn to Zeus* (1976), accessed February 5, 2008, at <www.utexas.edu/courses/citylife/readings/cleanthes_hymn.html>.

[54] See "Historical Sketch of Ethics: Stoicism and Paul," in *The International Standard Bible Encyclopedia*, ed. James Orr (1915; OakTree Software 1.0).

Christian texts. Citations, images and word pictures are quoted, adapted or appropriated from such pagans as Aeschylus, Sophocles, Plutarch, Tacitus, Xenophon, Aristotle, Seneca and other Hellenistic cultural sources. The sheer volume of such biblical reference suggests an interactive intercourse of Scriptural writings with culture rather than absolute separation or shallow manipulation of that culture.[55] Some Christians may react with fear that this kind of redemptive interaction with culture is syncretism, an attempt to fuse two incompatible systems of thought. Subversion, however, is not syncretism. And subversion is what Paul was engaged in.

Syncretism Versus Subversion

In subversion, the narrative, images and symbols of one system are discreetly redefined or altered in the new system. Thus Paul quotes a poem to Zeus but covertly intends a different deity. He superficially affirms the immanence of the Stoic "Universal Reason" that controls and determines all nature and men, yet he describes this universal all-powerful deity as personal rather than abstract law. He agrees with the Stoics that men are ignorant of God and his justice, but then affirms God will judge the world because of Christ's resurrection—two doctrines the Stoics were vehemently against. He affirms the unity of humanity and the immanence of God in all things, but he contradicts Stoic pantheism and redefines that immanence by affirming God's transcendence and the creature/Creator distinction. Paul did not reveal these stark differences between the gospel and the Stoic narrative until the end of his talk. Paul was subverting paganism, not syncretizing Christianity with it.

By casting his presentation of the Gospel in terms that Stoics could identify with and by undermining their narrative with alterations, Paul was strategically subverting through story. In his book *Engaging Unbelief*, Curtis Chang explains this rhetorical strategy as threefold: "1. Entering the challenger's story, 2. Retelling the story, 3. Capturing that retold tale with the gospel metanarrative."[56] Chang affirms the inescapability of story and image through history even in philosophical argumentation:

---

[55] *Dictionary of New Testament Background* (2000; OakTree Software 1.0).

[56] Curtis Chang, *Engaging Unbelief: A Captivating Strategy from Augustine to Aquinas* (Downers Grove, Ill.: InterVarsity Press, 2000), p. 26.

> Strikingly, many of the classic philosophical arguments from different traditions seem to take the form of a story: from Plato's scene of the man bound to the chair in the cave to Hobbes's elaborate drama of the "state of nature," to John Rawls's "choosing game." Stories may come in many different genres, but we cannot escape them.[57]

Many Christian apologists and theologians have tended to focus on the doctrinal content of Paul's Areopagus speech, and therefore miss the narrative structure that carries the message. There is certainly more proclamation in this passage than rational argument. Paul's narrative mirrors the beginning, middle and end of linear Western storytelling. God is Lord. He created all things, all people from one (creation), then determined the seasons and boundaries. Men became blind and are groping in the darkness, ignorant of their very identity as his children (fall). God raised a man from the dead and will judge the world in the future through that same man. Through repentance, people can escape their ignorance and separation from God (redemption).

Scholar N. T. Wright suggests that the way to handle the clash of competing stories is to tell yet another story; one that encompasses and explains the opposing stories yet contains an explanation for the anomalies or contradictions within those stories.

> There is no such thing as "neutral" or "objective" proof; only the claim that the story we are now telling about the world as a whole makes more sense, in its outline and detail, than other potential or actual stories that may be on offer. Simplicity of outline, elegance in handling the details within it, the inclusion of all the parts of the story, and the ability of the story to make sense beyond its immediate subject-matter: these are what count.[58]

The claim that we observe evidence objectively and apply reason neutrally to prove our worldview is an artifact of Enlightenment mythology. The truth is that each epoch of thought in history, whether medieval, Enlightenment

---

[57] Ibid, p. 30.
[58] N. T. Wright, *The New Testament and the People of God* (Minneapolis: Fortress, 1992), p. 42.

or postmodern, is a contest in storytelling. "The one who can tell the best story, in a very real sense, wins the epoch."[59] That's what Paul does with the Stoics.

The conventional image of a Christian apologist is one who teaches at a university, one who wields logical arguments for the existence of God and manuscript evidence for the reliability of the Bible, one who engages in debates about evolution or Islam. But in a postmodern world focused on narrative discourse, we need to take a lesson from the apostle Paul and expand our avenues for evangelism and defending the faith. We need more Christian apologists writing revisionist biographies of Darwin, Marx and Freud; writing for and subverting pagan TV sitcoms; bringing a Christian worldview to their journalism in secular magazines and news reporting; making horror films that undermine the idol of modernity; playing subversive industrial, rock and rap music. We need to be actively, sacredly subverting the secular stories of the culture, and restoring their fragmented narratives for Christ. If it was good enough for the apostle Paul on top of Mars Hill, then it's certainly good enough for those of us in the shade of the Hollywood hills now.

---

[59]Ibid., p. 29.

Chapter 7
Cultural Captivity

The New Testament book of Hebrews has long been recognized by Bible scholars as reflecting a subversive interaction with a worldview of the first century called Hellenism, a blending of Greek philosophy with Jewish thought. A famous Alexandrian Jewish writer of the time period, Philo, had attempted to integrate Platonic philosophy with Judaism. The result was a form of Hellenism that was very influential on the Jews and Christians of the day. One of the many doctrinal beliefs of this school was that the spiritual world of "ideas" was good and more real than the physical world, which was inherently evil and shadowlike. Hellenistic Judaism believed, with Plato, that the body is a prison house of the soul that longed to be released so it could become perfect and return to its maker, the Logos (Reason) or Sophia (wisdom). Since the physical world was bad and the spiritual world was good, a chasm separated humans from God.

Because of this ontological gap between man and God, Philo wrote of various mediators for man such as angels, Moses, Melchizedek, and the high priest. Hellenism posited that the world was created through the agency of the Logos, as the "firstborn son" who was also "light," a mediatory being on the borderline between Godhood and man.[1] The Hellenistic apocryphal book *The Wisdom of Solomon* speaks of Divine Wisdom mediating God's revelation, creating and sustaining the world, and reconciling men to God (7:21—8:1)—all elements related to Jesus in the book of Hebrews, but written to Hellenistic Jews.

The description of Jesus as Logos, Sophia and creator and sustainer of the world in the book of Hebrews, however, diametrically opposes these essential doctrines of the Platonic philosophy. The incarnation of Christ, God in the flesh (Heb 2:17) being tempted by sin (Heb 4:15) and experiencing suffering and other passions (Heb 5:7) was entirely incompatible with the Platonic notion of God's complete separation from humanity and physical reality. The writer of Hebrews

---

[1] Ronald Nash, *The Gospel and the Greeks: Did the New Testament Borrow from Pagan Thought?* (Phillipsburg, N.J.: P & R Publishing, 1992, 2003), pp. 81-82.

connects with certain Hellenistic notions of Logos and Sophia and then subverts them with the incarnational Logos of Scripture.

The book of Hebrews describes Jesus as superior to each of Philo's mediators one by one: angels (Heb 1:1-14), Moses (Heb 3:1-18), Melchizedek (Heb 5:1-10) and the high priest (Heb 5:1-10), thus subverting the Hellenistic notions of mediatorship.[2] Ronald Nash concludes in *The Gospel and the Greeks*,

> What becomes clear in a study of Hebrews is not that the writer was unfamiliar with Platonism, but that he self-consciously and intentionally set himself to contrast his understanding of the Christian message with the philosophy that he himself may have once accepted and that his audience may still have found attractive.[3]

So the book of Hebrews reflects the language, terms and concepts of Hellenism, but undermines them with new definitions of terms and usage. Similarly, the Gospel of John uses language that subverts Hellenistic mystery religion. In the very first chapter, John uses a word to define Jesus (*Logos*) that was well known in the dominant Hellenistic culture as a reference to Reason as the underlying structural order of all things. A look at a couple fragments from Heraclitus, the possible origin of the concept, will shed some light on just how the Greco-Roman pagans of John's era defined this "Logos."

> When you have listened, not to me, but to the [Logos], it is wise to agree that all things are one.
>
> For though all things come into being in accordance with this Logos, men seem as if they have never met it.[4]

One can read the first verses of the Gospel of John and see its obvious identification with this Greco-Roman concept of Logos.

> In the beginning was the Word [*logos*], and the Word [*logos*] was with God, and the Word [*logos*] was God. He was in the beginning with God. All things came into being through Him,

---

[2] Nash, *Gospel and the Greeks*, pp. 94-98.
[3] Ibid., p. 90.
[4] James B. Wilbur and Harold J. Allen, *The Worlds of the Early Greek Philosophers* (Buffalo, N.Y.: Prometheus Books, 1979), pp. 64-65.

> and apart from Him nothing came into being that has come into being. In Him was life, and the life was the Light of men. The Light shines in the darkness, and the darkness did not comprehend it.... And the Word [logos] became flesh, and dwelt among us, and we saw His glory, glory as of the only begotten from the Father, full of grace and truth. (Jn 1:1-5, 14)

John's definition of the Logos, however, shows a subversion taking place. For Greek philosophy, the Logos affirmed the oneness of all things out of which all things were created and separated. Men were ignorant of this knowledge but enlightened by it because the Logos was pure thought itself as an intelligent guiding force.[5] When John wrote his Gospel, he started with Logos rather than the Hebrew name YHWH or the Greek equivalents *kyrios* or *theos* as the creator of the universe. He echoed the Greek philosophical language of ultimate origin; immanence, lightness and darkness, human ignorance and the "fullness" of truth, but he gave it a Hebrew spin. John's Logos is not an abstract force but a rational person. The Greek understanding of ultimate reality is shown to be inadequate in light of Christianity.

The apostle Peter subverts Hellenistic imagery when he writes about the cataclysmic spiritual events surrounding God's judgment in the Noachian flood.

> God did not spare angels when they sinned, but cast them into hell and committed them to pits of darkness, reserved for judgment. (2 Pet 2:4)

What is important to realize is that the word translated as "hell" in this English translation is not the usual Greek word, *gehenna*, but *tartarus*, a well-known Greek mythic location written about by Plato:

> The very wicked are cast for ever into Tartarus, the traditional place of punishment in Hades surrounded by a brazen wall and encircled by impenetrable darkness. Here, they receive terrible torture (Republic 626).[6]

---

[5] Ibid., p. 63.

[6] "Resurrection," in *New International Dictionary of New Testament Theology*, ed. Colin Brown (Grand Rapids: Zondervan, 1975, 1986; OakTree Software 1.0).

The Greek poet Hesiod, writing around 700 B.C., described Tartarus as the underworld pit of darkness and gloom where the Olympian Titan giants were banished following their war with Zeus.[7] Obviously, Peter does not affirm Greco-Roman polytheism by referring to Tartarus, but he is clearly using a Hellenistic word that his readers, believer and unbeliever alike, would be very familiar with, and he redefines it within his Christian faith.[8]

Gospel Versus Empire

The Roman Emperor was considered deity, and all Roman subjects were required to pay homage in worship to him. And when an emperor would conquer a particular ruler, he would strip that ruler of his weapons and armor and drag him in chains, along with the captured spoils of war, in a "triumphal procession" through the streets of the city.[9] Paul describes the spiritual victory of Christ's atonement in exactly these imperial terms:

> When He had disarmed the rulers and authorities, He made a public display of them, having triumphed over them through Him. (Col 2:15)
>
> But thanks be to God, who always leads us in triumph in Christ. (2 Cor 2:14)

In these passages, Paul is claiming for Jesus the prerogatives of Caesar, reducing Caesar's own power to mere parody of Christ's greater authority. N. T. Wright points out that even preaching the Gospel is presented in the Scriptures as a "herald of good news" (Lk 16:16) of Christ's kingdom and rule over all other human authorities on the earth. This reflects not only the Hebrew concept of "good news" (Is 52:7) but a subversion of Roman practice: a herald announcing "as good news" the birth or rule of the emperor as a savior to all the world.[10]

---

[7] "Polytheism, Greco-Roman," in *Dictionary of New Testament Background* (Downers Grove, Ill.: InterVarsity Press, 2000; OakTree Software 1.0).

[8] Some scholars suggest that the Greek notion of giants in Tartarus is actually a distorted pagan retelling of the much earlier biblical story of the imprisonment of giants or fallen angels during the Noachian flood (Gen 6:1-7). This would then be an example of paganism subverting Judeo-Christianity, which Peter then subverts right back.

[9] *Barnes' Notes on the New Testament*, derived from an electronic text from the Christian Classics Ethereal Library (www.ccel.org), formatted and corrected by OakTree 1.0.

[10] N. T. Wright, *What Saint Paul Really Said* (Grand Rapids: Eerdmans, 1997), pp. 42-45. Wright quotes a

When Paul wrote that "our citizenship is in heaven, from which also we eagerly wait for a Savior, the Lord Jesus Christ" (Phil 3:20), he was subversively defying the concept of Roman citizenship as the ultimate obligation on occupied territories. Ancient Roman sources call Caesar "the savior and benefactor of the inhabited world,"[11] the one who brought a new world of salvation, justice and peace.[12] Jesus is subversively portrayed in the image of the Roman Emperor, in effect, stealing Caesar's thunder.[13]

It is important to understand that this application of imperial language and imagery to Jesus was not mere mimicry or analogy but subversive defiance against the emperor. In ancient Middle Eastern monarchical and imperial culture, claiming the attributes and privileges of the king was tantamount to treason. The Jews understood full well the messianic claims of Jesus were claims of kingship. It was after all, the prophesied attribute of the Messiah in the Old Testament that he would be the king who will "set up a kingdom which will never be destroyed, and that kingdom... will crush and put an end to all these kingdoms, but it will itself endure forever" (Dan 2:44). This might be akin to a small cult of people in America going around claiming that their cult leader is president of the United States and the Supreme Court, and will ultimately crush America and its leaders. Of course, Jesus—the stone "cut without hands" (Dan 2:44-45)—did crush the Roman Empire, yet not overnight like the Jews expected.[14] The first-century Jews understood Jesus to be clearly defying the emperor's claim to universal power and authority when they said of the Christians, "They all act contrary to the decrees of Caesar, saying there is another king, Jesus" (Acts 17:7). And when the chief priests called for Christ's crucifixion, they repeated their submission to Roman rule with the oath, "We have no king but Caesar" (Jn 19:15). To call Christ a higher king

---

Roman inscription of 9 B.C. that refers to the birth of Emperor Augustus as providence sending "a saviour for us and those who came after us, to make war to cease, to create order everywhere . . . the birthday of the god [Augustus] was the beginning for the world of the good news that have come to men through him."

[11] Accessed February 5, 2008, at <www.bsw.org/project/biblica/bibl79/Comm05m.htm>.

[12] Richard A. Horsley, ed., *Paul and Empire: Religion and Power in Roman Imperial Society* (Harrisburg, Penn.: Trinity Press International, 1997), pp.140-41.

[13] N. T. Wright, *Paul's Gospel and Caesar's Empire,* accessed February 5, 2008, at <www.ctinquiry.org/publications/reflections_volume_2/wright.htm>.

[14] The Pauline concept of this "now and not yet" kingdom is that Christ's death and resurrection was the inauguration of this conquering kingdom in its initial breaking of the powers of darkness (Col 2:14-15). But the outworking of this initial beachhead of victory would take time through history, step by step, conquered foe by conquered foe, until the end when Christ returns and hands the kingdom over to the Father (1 Cor 15:22-28). This explains Hebrews' ironic pronouncement that "all things are in subjection under his feet. . . but now we do not yet see all things subjected to him" (Heb 2:8).

than Caesar, let alone another king, was treason to the imperial decree, an action that called for crucifixion.

The gospel message of the cross of Christ became an image of reverse propaganda. In the Roman Empire, crucifixion was an effective image displaying the might of imperial justice and deterrence. We must not forget that what is to us a religious spiritual symbol (the cross) was to Roman subjects an image of brutality and terror. So it would be truly "foolish" at that time to speak of crucifixion in terms of any kind of victory. It would be like saying someone executed on the electric chair was victorious. But New Testament writers like Paul turned the imagery against itself by declaring the cross an act of triumph over rulers and authorities (Col 2:15).[15]

Thus, in 1 Corinthians, Christ's resurrection from the dead concludes in his imperial reign from heaven in the present day, putting his enemies one by one "under his feet," much like the colonizing of Rome (1 Cor 15:25) until he "comes" to "abolish all rule and authority and power," a subversive attack on the absolute power of Rome, including what Paul called earlier "the rulers of this age" (1 Cor 2:8). Even Paul's description in Ephesians of spiritual armor against the "rulers, powers and world forces of this darkness" is the imagery of an imperial army (Eph 6:12-17). As Neil Elliott concludes, "it is the resurrection of Christ the crucified that reveals the imminent defeat of the Powers, pointing forward to the final triumph of God."[16] The "coming" (Greek: *parousia*) of Christ referred to in 1 Thessalonians,[17] and our "meeting" (*apantesis*) of him with trumpets and glorious fanfare (1 Thess 4:16-17) is a reflection of the imperial arrival of Caesar to a Roman city, where the inhabitants come out to meet him in honor.[18]

Ironically, the entry into the city gates by the Roman Emperor is deliberately subverted in Christ's entry into Jerusalem on a donkey (Mt 21:1-5). The imperial visit, also referred to as Caesar's "adventus," included a parade of armed forces, followed by a golden chariot or throne carrying the emperor, crowned and carrying a palm branch. The citizens would shout

---

[15] Imperial order was very hierarchical, stressing rulers and authorities on all levels. Neil Elliott, "The Anti-Imperial Message of the Cross," in Horsley, ed., *Paul and Empire*, pp. 167-83.

[16] Ibid., p. 181.

[17] See 1 Thess 1:10; 2:19; 3:13; 4:15; 5:23.

[18] Helmut Koester, "Imperial Ideology and Paul's Eschatology in 1 Thessalonians," in Horsley, ed., *Paul and Empire*, pp. 158-66. See Josephus Antiquities 11.327ff. for a primary source of this imperial parousia and apantesis.

salutations in awe of his godlike stature and salvific powers.[19] In the Gospel version, Jesus arrives amid Hosannas ("Save, we pray") and palm branches. But his humble status, "gentle, and mounted on a donkey, even a colt, the foal of a beast of burden," subversively undermines worldly military or political power and glory. In fact, God's contempt for this ironic contrast is best described as mockery (Ps 2:1-9, esp. v. 4).

The early Christians picked up this technique of irony used in the Gospels and implemented it into their art in order to further their subversion of the Roman Empire and its pantheon of gods. Christian art from as early as A.D. 300 depicts Christ in poses that resemble the emperor or Roman deities as depicted on coinage and other Roman art. Christ is often pictured as enthroned among his apostles like a deity in a pantheon and the emperor on his throne;[20] complete with gold paint and halos, Roman images used for deity.[21] Compositions are often symmetrical and frontal in display, a likeness of imperial art and glory;[22] funerary tables of the mighty Hercules were replaced with funerary tables of the gentle Good Shepherd;[23] a predominance of art illustrating Christ's miracles, more common than any other images in this time period, indicated a "war of images" with the ineffectual pagan magic so common in the ancient world.[24] Early Christian art was subversive of Roman Empire and Roman magic religion.

Yet another way in which the New Testament writers may have subverted the prevailing Imperial culture is in the notion of Christian assemblies or local churches. The Greek word for "church" in the New Testament is *ekklesia.* But translating the word as "church" misses an important context for the first-century Christians. The "primary meaning of *ekklesia* in the Greek-speaking eastern Roman empire was the citizen 'assembly' of the Greek polis,"[25] a term which had evolved from the Greek idea of local democratic cities ruled by kings[26] into the Roman idea of local communities centered around patron gods festivals and customs under the supreme authority of Caesar. Diana, for

---

[19] Thomas F. Mathews, *The Clash of the Gods: A Reinterpretation of Early Christian Art* (Prince-ton, N.J.: Princeton University Press, 1993, 1995), pp. 24-27.
[20] Ibid., pp. 3-5, 107-8.
[21] Ibid., p. 101.
[22] Ibid., p. 14.
[23] Ibid., p. 8.
[24] Ibid., pp. 59, 65-67.
[25] Horsley, *Paul and Empire*, pp. 208-9.
[26] "Polis," accessed at Wikipedia, February 5, 2008, at <http://en.wikipedia.org/wiki/Polis>.

example, was the patron goddess of Ephesus around whom the economic, political and religious cult thrived (Acts 19:23-41). The power of Rome prospered in allowing city-states their local deities and customs, so long as they rendered unto Caesar worship as the supreme head over all. So the apostolic emphasis on the Christian *ekklesia* as an alternative community apart from the local deities and without worship of Caesar was a decided subversion of the Roman imperial order of assemblies. This alternative Christian community awaiting the apocalyptic overthrow of imperial hegemony ultimately disturbed the *Pax Romana* ("Peace of Rome"), resulting in the tribulation and persecution of Christians under Emperor Nero, during which Christians were accused of being "haters of the human race" by imperial inquisitors.[27] Of course, the Jews engaged in persecution of the Christians as well for their subversive defiance of their own traditions.[28] The notion of Christian *ekklesia* ("assembly") had its primary origins in the ancient Hebrew Old Testament concept of the "assembly of the LORD" (1 Chron 28:8). The synagogue was the basic local unit of Jewish cult that met on the Sabbath, so the Jewish Christians having their own synagogue on Sunday in celebration of Messiah's resurrection was a subversive alteration of Jewish culture (Mk 16:9; Acts 20:7). So in a way, Christian *ekklesia* was subversive not only of Rome but also of Jerusalem. Which leads us to the next point.

Subversion of Jewish Culture

It is important to remember that the Gospels are not merely subversive of pagan imagery and culture, they are first and foremost subversive of ancient Jewish culture itself! The Jewish expectation of a conquering military messiah is not only reflected in the Dead Sea Scrolls of the Qumran community[29] and the manifold revolutionary sects of the first century[30] but also in the hostile reaction of the Jews toward Jesus' claim to be Messiah. Although Messiah as suffering servant and spiritual victor is not a redefinition of the Old Testament prophecies (Is 53), it is certainly undermining of the prevalent expectations of

---

[27] Kenneth L. Gentry Jr., *The Beast of Revelation* (Powder Springs, Ga.: American Vision, 2002), p. 51. Gentry is referring to the primary source of Roman historica, Tacitus, in his Annals 1544.

[28] John 20:19; Acts 8:1-3; Mark 7:5.

[29] See for instance, Theodor H. Gaster, trans., *The Triumph of God: Descriptions of the Final Age, in The Dead Sea Scriptures, 3rd ed.* (New York: Doubleday, 1976), pp. 383-428.

[30] Flavius Josephus, *The Wars of the Jews*, in *The Works of Josephus* (Peabody, Mass.: Hendrickson, 1987, 1992).

first-century Jews who had misunderstood the Scriptures and were looking for worldly deliverance from the Romans as God's promised victory.

N. T. Wright has pointed out that the narrative of Luke reflects not only a Hellenistic biographic approach (thus casting it in terms understood by his pagan readers) but also a retelling of the Davidic story of kingship.[31] Both David's and Jesus' stories are outlined with a prior herald's birth (Samuel and John the Baptizer), a mother's song of praise and gratitude, judgment on Israel for rejection of God's word, the life of an outcast with a motley crew of followers in the desert, an anointing of kingship by the herald, a Spirit anointing, a declaration of sonship,[32] a battle with a monster in the desert, further wandering in the desert, and a triumphal arrival in Jerusalem.[33] Jesus' life was retold as a Davidic story—the Son of David to sit on his throne (Lk 1:32)—to subvert the Jewish expectation of a revolutionary political military ruler of violence with a Messiah of suffering and a kingdom of spirit without physical weapons.

Luke is not the only one to subvert with his Gospel. Matthew subverts the Jewish exile and return story of Israel, and retells it as believers in Jesus forming the true descendants of Abraham, Isaac and Jacob. Jesus is the "Joshua" that brings the Jews into the land of blessings and curses promised in Deuteronomy 30:15-20.[34]

Mark's Gospel subverts the apocalyptic unveiling of mysteries and secrets of the kingdom of God by reversing the Jewish expectations of justice. As Wright explains, in Mark's subversion,

> The coming of the kingdom does not mean the great vindication of Jerusalem, the glorification of the Temple, the real return from exile envisaged by the prophets and their faithful readers. It means rather, the desolation of Jerusalem,

---

[31] "I will raise up your descendant after you, who will come forth from you, and I will establish his kingdom. He shall build a house for My name, and I will establish the throne of his kingdom forever. I will be a father to him and he will be a son to Me" (2 Sam 7:12-14); "And so, because he was a prophet, and knew that God had sworn to him with an oath to seat one of his descendants upon his throne" (Acts 2:30).

[32] "I will be a father to him and he will be a son to Me" (2 Sam 7:14); "And a voice came out of heaven, 'You are My beloved Son, in You I am well-pleased'" (Lk 3:22).

[33] N. T. Wright, *The New Testament and the People of God* (Minneapolis: Fortress, 1992), pp. 378-83.

[34] Ibid., p. 388. "Jesus" is the Greek translation of "Joshua."

the destruction of the Temple, and the vindication of Jesus and his people.[35]

The Gospel of John uses language that seems to subvert Hellenistic mystery religion. But conservative scholars have recently suggested that the opening of John's Gospel about the Logos (indeed the whole of the Gospel) reflects a subversion of "wisdom" that is more Hebraic than Hellenistic.[36] And that Hebraic concept is reflected not only in Genesis, but in the apocryphal books and Dead Sea Scrolls leading up to the New Testament:[37]

> Wisdom will praise herself, and will glory in the midst of her people. In the assembly of the Most High she will open her mouth, and in the presence of his host she will glory.... Then the Creator of all things gave me a commandment, and the one who created me assigned a place for my tent. And he said, "Make your dwelling in Jacob, and in Israel receive your inheritance." From eternity, in the beginning, he created me, and for eternity I shall not cease to exist.... All this is the book of the covenant of the Most High God, the law which Moses commanded us as an inheritance for the congregations of Jacob. (Ben Sirach 24:1-24)

In this Hebrew scroll we see wisdom with God in the beginning, just as Logos was with God in the beginning in John. Wisdom is given a tent, just like Jesus "pitched his tent" in John 1:14. Wisdom has glory just as Jesus has glory (Jn 1:14). The law comes through Moses in Ben Sirach, just as it is affirmed in John 1:17, but expanded to add grace and truth being realized through Jesus Christ. The parallels are strong, as they are with Hellenism, reflecting perhaps more accurately that the kind of language John used was universal within the culture, concepts utilized by most religious and cultural communities of the era for their own purposes. Everyone used a similar vocabulary of light

---

[35] Ibid., p. 395.

[36] Ibid., pp. 410-17.

[37] James H. Charlesworth, ed., *John and the Dead Sea Scrolls* (New York: Crossroad, 1991). C. K. Barrett, *The Gospel According to St. John: An Introduction with Commentary and Notes on the Greek Text*, 2nd ed. (Philadelphia: Westminster Press, 1978).

and darkness, wisdom and word, life and death, spirit and flesh, and simply subverted those terms within their own thought forms.[38]

Jesus himself was a master subversive storyteller who entered the Jewish history of hope, and retold that story of exodus, exile and return in terms that turned the Jewish expectations upside down. His parables are strong indictments against the "chosen people" who reject their own messiah and instead receive judgment upon themselves, while the "rejected ones" (Gentiles, Samaritans, tax collectors, prostitutes and other sinners) enter into the kingdom (Mt 21:31-32). The parables of the vineyard (Mt 21:33-43), the tree barren of fruit (Lk 13:6-9), the unfaithful servant (Mt 24:45-51), the prodigal son (Lk 15), the Pharisee and tax collector (Lk 18:9-14), the ten virgins (Mt 25:1-13), the hidden talents (Mt 25:14-30), the sheep and the goats (Mt 25:31-46) and the wedding feast (Mt 22:1-14; 8:11-12) are all subversive stories of images that illustrate the false assumption of the Jewish people as righteous before God.

Jesus' healings of the blind, deaf and dumb, lepers, cripples, the possessed, Gentiles, Samaritans and other ritually "unclean" persons bore witness to "the inclusion within the people of YHWH of those who had formerly been outside,"[39] a reconstitution of the people of God by gathering the outcast into God's new community, the kingdom of heaven. His parables of God seeking and saving the lost like a woman for a coin or a shepherd after a lost sheep or the prodigal son (Lk 15) were implicit defiance of the Jewish community's rejection of the "other" as embodied in the Gentiles or "sinners."

Wright points out that Jesus' parables were not merely tales of "timeless dogma or ethics" but rather an entire retelling of the story of Israel with a new agenda much in the same way as someone might undermine the received history of a country's heroic growth of freedom by retelling it in terms of exploitation and power. The Olivet Discourse in Matthew 23—24 and Luke 21, as well as the book of Revelation, are prophecies of judgment upon first-century Israel for rejecting the Messiah. The destruction of Jerusalem and the Temple that occurred in A.D. 70 is then described as a result of such rejection.[40] As Jesus clearly states to his hearers of the first-century generation:

---

[38]D. A. Carson, *The Gospel According to John* (Grand Rapids: Eerdmans, 1991), pp. 59-60.

[39]N. T. Wright, *Jesus and the Victory of God* (Minneapolis: Fortress, 1996), p. 192.

[40]I highly recommend the following books for more information on the Olivet Discourse prophecies: Gary DeMar, *Last Days Madness: Obsession of the Modern Church* (Atlanta: American Vision, 1997), Kenneth L. Gentry Jr., *The Beast of Revelation* (Powder Springs, Ga.: American Vision, 2002).

> "Jerusalem, Jerusalem, who kills the prophets and stones those who are sent to her! How often I wanted to gather your children together, the way a hen gathers her chicks under her wings, and you were unwilling. Behold, your house is being left to you desolate!"... Jesus came out from the temple and was going away when His disciples came up to point out the temple buildings to Him. And He said to them, "Do you not see all these things? Truly I say to you, not one stone here will be left upon another, which will not be torn down." (Mt 23:37—24:2)

Perhaps Jesus' most indicting subversion of Israel is his parable of the vineyard in Matthew 21, where he likens Israel's rejection of his Messiahship to the rejection and killing of a vineyard owner's son, resulting in the destruction of those vine-growers and the renting out of the vineyard to others. This parable, a retelling of Isaiah's similar parable (Is 5), ends with the ultimate subversion from Jesus' own lips, "Therefore I say to you, the kingdom of God will be taken away from you and given to a people, producing the fruit of it" (Mt 21:43).

In all these parables and images, this presumption of Jewish righteous standing is turned on its head by God who rejects such arrogance in favor of the "outcast," the repentant sinner. Wright concludes, "This ties in, of course, with the use of apocalyptic, which (as we now know) is at least in part to be understood as the literature of subversion, of the cryptic undermining of a dominant and powerful worldview, and the encouraging and supporting of a revolutionary one."[41] God scandalously chooses the "unchosen" to be his people—much to the shock and chagrin of those who considered themselves chosen through family birth:

> As He says also in Hosea, "I will call those who were not My people, 'My people,' And her who was not beloved, 'beloved.'"
> "And it shall be that in the place where it was said to them, 'you are not My people,' There they shall be called sons of the living God." (Rom 9:25-26)

As the Temple served as a metaphor for the covenant along with the language of creation of the universe, so its destruction was described in the

---

[41] Wright, *Jesus and the Victory of God*, p. 179.

metaphoric image of the end of the universe. Now we see in the New Testament the subversion of Temple imagery. Following Jesus, the apostle Peter redefines a host of Old Testament imagery in terms of New Testament covenant, along the way describing the body of Christ as the rebuilt temple:

> And coming to Him as to a living stone which has been rejected by men, but is choice and precious in the sight of God, you [Christians] also, as living stones, are being built up as a spiritual house for a holy priesthood, to offer up spiritual sacrifices acceptable to God through Jesus Christ. (1 Pet 2:4-5)

Peter then images Jesus as that cornerstone of the new Temple:

> For this is contained in Scripture: "Behold, I lay in Zion a choice stone, a precious corner stone, And he who believes in Him will not be disappointed." This precious value, then, is for you who believe. (1 Pet 2:6-7)

Lastly, Peter subverts the Old Testament language used of ethnic Jews ("chosen people," "holy nation," royal priesthood") and applies that terminology to all believers in Jesus:

> But you are a chosen race, a royal priesthood, a holy nation, a people for God's own possession, so that you may proclaim the excellencies of Him who has called you out of darkness into His marvelous light; for you once were not a people, but now you are the people of God; you had not received mercy, but now you have received mercy. (1 Pet 2:9-10)

Christianity, though it was the intended messianic fulfillment of the Old Covenant promises, was nevertheless a subversion of a first-century Jewish worldview that had strayed from the Scriptures into rabbinic distortion, thereby missing the very Messiah they looked for. With this radical subversion of Jewish expectations and the transformation of the entire symbolic system of Temple, Torah, blood and soil, into Jesus and his followers, it is no wonder the apostles of that subversive message were all martyred, save one.[42]

---

[42] N. T. Wright, *The New Testament and the People of God* (Minneapolis: Fortress, 1992), pp. 450-51.

Recent Christian Heroes of Subversion

Rather than separating himself into the Christian enclave of "holy subculture," Paul and the other biblical writers interacted redemptively with their Jewish and pagan surroundings. They assimilated Jewish and pagan imagery into a Christian worldview and redefined it. They found points of connection and truth, and affirmed them. They also pointed out where Christianity was distinct and antithetical. But they interacted with the culture. They did not avoid it. So Christians today should expose themselves to and even participate in the music, movies and television of today with an eye toward the truth—*within* the media as well as the truth *without* it.

An excellent example of Christian appropriation of pagan mythology and images are the famous Christian fantasy writers C. S. Lewis and J. R. R. Tolkien. Their love of pagan Nordic mythology united them in their early club, The Coal Biters. Later, this influence showed up in their writing, such as Tolkien's Lord of the Rings trilogy and Lewis's seven-volume Chronicles of Narnia. Tolkien's stories abound with the mythical Norse characters of wizards, dwarves, elves, giants, trolls and others.[43] Lewis's stories are saturated with beasts from assorted pagan mythologies. *The Lion, the Witch, and the Wardrobe* alone contains the phoenix of Egyptian origin; Bacchus, the Roman god of wine; minotaurs, fauns, centaurs, unicorns, and gryphons from Greco-Roman paganism. And then there are the witches, as well as animistic tree nymphs, wood nymphs and water nymphs.

For years I struggled with the notion of using such fantasy characters of pagan origin in Christian art. The strongest example of this is the use of witches. I labored over the use of witches in non-Christian stories like the Harry Potter series as opposed to the use of such creatures of magic in the Christian fantasies of Lewis and Tolkien. On the one hand, Harry Potter seems to "normalize" witchcraft and support the possibility of good and bad witches. Contrarily, the Bible condemns all forms of witchcraft as evil (Deut. 18:9-14). There is no such thing as good or evil witches in the Bible. There is only one kind of witchcraft and that is the evil kind.

And yet how different are Lewis and Tolkien's witches or for that matter, their "magic"? Yes, Lewis's White Witch is evil, which is consistent with Scripture, but the other mythological creatures, good and evil, are equally as

---

[43]See Andy Orchard, *Cassell's Dictionary of Norse Myth and Legend* (London: Cassell, 2002).

pagan (wizards, satyrs, fairies, and centaurs). And Tolkien's good and bad wizards are simply male witches. So there is not all that much difference in that sense between Potter and Narnia or Middle Earth.[44]

Reflecting on biblical passages that not only referenced pagan myths and images but used them in the service of Christianity helped me to realize that images that originate in pagan beliefs such as animism can be put to good Christian use if they are redeemed imaginatively. This is exactly what the godly Jotham did in the Bible when he confronted Judah with a parable of talking trees that seek a king and end up convincing a bramble bush to rule over them (Judg 9:7-15). Throughout Scripture we read of rivers and trees clapping their hands in praise of God and mountains singing songs of joy (Is 55:12; Ps 98:8) or having envy (Ps 68:16) as if these inanimate objects had souls and could relate to God. Jesus used talking sheep and goats as an allegory of the final judgment (Mt 25:36-41). And Balaam's donkey argued with his master over his failure to trust his beast of burden's spiritual insight (Num 22:28-30). The many-headed beast of Revelation 13:5-6 is a foul-mouthed monstrosity, while the flying talking eagle of Revelation 8:13 is a righteous prophet. Even the holy union of Christ with the church is represented as a woman (the bride) marrying an animal (the Lamb) in Revelation 19:6-9. These are all scriptural examples of animism used metaphorically in the service of God.

In like manner, Lewis and Tolkien seem to use magic and witchcraft more as a metaphor for something else than as a sign of real-world gnostic manipulation of reality. Lewis's "deep magic" is an allegorical metaphor for the Law of God and the order he has ordained for reality. The pagan mythological characters in the Chronicles of Narnia are simply various images reflecting man's misguided imaginative perceptions of God—an acknowledgment of the universal reality created by God and distorted by the Fall.

Tolkien's entire Middle Earth mythology of magic was a metaphor for the loss of the sacred in modernity. He saw Enlightenment scientific rationalism and its spawn, the Industrial Revolution, as the killer of the spiritual side of man.[45] This was the result not of modernist environmentalism but of his

---

[44] A bigger problem, as I see it, with Harry Potter is not so much that author J. K. Rowling classifies good and bad witches but that some of the Potter stories tend to justify the pragmatic morality of situational ethics. Lying, disobedience to authority and breaking rules are justified in the first book when they result in good being accomplished. This "ends justifying the means" is unbiblical and detrimental to the spiritual well-being of the children who absorb it (Rom 3:8; 1 Cor 15:33). On the other hand, there are also strong themes of loyalty, friendship, courage and other Christian values in the Potter series, which makes it a mixture of good and bad.

[45] *The Rough Guide to the Lord of the Rings* (Strand, U.K.: Penguin, 2003), pp. 277-78.

Roman Catholic medieval unity of knowledge and life before God. Tolkien's method is similarly employed in the horror genre in art, novels and films. Horror communicates a very clear picture of the world as containing real evil. In this era of postmodern relative morality where people actually try to justify atrocities by appealing to moral equivalency (ie: "one man's terrorist is another man's freedom fighter"), this elementary notion of good and evil is rather profound. In horror, one man's serial killer is really a serial killer and his evil is undeniably without moral equivalency. Christian filmmaker Scott Derrickson's *The Exorcism of Emily Rose* uses the horror genre to communicate a strong spiritual reality to a modernist world of positivistic science. My own film adaptation of Frank Peretti's Christian horror novel *The Visitation* sought to use demonic deception as a corollary to a lack of true understanding of Christ. A look at the origins of modern horror from the Romantic period *(Frankenstein, Dracula, Dr. Jekyll and Mr. Hyde)* reveals a rather Christian influence in revealing the negative ramifications of man's hubris and immorality.[46]

Subverting Christianity

Sadly, one of the most powerful recent examples of subversion was in fact a non-Christian movie trilogy, *The Matrix*, that subverted Christian themes. The cinematic equivalent of Friedrich Nietzsche's book *Thus Spake Zarathustra* or Jean Baudrillard's *Simulacra and Simulation*, The Matrix trilogy runs multiple religious images—mostly from Christianity—through a Nietzschean interpretation that deconstructs all these faiths into Gnostic salvation of redemption through self-enlightenment. The series marked a turning point in mainstream society from modernism to postmodernism.

The movies shown in figure 7.1 below were all successful popular movies about heroes who in real life were Christians, whose faith influenced their exploits. Yet, every one of these movies either entirely ignored that faith or downplayed it to virtual irrelevancy. Paul Rusesabagina was the man profiled in *Hotel Rwanda*; his Christian faith caused him to reach out and help those who were being slaughtered in the 1990s Rwandan genocide. But you would never know that because the filmmakers did not depict his faith.

The protagonist of *The Pursuit of Happyness*, Chris Gardner, was helped by the values of his faith, such as the Protestant work ethic, that helped him

---

[46]E. Michael Jones, *Monsters from the Id: The Rise of Horror in Fiction and Film* (Dallas: Spence Publishing, 2000).

overcome his poverty. But you would never know that because filmmakers successfully hid his faith.

The film *Becoming Jane* fictionalizes Jane Austen's life. Along the way it eliminates her Christian faith, depicting her as a humanistic proto-feminist romantic instead.

Figure 7.1

The real Anna Leonowens who married the King of Siam was a Christian missionary whose faith informed her values. But you wouldn't know that because her faith was non-existent in *Anna and the King*.

Two movies about Pocahontas—*The New World* and *Pocahontas*—deliberately ignore the woman's conversion to Christianity, and even go so far as to romanticize the Native American animism that she rejected.

In the second half of his life, after his encounter with God in a cave, Johnny Cash was all about Jesus. But you wouldn't know that from *Walk the Line*, because this movie stops chronologically before the most profound redemption and character arc takes place. The movie portrays Cash being saved by June Carter, rather than by Jesus Christ.

In real life, the protagonist that *Hardball* was based on, Daniel Coyle, brought redemption to inner-city kids through his faith in Jesus Christ. But you wouldn't know that because the movie depicted him as a profane, foul-mouthed jerk who becomes a humanistic humanitarian.

The hero that the film *The Patriot* was based on, Francis Marion, was fueled in his ambition for American independence by his Christianity, a fact almost entirely ignored in the movie, save for a trivial shot of prayer.

Other movies, such as *Inherit the Wind* (1960), 1492 (1992), *Titanic* (1997), *King Arthur* (2005), *Kingdom of Heaven* (2005), *Children of Men* (2006), and *Beowulf* (2007) are successful movies that took the Christian themes of the original material and twisted them into anti-Christian themes, thus in effect raping the faith of the original authors. These movies are examples of how powerful subversion can be. In essence, these Christian stories have been captured and retold through paradigms of "good works" or the "power of the human spirit" or some other humanistic fiction rather than through the living vital faith of the heroes.

Those who capture the culture not only tell their own stories but reinterpret the stories of their opponents through their own worldview. This is not necessarily dishonest; we all interpret and reinterpret history through our worldviews. Christians should tell their own stories of martyrs or missionaries, but we should not neglect to retell the stories of atheists and humanists like Darwin, Stalin, Marx, Nietzsche and Freud and others through our worldview. Subversion is the nature of storytelling, and storytelling is how anyone wins a culture.

Chapter 8
What Art Would Jesus Do?

The Church of Jesus Christ has had a troubled relationship with the arts throughout history. Perhaps one of the reasons why lies in the very nature of creativity, which is driven to discover new and original ways of communicating or seeing things.

This search for newness often results in new styles of art that challenge the status quo with revolutionary implications on the way we see the world. While many Christians today find Impressionism an acceptable painting style, they rarely realize that it was originally received with derision, due to its origins in the philosophy of naturalism.[1] This belief—that there is no spiritual reality and everything is reducible to sense impressions—was taken to its logical conclusion: reality itself is merely reflections of light in our eyes.

From rock music to abstract expressionism to horror movies, Christians have often reacted with hostility to the surface elements of artistic styles in music, painting, theater, film, and literature rather than understanding the worldview below the surface. To these reactionary Christians, because abstract expressionists like Jackson Pollock painted chaotically, all abstract expression becomes godless. Because some horror movies exploit fear and violence, all scary movies become "demonic."

Such reactionism is biblically unwarranted. A survey of the styles of art and literature in the Bible unveils a plethora of genres, including abstract art and horror, that have been used for both evil and good in the history of art. What makes the art evil or good is not the style but the worldview that the style is servicing. Abstraction may appear ugly to some people, but even so, ugliness is part of the biblical painting of the world in the Fall. Representational or realistic art can be used to express the beauty of creation or a godless

---

[1] H. R. Rookmaaker, *Modern Art and the Death of a Culture* (Downers Grove, Ill.: InterVarsity Press, 1971), pp. 82-87.

philosophy of naturalism. Horror can be used to exploit fear and sexuality or to prove the real existence of evil to a world that believes in relativism.[2]

Rules of Beauty

Christians who are influenced by modernity are conditioned to seek for absolute rules of good and bad art. Rap isn't real music, abstract expressionism isn't real painting, and so on. The problem with this categorizing agenda is that, while there may be some rules regarding the nature of how art affects the viewer, rules for art that are traditionally recognized in conservative circles are too often unbiblical. When observed in the light of Scripture, these absolutes dissolve into a sea of a thousand biblical qualifications. Let's take a closer look at some of these rules to see how absolute and unbiblical they really are.

Realism over Nonrealism

Realistic art is often elevated in Christian circles above other artistic styles. There is a marked tendency to consider fantasy, myth, abstraction, symbolism and other non-representational styles as less legitimate than realism or representational art. The more literal, the better; the more obvious the better; the more "like real-life" the better. This is often linked to a desire for "literalism" in interpreting the Bible. Some say a realistic story meets a person where they are; a literal picture of reality is more easily understood than symbol; representations of things in the world are safer than flights of fantasy.

Unfortunately these well-meaning Christians do not realize that this elevation of realism springs from the naturalistic scientific claim that the empirical world—what we see with our senses—is all there is. It hides the central conceit of modernity that reality can be known objectively and without prejudice or bias by our mere observation. In this context, realism is anything but real. It is the claim that the way things appear is the way they really are, that there is no underlying reality.

Taken this way, realism becomes a façade for nihilism, the belief that there is no meaning, purpose or value to life. There is just "what happens," and "that's reality, baby." Realism becomes a life lived in the Matrix.

---

[2]See my book *Hollywood Worldviews* for a discussion of how worldviews are communicated through film.

Christianity is realistic in that it portrays the way things really are, but not often in a realistic style. Vast metaphors, symbols, analogies and poetry are used to describe the spiritual or metaphysical reality beneath the outward appearance of human experience. I know a lot of nice people who are not Christians and don't seem bad as human beings. They do good, they seem to be free and open to truth, and some of them are even well-adjusted and fulfilled. But is this reality? Like Morpheus explaining to Neo, so Jesus and the apostles unveil an apocalyptic reality quite different from the way things appear: no one is ultimately good (Lk 18:19); all unbelievers are rebels against God (Rom 3:9-12), slaves to their sin (Jn 8:34), blind (2 Cor 4:4), spiritually dead (Eph 2:1) and without hope (Eph 2:12).

Realism is not the full picture.

Harmony over Disharmony

Often religious folk have the belief that songs that do not have a harmonious order, paintings that are messy and disturbingly imbalanced, and movies that are "dark and negative" reflect an ungodly viewpoint in the artist or work. "Family-friendly" arts and entertainment that stress harmony or order and positivity are to be preferred over those showing disharmony or negativity. After all, "God is not a God of confusion, but of peace" (1 Cor 14:33).

To be sure, the Bible is a book that communicates an ultimate harmony and ultimate order for God and the universe. But because it is a fallen world, we are not there yet, so the Bible deals very openly with the disorder around us. The nature of the entire Bible is one of conflict between light and darkness. There are periods of great darkness (Judges), and spiritual apostasy (minor and major prophets). God often gives disturbing visions and images in order to bring back the harmony or order that was lost (Revelation).

Moreover, sometimes harmony can be idolatrous. In the pagan culture of unified harmony and peace under Caesar or Nebuchadnezzar, to stand apart and be out of harmony with the prevailing order would be in fact the godly thing to do. Sometimes art needs to be disturbing and out of order with the times if the times are indeed evil as the Bible says they are (1 Cor 2:6; Col 2:20-21).

Linearity over Nonlinearity

Some Christians think that nonlinearity is ungodly in art. They believe that a story out of chronological sequence is irrational and therefore not good.

Nonlinearity is an offense to rationalism because it appears to deny the order of reality.

The Bible's overall narrative is linear in its organization: Genesis (beginning), redemptive history (middle), and eschaton (end). But within this overarching order there are cyclical histories (1-2 Kings), multiple perspectives (four Gospels), as well as nonlinear chronology (Isaiah, Jeremiah, Revelation). And the major and minor prophets are certainly not placed in their respective linear chronology within the text. The Scriptures are inherently multi-perspectival, being written by kings and slaves, princes and paupers, from God's perspective as well as from the perspective of saints and sinners. The nonlinearity and perspectivalism in the Bible serve a higher, God-directed purpose and ought not be feared.

Styles of Art in the Bible

Francis Schaeffer's classic little book *Art and the Bible* contains a survey of art used in the Bible.[3] In addition to representational art for the tabernacle and temple (Ex 25:18,31), God also commands abstract art (Ex 28:33), symbolic art (Ex 28:15), art as sacrament (Num 21:8) and art for beauty's sake (Ex 28:2). In the Scriptures, there is not merely religious art such as sacred poetry (Psalms), but so-called secular art: friendship poetry (2 Sam 1:19-27), erotic romance novels (Song of Solomon) and civic sculpture (1 Kings 10:18-20). God employs the genres of epic (Exodus), romance (Ruth and Esther), erotic thriller (Prov 7), horror and fantasy (Dan 7), and absurdist drama (Ecclesiastes). God clearly enjoys loud music, singing (1 Chron 23:5) and dancing (Ps 149:3), as well as their opposites: chanting (Ezek 32:16), silence ("selah" throughout Psalms) and stillness (Ps 4:4).

God had his prophets put on war dramas (Ezek 4:1-3), engage in shocking performance art (Is 20:2-4), tell parables (Mt 13:3), allegories (2 Sam 12:1-7), symbolic fantasies (Judg 9:7-15), zombie stories (Gen 41:19-21) and other monster and sci-fi horror epics (Revelation). Jesus' fictional parables run the gamut of genres with gangster stories (Mt 18:6), macabre horror (Mt 18:8-9), family drama (Lk 15:11-32), thrillers (Mt 18:23-35), courtroom dramas (Lk 18:1-8), revenge stories (Mt 21:33-41), corporate espionage (Lk 16:1-9), animal tales (Mt 25:36-41), tragedies (Mt 24:45-51) and comedies (Lk 15:3-10).

---

[3]Francis Schaeffer, *Art and the Bible* (Downers Grove, Ill.: InterVarsity Press, 1973).

The fact that most of these examples from Scripture are literary styles does not restrict the analogy to literature. Abstraction, realism, symbolism and others exist in all creativity, including music and the visual arts. There are simply so many styles that God has used or approved of that it would be ludicrous to try to condemn any particular style of art simply because godless people are using that style to communicate an aspect of their godless worldview. Scripture often employs these same styles of art that modern Christians bristle at. It is not the form that necessarily makes the art immoral, it is the content.

Each genre or style of art contains a particular angle that can be used in the service of truth or falsehood as well as employed to exploit evil or expose sin biblically. Consider the "family friendly" cartoons of Disney that teach antibiblical values such as disobedience to parents *(The Little Mermaid, Mulan)*, Christianity as the enemy of progress *(The Hunchback of Notre Dame, Beauty and the Beast)*, evolution *(Dinosaur)*, and the lie of the "noble savage" *(Pocohantas, Tarzan)*. Even biblical epics can be a twisting of the truth into a lie (the movies *Noah* and *Exodus: Gods and Kings*, the novel *The Red Tent*, Salvador Dali's painting *The Last Supper*). Some so-called Christian movies actually teach a modern "love-gospel" that is far more spiritually detrimental than any slasher flick or erotic thriller.[4]

R-Rated Bible

Another aspect of style that afflicts Christian decision-making about the arts is the depiction of sin or the dark side of humanity. Many Christians are rightfully concerned about the increasing amounts of sex and violence in the arts, specifically pop music, television and movies. But when they make sweeping condemnations such as "All R-rated movies are sinful or bad" or "Any sexual reference in music is wrong," they are unwittingly fostering an unscriptural worldview that would condemn their own Bibles. I have spoken at Christian colleges that forbid their students from watching R-rated movies. Where they find this rule in the Bible is yet to be revealed, but ironically, there is no simultaneous restriction on reading R-rated literature. Perhaps this oversight

---

[4] The movie *Joshua* depicts a priest who refers to the Law of God and admission of sin as a Pharisee. The Christ figure in the film claims God is only about love, not law or judgment of sin. This "love gospel" has its roots in the ancient heresy of Marcionism, the belief that the God of the Old Testament was harsh and judgmental, while in contrast, the God of the New Testament is loving. The dichotomy of love and judgment in God's character is not biblical. In both Old and New Testaments, God is judge, jury (Ps 7:11; Heb 13:4), executioner (Dan 4; Mt 22:1-14), defense attorney (1 Jn 2:1) and kinsman redeemer (Heb 4:15).

was deliberate in order to allow the students to read and study their R-rated Bibles. Consider the R-rated books of Judges, 1 and 2 Kings and Chronicles, or the erotic poetry of Song of Solomon.[5]

Another irony is that this prohibition against R-rated material precluded students at one school from seeing *The Passion of the Christ,* one of the most powerful biblical movies in history, because of its R-rating. Some schools made an exception for *The Passion* because it is about redemption through the violence of the cross. What they fail to understand in their double standard is that the same kind of redemption, even substitutionary atonement (which is part and parcel of the Gospel), is found in other violent R-rated movies as well, such as *Braveheart, Collateral, Last of the Mohicans, Man on Fire, Return to Paradise, To End All Wars, Schindler's List* and *The Addiction.*

One of the most common anthropomorphic images in Scripture is that of God as lover or husband to his people. Over and over again, in both Old and New Testaments, God refers to Israel, his people, as a bride or wife (e.g., Jer 31:32; Rev 19:17).

Many Christians try to ignore or deny the erotic poetry of the Song of Solomon by reducing it to an allegory of Christ's love for the church. But even if it is an allegory, it still remains *erotic sexual love poetry,* something most churches would never read to their children, and certainly not in Sunday School.

The metaphor of marriage between God and his bride (the people of God) becomes a springboard for God's imagination when he deals with disobedience or spiritual apostasy. God uses many graphic sexual images to describe unfaithful or hypocritical faith. Just a sampling of such explicit metaphors are adultery (Hosea), prostitution (Hosea, Nahum 3), promiscuity (Ezek 16; 23), bestiality (Jer 13:25-27; Ezek 23:20), sex with inanimate objects (Jer 3:1-9; Ezek 16:17), gang rape (Ezek 23:28-29), indecent exposure (Jer 13:25-27; Nahum 3:5), and even the throwing of feces (Nahum 3:6). The Bible is simply not G-rated literature for family-friendly programming. Parental discretion is advised.

---

[5]In my book *Hollywood Worldviews: Watching Films with Wisdom and Discernment,* I chronicle and exegete Scriptural passages that prove the Bible is explicit about depravity and not at all shy in describing some sins in morbid or even erotic detail. Parental discretion is advised.

Sarcasm

Another kind of creative expression that is not as readily embraced in some parts of Christendom is sarcasm. Some Christians feel that sarcasm or satire is harsh and unloving—not befitting a Christ-like treatment of people. And a cursory look at American culture confirms that concern. We are drenched in sarcastic humor that often approaches cynical cruelty. Comedians ruthlessly mock everything from the sanctity of sex to the holiness of God. Chic nihilism reigns in music, movies and television. But does all this sophistry preclude a proper use of sarcasm? What is the Christian's responsibility regarding this dark angle on humor? It turns out that an examination of the Bible yields a rather startling revelation: God uses sarcasm and mockery as an important tool of truth-telling.

God is often sarcastic in his humor. And particularly in relation to sin. In response to the foolishness of sinners gathering together, plotting against God and his anointed Son, King David writes, "He who sits in the heavens laughs, The Lord scoffs at them" (Ps 2:4-5). God scoffs. He mocks the folly of wicked men (Ps 37:12-13), He mocks nations of sinners who "howl like dogs," and "belch forth with their mouths" (Ps 59:6-8). Arrogant rebels deserve to be mocked when comparing them to the glory of God.

But God does not reserve his acerbic wit for the reprobate alone. He also employs it against his own regenerate children when they get out of line. When Job's sincere desire to accept the deep ways of God turns into a questioning demand to account for alleged injustice, God responds with eighty-plus sarcastic questions meant to humiliate Job in his hubris. And God prefaces those questions by mockingly saying, "I will ask you, and you instruct Me!" (Job 38:3). As if God has anything to learn from the brightest star of human intelligence. As if God is obligated to give an account of his ways to man (Job 33:13). Questioning God deserves to be scorned, especially when it is engaged in by a believer who ought to know better.

Sarcasm is not below God's character, and neither is it below his people's character. The same laughing derision that God himself employs toward the wicked is also played out dramatically through God's appointed mockers—I mean messengers.

Elijah

When Elijah engages the false prophets of Baal on Mount Carmel in 1 Kings 18, both he and the enemy prophets place cut-up oxen on an altar of wood without fire. The challenge: Each will call upon their own God. And whichever God answers with fire from heaven upon the altar, he is God.

The Baal prophets call and call and cut themselves like a bunch of spiritual idiots. But surprise, no fire from heaven. Elijah responds with dripping sarcasm that can only come from the mouth of an anointed servant of God:

> Elijah mocked them and said, "Call out with a loud voice, for he is a god; either he is occupied or gone aside [to the toilet], or is on a journey, or perhaps he is asleep and needs to be awakened." (1 Kings 18:27)

Yahweh, of course, responds with fire from heaven. So the ridicule is clear. A god who is finite and who needs to travel or go to the bathroom or sleep is no god at all but a figment of men's idolatrous imaginations. And that is truly a laughing sight worthy of the highest scorn. The Comedy Channel, eat your heart out.[6]

Isaiah

In Isaiah 44 the prophet mocks those who worship idols made of the same wood used for common household tasks. One can hear the sarcasm bellowing in the words put into the idolater's mouth by Isaiah:

> "Aha! I am warm, I have seen the fire." But the rest of it he makes into a god, his graven image. He falls down before it and worships; he also prays to it and says, "Deliver me, for you are my god." (Is 44:16-17)

And atheists think they have a corner on mocking religion. God has the longest-running gag about religion yet—false religion, that is.

---

[6]Dennis Miller is a comedian, formerly of *Saturday Night Live,* who earned his reputation for quick, sophisticated sarcastic humor.

Paul

In 2 Corinthians Paul lays it on heavy with his own children in the faith. He sarcastically chides the Corinthians for their ignorant and foolish acceptance of false apostles, whom he mockingly calls "super-apostles":

> For you, being so wise, tolerate the foolish gladly. For you tolerate it if anyone enslaves you, anyone devours you, anyone takes advantage of you, anyone exalts himself, anyone hits you in the face. To my shame I must say that we have been weak by comparison. (2 Cor 11:19-21)

He calls them "wise" when they obviously are not. He intimates that it is sheer stupidity on the Corinthians' part for failing to recognize Satan's minions even when they're outright slapping them in the face (2 Cor 11:13-14)!

Paul concludes by asking them to forgive him for *not* being a financial burden to them (2 Cor 12:13), as if money-grubbing is the sign of a true apostle and preaching for free was not. This is mockery par-excellence. Here is some material for an ancient version of *Late Night with the Apostle Paul*.

Jesus

But what about Jesus? The man of love and kindness—surely he never used sarcasm or mockery to get a point across.

As the prophet Micaiah would say, go ahead and believe what you want. But here's the truth: Jesus mocked.

In Luke 13:32, for example, Jesus called King Herod a "fox." In ancient Jewish literature, the image of a fox was not only used as a derogatory metaphor for lowly cunning, but more particularly was a reference to people who were of little importance. The fox was a political nuisance who, like the jackal, would scavenge off the kill of a lion (imagery for truly powerful people) and try to dodge the consequences.[7] By using the image of a fox for Herod, Jesus is insulting him in the same way we might today insultingly refer to politicians as "publicity hounds," "weasels," or "sleazebags."

---

[7] "Animals: Fox or Jackal," in *The Dictionary of Biblical Imagery*, ed. Leland Ryken, James C. Wilhoit and Tremper Longman III (Downers Grove, Ill.: InterVarsity Press, 1998), p. 30.

But that's not all. By using the feminine form of the word Jesus is actually calling Herod a "vixen," a female fox, insinuating he was dominated by his unlawful wife Herodias.[8]

The Punchline

Of course, these biblical examples do not justify *all* sarcasm. We may not receive actual visions or direct words from God like they did, but we can draw on the principles found in their behavior and act accordingly. For example, we might draw the principle that satire may be appropriate when applied to public sins or evil done by men who openly defy God's law (Lk 13:32; 1 Kings 18:27) but not necessarily to the private sins of individuals with whom we have personal relationships (Mt 18:15). It may be appropriate to ridicule false religions and idolaters for their foolishness (Is 44:16-17), but not necessarily the moral failures of otherwise godly men (Gal 6:1). Condemning hypocrisy is biblical (Mt 23:13-29), hypocritical condemnation is sinful (Mt 7:1-5). We should degrade false teachers–even by name–in scathing terms (2 Tim 2:17-18) but we should be patient and kind with merely errant or misguided teachers (Phil 1:15-18). We may even chide the body of Christ if it has become hardened of heart, dense-headed or easily fooled, but only with a humble heart and redeeming motives (2 Cor 11). And of course, it is never appropriate to make jabs at God or his word, unless one is begging to be cursed (Job 40).

The danger of using sarcasm notwithstanding, it is certainly one of the most potent tools to make a moral point and expose sin, lies and hypocrisy with an edge of humor. The essence of comedy is precisely that we laugh at our faults and frailties, and yes, even at our sins, which elevates the excellent and the virtuous as superior. Sarcasm reinforces the values we believe in by showing the absurdity of those values that we don't. God is the original satirist. And he has built his comedy on the foundation of his apostles and prophets.

---

[8] Greg Bahnsen, *Theonomy in Christian Ethics* (Phillipsburg, N.J.: Presbyterian and Reformed, 1984), pp. 391-92.

Chapter 9: Afterword
In Good Company

I began this story explaining how I was driven by the pursuit of reason into a hunger for ideas and rational certainty but ended in the despair of dehumanized abstraction and an intellectualized faith that lacked imagination. My love of the arts and of creativity ruled my career and my personal interests, but my faith was dominated by rationality. I had been living in a struggle over my soul between reason and imagination—a struggle that originated in the modern scientific rationalistic way of looking at the world taught to me by my culture.

Since becoming aware of this cultural bias with its blessings and curses as well as the Bible's imaginative approach to truth and God, I have continued on my journey to seek a better balance between my intellect and emotions, between my reason and my imagination. But it remains a difficult task. I don't consider myself as having arrived or even living out my revelations as consistently as I would like. Old habits die hard. And doubts remain, accusing me of starting down the slippery slope to heterodoxy, of swinging the pendulum to another extreme, of worshiping images! Or maybe these accusations are just the toxic residue of the unbiblical paradigm of modernism that I've unveiled in my soul and sought to remove.

In light of these uncertainties, it was an amazing encouragement and affirmation to discover quite recently that a personal hero of mine, C. S. Lewis, had not only gone through this same struggle but experienced a similar transformation in his own intellectual and creative life. Apparently Lewis, famous for both his apologetics and his fantasy fiction, had struggled for many years over his imagination and intellect. Author Peter Schakel chronicles this struggle in his book *Reason and Imagination in C. S. Lewis: A Study of "Till We Have Faces."* Lewis's poem "Reason," probably written before he was a Christian, describes his internal tension as an ancient battle between science and mythology, between the so-called clarity of reason and dark obscurity of imagination.[1]

---

[1] Peter J. Schakel, preface to *Reason and Imagination in C. S. Lewis: A Study of "Till We Have Faces"*

REASON

>Set on the soul's acropolis the reason stands
>A virgin, arm'd, commercing with celestial light,
>And he who sins against her has defiled his own
>Virginity: no cleansing makes his garment white;
>So clear is reason. But how dark, imagining,
>Warm, dark, obscure and infinite, daughter of Night:
>Dark is her brow, the beauty of her eyes with sleep
>Is loaded, and her pains are long, and her delight.
>Tempt not Athene. Wound not in her fertile pains
>Demeter, nor rebel against her mother-right.
>Oh who will reconcile in me both maid and mother,
>Who make in me a concord of the depth and height?
>Who make imagination's dim exploring touch
>Ever report the same as intellectual sight?
>Then could I truly say, and not deceive,
>Then wholly say, that I BELIEVE.[2]

At this early point in his life Lewis's love of imagination seemed a contradiction to his highly rational mind. Nevertheless, imagination appeared to touch the infinite in a way that reason could not, and it haunted him.

Lewis had his confidence in the ability of reason to establish the existence of God shaken in a public debate with G. E. M. Anscombe. Apparently, Anscombe's critique was effective in challenging Lewis's privileged status as apologist. Ironically, since Anscombe was a Catholic, she was disagreeing with Lewis not over God's existence but merely on his arguments for God's existence. It was shortly after this incident that Lewis became more focused on writing fiction and less on abstract argumentation.[3]

Michael Ward, writing on the creative genius undergirding the Narnia Chronicles, argues that Lewis's turn to fiction and specifically the "Narniad" was "a deliberate engagement with, rather than a retreat from [Abscombe's]

(Grand Rapids: Eerdmans, 1984), accessed March 11, 2009, at
<http://hope.edu/academic/english/schakel/tillwehavefaces/publishing.html>.

[2]C. S. Lewis, *Poems* (Orlando: Harcourt, 1964, 1992), p. 81. Quoted in ibid.

[3]Schakel, *Reason and Imagination*, accessed March 11, 2009, at <http://hope.edu/academic/english/schakel/tillwehavefaces/chapter13.html>.

critique of his theology."[4] It wasn't that Lewis ditched the double-sided razor-sharp contours of reason and "fled" to the esoteric safety of ambiguous creative writing. It was more an application of a growing realization of the danger of an intellectualized faith that he would write about in a later essay:

> I have found that nothing is more dangerous to one's own faith than the work of an apologist. No doctrine of that Faith seems to me so spectral, so unreal as one that I have just successfully defended in a public debate. For a moment, you see, it has seemed to rest on oneself: as a result, when you go away from that debate, it seems no stronger than that weak pillar. That is why we apologists take our lives in our hands and can be saved only by falling back continually from the web of our own arguments, as from our intellectual counters, into the Reality—from Christian apologetics into Christ Himself.[5]

Lewis was pulling away from his unshakable modernist faith in the powers of abstract reason and seeking the uncertain experiential reality of relationship with God. In *A Grief Observed*, Lewis expresses his doubt in the ability of scientific observation—and its finite counterpart the rational intellect—in truly comprehending reality:

> Five senses; an incurably abstract intellect; a haphazardly selective memory; a set of preconceptions and assumptions so numerous that I can never examine more than a minority of them—never become even conscious of them all. How much of total reality can such an apparatus let through?[6]

It would be wrong to conclude that Lewis was swinging the pendulum from an intellectual faith to an anti-intellectual faith. More accurately, he was recognizing the limitations of the very organs of knowledge that he had relied upon. Reality was much bigger and more allusive than he had previously so presumptuously assumed. And it was imagination that he had previously

---

[4] Michael Ward, *Planet Narnia: The Seven Heavens in the Imagination of C. S. Lewis* (New York: Oxford University Press, 2008), p. 4.

[5] C. S. Lewis, "Christian Apologetics," in *God in the Dock: Essays on Theology and Ethics*, ed. Walter Hooper (Grand Rapids: Eerdmans, 1970), p. 103.

[6] C. S. Lewis, *A Grief Observed* (New York: HarpeCollins, 1961), p. 64.

considered "dark and obscure" that was actually able to access reality in ways reason could only dream of. The battle in his soul was turning in favor of imagination. Quoting a letter from Lewis to a literature society in the last years of his life, Schakel illustrates Lewis's journey and revelation of the superiority of imagination in his spiritual literary endeavors:

> The imaginative man in me is older, more continuously operative, and in that sense more basic than either the religious writer or the critic. It was he who made me first attempt (with little success) to be a poet. It was he who, in response to the poetry of others, made me a critic, and, in defense of that response, sometimes a critical controversialist. It was he who after my conversion led me to embody my religious belief in symbolical or mythopeic forms, ranging from *Screwtape* to a kind of theologised science fiction. And it was of course he who has brought me, in the last few years, to write the series of Narnian stories for children; not asking what children want and then endeavouring to adapt myself (this was not needed) but because the fairy tale was the genre best fitted for what I wanted to say.[7]

Lewis went from being an imaginative youth, to a rational adult who subordinated imagination to reason, to a writer who tried to integrate his imagination rationally, to an artist who returned to his youthful imagination. Like Jesus telling parables, Lewis came to believe that some aspects of truth, reality and God can only be captured through stories of the imagination.

Lewis's worship and awe of God's majesty through the powers of imagination in a universe of images can perhaps be best expressed through imaginative prose. Here Ransom, the protagonist of his novel *Perelandra*, looks out on the night sky and muses on his own enlightenment of freedom from the deadness of Enlightenment science and reason:

> A nightmare, long engendered in the modern mind by the mythology that follows in the wake of science, was falling off

---

[7] Letter from C. S. Lewis, quoted in Schakel, *Reason and Imagination*, accessed March 11, 2009, at <http://hope.edu/academic/english/schakel/tillwehavefaces/chapter13.html>.

him. He had read of "Space": at the back of his thinking for years had lurked the dismal fancy of the black, cold vacuity, the utter deadness, which was supposed to separate the worlds... but now that very name "Space" seemed a blasphemous libel for this empyrean ocean of radiance in which they swam. He could not call it "dead"; he felt life pouring into him from it every moment. How indeed should it be otherwise, since out of this ocean the worlds and all their life had come? He had thought it barren: he saw now that it was the womb of worlds. No: space was the wrong name. Older thinkers had been wiser when they named it simply the heavens—the heavens which declared the glory—the "happy climes that ly. Where day never shuts his eye. Up in the broad fields of the sky."[8]

What Lewis had learned, what I am learning, at the outer limits of our engagement with Christian faith through reason alone, is good news: God is bigger than rationality, bigger than imagination, and he is Lord of both. His invitation through Isaiah still rings true as we move gradually from the Age of Reason to the Media Age and as we oscillate back and forth between these paradoxical priorities of word and image:

> "Come now, let us reason together," says the LORD. "Though your sins are like scarlet, they shall be as white as snow; though they are red as crimson, they shall be like wool." (Is 1:18)

---

[8] C. S. Lewis, *Out of the Silent Planet* (New York: Scribner, 2003), p. 34.

Chapter 10: Appendix
Answering Objections

Word-oriented Christians often react with hostility to the suggestion that *image* is just as legitimate a means to the God of communication as *word* is. They cannot conceive that a movie or a painting can possibly have as much value or influence as a preached sermon or written systematic theology. Some decry the rise of the image and the fall of the word in our culture and lament for "better days" when print culture ruled the day and image was "in its place" as a subordinate and mistrusted medium. They are concerned about the negative effects on civilization that image brings. And they have some good arguments, arguments that I would like to explore in this appendix. I'll subtitle the arguments, spell them out briefly, and try to answer them equally as brief.

Objection 1:
Words Are Invisible Like Spirit; Images Are Visible Like Flesh

Many people assume that "image" refers only to things that are visible and "word" refers only to abstractions—things that are, in effect, "invisible." For ease of reference, I will refer to this dichotomy as the "visible/invisible fallacy." But as I explained from the start, we are talking about the *categories* of rationality (word) and imagination (image).

Visual images and printed words both affect the way we think and perceive the world. Many communications theorists agree that the dominance of the printed word has produced a certain kind of abstract thinking.[1] But as author Mitchell Stevens notes, written words' great limitation grows out of this great strength of abstraction. He writes that writing...

> is a system of representation, or code, that represents another system of representation, another code: spoken language. The written word *face*—to oversimplify a bit—calls

---

[1] Mitchell Stevens, *the rise of the image the fall of the word* (New York: Oxford University Press, 1998), pp. 20-21.

to mind the sound "fās." It is, therefore, two steps removed from that expressive skin sculpture itself.... Increasingly in the five thousand years since the development of writing, [our eyes] have been reduced to staring at letters of identical size and color, arranged in lines of identical length, on pages of identical size and color. Readers, in a sense, are no longer asked to see; they are simply asked to interpret the code.[2]

The category of visible and invisible are not so exclusive to image and word as some think. Consider the visual nature of words. If you look at the picture in just below, what do you see? You see the image of a shepherd.

Now, what do you see in the words just below? You see a shepherd.

A SHEPHERD

The first figure (the image) is representational, the second figure (the word) is symbolic. Technically, written words are just as much images as any painting or other visual image. The main difference is that they are symbolic as opposed to representational. So, in a way, the privileging of written words over visual images is really the privileging of one kind of image (symbolic) over another kind of image (representational). Printed words are actually symbolic images.

---

[2] Ibid., pp. 63-64.

But aren't mental images that we get from reading words different from physical images that we see with our eyes? Yes, they are different, but not so different as some would like to assert. When you see a visual picture of a shepherd, you are viewing an external public image. But when you read the word *shepherd,* you merely displace the *location* of the image from external and public to internal and private. You are privileging mental visual images over physical visual images. Thus a Scripture like Psalm 89:13, "God has a strong right arm," is rightly considered imagery because it is a "word-picture," words that paint a picture in the mind rather than appeal to some kind of abstract reasoning.

Sometimes words are invisible, as in speech, sometimes they are visible images, as in written words. Sometimes imagery is visible as in visual pictures, sometimes it is invisible, in the mind. Imagery can involve more empirical senses than the eye, such as a movie, but word also involves the eye in reading, or the ear in hearing, and in that way has a sensate aspect to it. Reading words is the same thing as seeing images, and both involve our empirical senses.

This is not to say, however, that words are merely reducible to images. For much of imagination involves words, reason and propositions as well. For example, a story about Moses includes propositions about his life or what God has said. When we talk about a painting or a movie, we use analytical discourse in our interaction with the medium. A musical composition follows an underlying rational structure of order. Words and images are not reducible to each other, they are interdependent concepts that can be distinguished but not always separated.

Objection 2:
This Book Is Written in Rational Propositional Words

This very book, arguing as it does for assigning a high value to imagery, is itself predominantly rational and propositional in method. Doesn't that seem like a contradiction?

Not at all. The Bible values words, books, rationality, propositions and logic, and therefore, so do I. I am not suggesting in the least that we scrap words and rationality because of the failure of modernity to measure up to biblical balance. Nor am I suggesting a pendulum swing of the superiority of image over word. I am suggesting that image has been devalued, thus we are impoverished in our biblical understanding of truth *and* God, and we need to have an equal ultimacy of both word *and* image in our cultural vocabulary.

I have been engaged in visual and dramatic imagery as an artist for many years. The fact that I also write propositional words reinforces my call to unity of engaging in both. We must have sermons and rational argumentation, but we must also have story, drama and other tactile imagery in our theological exploration of God or we miss God's fullness.

Objection 3:
God Left Us No Canonical Works of Art

Some might argue that God gave us only words in the Scripture, not pieces of art. If God considered images or art to be as valid as words, he would have left us with some. Since he did not, then imagery must not be as important as words.

This entire book has been a verification that the Bible itself is a work of art. The nature of narrative, parables, verbal imagery, metaphors and stories of visions, miracles and dreams is precisely a literary *art form* and not a scientific or rationalistic discourse. Just because it is written in words does not negate its artistic nature and does not reduce it to logocentricity.

If God used image to reveal himself and truth (such as in dreams and visions), then image is *not* a second-class means of communication. It's just as important a part of the process. Second Timothy 3:16 says that "all Scripture is inspired by God," or "God-breathed" words. But does this mean that the images, visions and dreams that God gave were not also "God-breathed"? Of course not. Both images *and* words are God's "Word," or as we indicated earlier, God's message. A person's *testimony* of what God has done in their life is not more important than what God *actually* did in their life.

Biblical apologists defend the inerrancy of Scripture by appealing to the "original autographs" as being without flaw, as opposed to the copies or translations that we have.[3] In a similar sense the written words are the translation of the experience or original vision from God. So the biblical legitimacy of the final written words does not eliminate the biblical legitimacy of the images upon which they are based. Both word and image are equally

---

[3] This strikes me as a questionable procedure: Attempting to prove the perfection of something that we do not have. I can understand this as a faith commitment, but not an evidential proof.

God-breathed communication. To pit one against the other is to pit God's Word against God's Word.

It is true that without words, we could not have the Bible as we now have it. But it is equally true that without dreams, visions, and other incarnate *imagery*, we could not have the Bible as we now have it. God's use of words surely legitimates words as a sufficient, but not exhaustive, means of communication. In the same way, his use of images surely legitimates imagery as a sufficient, but not exhaustive, means of communication.

Objection 4:
Images Need Words, Words Don't Need Images

Words, it is argued, can instruct without images, but images must be interpreted with words or they are arbitrary or unknowable. In this view image is subordinate to word. God's visions and dreams all had to be interpreted with words. If they did not, then they would be meaningless or confusing, with a hundred different possible interpretations. The prophet walking around naked without explanation would be no different than a lewd criminal streaking through the city. Words give meaning, images confuse or are too ambiguous.

Consider the vast amount of imagery we have already shown to be the foundation of God's revelation. However, is it not unbiblical speculation to argue that God *could have* communicated his truth in words alone without images, or for that matter, in images alone without words? The fact is, he didn't choose words alone. And if he didn't, then that should cause us to be cautious about suggesting that one of God's chosen means of communication (image) is inferior to another (word).

Meanwhile, any perusal of a dictionary will illustrate that words often have dozens of shades of differing potential meanings. As Mitchell Stevens points out, "Writers can never be sure that their words have only one possible interpretation. As our literary theorists have spent a third of a century pointing out, readers bring different experiences and interests to the sentences they read and therefore take different meanings from them."[4] Words are often just as confusing or unclear as images.

Words are inescapable, true enough. But it is also true that images are inescapable. Many biblical concepts cannot be described in mere words of

---

[4] Stevens, *rise of the image*, p. 67.

abstraction without imagery. Take for instance, the kingdom of God. Jesus almost exclusively used parables for the kingdom because of the inadequacy of abstract rationality alone to convey it. The Old Testament also uses images—allegorical, symbolical and metaphorical—to express the kingdom of God: wolves and lambs grazing together (Is 65), nations streaming to a mountain (Is 2; 11) that grows and fills the earth (Dan 2), an uncrossable river (Ezek 47:1-12). Without words of explanation what would biblical images mean? But without incarnate images and experiences from God, what would the biblical authors have to say? Abstract rational propositions of the eternal truths of reason? As proven earlier, *no way*. Language is necessary to our identity as human beings created in the image of God, but God did not create us as disembodied intellects. Language has many forms; spoken, written, or imaged, abstract or concrete. Blessed is he who uses all those forms as much as possible.

Objection 5:
Images Manipulate Emotions

Another criticism of image as a legitimate means of communication and persuasion is that images are more emotion-driven than words. People are manipulated because their rational faculties are diverted with the nature of image-oriented mediums. We've all complained about how advertising manipulates people to buy things they don't want or need. We've complained how the techniques of filmmaking and television news bypass rationality and form attitudes in people by selective visuals, out-of-context presentations or outright visual fabrication.

In his book *The Vanishing Word*, Arthur Hunt makes the argument that an image-orientation in our culture disarms our analytical and critical faculties. It diffuses our "mental defenses to arm ourselves against demagoguery" and makes us more susceptible to tyranny. It supplants the idea of Christianity as a religion of the book.[5] No doubt these dangers are real for imagocentrism. But they are also real dangers of logocentrism as well. Mormons, Jehovah's Witnesses and Muslims are word-oriented "people of the book," yet many nonetheless ignorantly follow demagogues and tyrants like lemmings into the sea. Books, words and

---

[5] Arthur W. Hunt III, *The Vanishing Word: The Veneration of Visual Imagery in the Postmodern World* (Wheaton, Ill.: Crossway Books, 2003), pp. 25, 213-40.

reading haven't rescued them from their ignorance, they have reinforced it. Word has the same potential for good or bad as image does.

Images cut out of context can make lies look like truth or visually connect opposing ideas as if they were consistent. So for instance, a news story about the war on terrorism followed by a series of commercials about toothpaste and soda will tend to trivialize the importance of the war as just another product being sold. The old Nazi propaganda trick of dissolving images of rats into images of Jews carries the same sort of deception of image. Neil Postman, in his classic *Amusing Ourselves to Death*, laments the modern inability to detect lies because of the fragmentary nature and soundbite editing of television visuals.[6]

This potential of image toward irrationality and contradiction is certainly a valid concern. But yet again, this concern can be equally applied to word and rational discourse itself. Postman himself uses newspapers—*word-oriented communications*—as an example of soundbites and fragmentation, thus affirming the manipulative power of the word. Words often promote irrationality (Friedrich Nietzsche's books) and regularly manipulate emotions (sermons of politicians and TV evangelists). The image rhetoric of Joseph Goebbels's propaganda were no more manipulative than the logical rhetoric of Hitler's book *Mein Kampf* or his sermonic oration. Michael Moore's films are no more logically or emotionally manipulative than his interviews. The problem is not so much with the medium being manipulative as it is with people being manipulative with whatever medium they use to communicate.

It is important to note that in ancient times, the change from a verbal culture to a written culture was attended with the same exact fears that moderns now have of the change from a word culture to an image culture. Plato writes of the Egyptian king Thamus bemoaning the perils of written words being the same as the peril of painting pictures, in that there is a lazy submission of man's mind to the form of written words:

> This discovery of yours [written words] will create forgetfulness in the learners' souls, because they will not use their memories; they will trust to the external written characters and not remember of themselves… you give your disciples not truth, but only the semblance of truth; they will be hearers of many things and will have learned nothing; they

---

[6]Neil Postman, *Amusing Ourselves to Death: Public Discourse in the Age of Show Business* (New York: Penguin Books, 1985), pp. 107-13.

will appear to be omniscient and will generally know nothing; they will be tiresome company, having the show of wisdom without the reality.[7]

With the invention of the Western printing press in the sixteenth century and subsequent mass production of written words, critics mouthed the same exact concerns about written words that are now exclaimed of moving images: that printed words would "scatter prejudice and ignorance through a people," that the dissemination of printed matter would be the "most powerful of ignorance's weapons," that eighteenth-century newspapers reduced politics to acting and facts to soundbites, that books were mindlessly addictive and left the reader with an emptiness of soul. Such critiques came from learned men like Alexander Pope, Leo Tolstoy and Ralph Waldo Emerson.[8] In many ways, these men's fears were proven correct. The printed word has spread ignorance, prejudice and irrationality, just as much as it has spread literacy, education and rationality.

In the 1960s, the era when Marshall McLuhan began warning us of the medium being the message and all the worry warts were fearing the dumbing down nature of visual communications like television, Edmund Carpenter reversed the charges against reading:

> When we read, another person thinks for us: we merely repeat his mental process. The greater part of the work of thought is done for us. This is why it relieves us to take up a book after being occupied by our own thoughts. In reading, the mind is only the playground for another's ideas. People who spend most of their lives in reading often lose the capacity for thinking, just as those who always ride forget how to walk. Some people read themselves stupid.[9]

With all the dangers of image-worship in our culture toward emotional manipulation and irrationality, there is just as much danger of word-worship

---

[7]Plato *Phaedrus* 275, in *Great Books of the Western World* (Chicago: Encyclopaedia Britannica, 1971, 6:138-39.

[8]Stevens, *rise of the image*, pp. 34-36.

[9] Edmund Carpenter, "The New Languages," in *Mass Media: Forces in Our Society*, 2nd ed., ed. Voelker (New York: Harcourt, Brace Jovanovich, 1975), pp. 373-74. Thanks to Azusa Pacific University communications professor John Hamilton for this reference.

toward emotional manipulation and irrationality *as well as* intellectual manipulation and dehumanization.

In fact, one could argue that more damage has been done to humanity in the twentieth century alone, through the manipulative *words* of Karl Marx, Charles Darwin, Sigmund Freud and Friedrich Nietzsche, than all the ancient image cultures combined.

Objection 6:
Images Distort Reality Through Illusion

Image-orientation is accused of distorting reality through artifice. As author Richard Lints complains, storytelling is a questionable "vinyl narrative" of unintended consequences because

> it is an artificial medium whose primary intent is to amuse. Its hidden assumption is that the world unfolds before the audience as the human author imagined it. Its message is that the world can be like this if you want it to be.... Drama is a medium that reinforces the artificial character of truth.[10]

This criticism has a long and distinguished history, from Plato's concern about painted pictures deceiving through the "imitation of appearance" over "real things," all the way through historian Daniel Boorstin's 1962 prophetic book *The Image*, declaring images as the "menace of unreality."

But this is another case where the same danger is inherent in word-orientation. Writing uses the same techniques of selectivity (as in Charles Darwin's writing), pulling out of context (as with Karl Marx), and outright lying (as with notorious cases from such "trustworthy" sources as the *New York Times* and veteran news anchor Dan Rather) that Lints is concerned about regarding images. Words distort reality through artifice, assume that the world "unfolds as the human author imagined it" and "reinforce the artificial character of truth." Just read any book by the titans of modernity and you'll get a five-course meal of the "menace of unreality" and artificial pictures of the world they paint with their words. As stated earlier, the twentieth century is littered with a hundred million corpses and millions of eternally damned souls due to

---

[10]Richard Lints, "The Vinyl Narratives: The Metanarrative of Postmodernism and the Recovery of a Churchly Theology," in *A Confessing Theology for Postmodern Times*, ed. Michael Horton (Wheaton, Ill.: Crossway Books, 2000), p. 95.

the "unintended consequences" of words, books and propositions of these word-oriented thinkers and movements.

One Christian cultural critic says the following in criticizing televised images:

> For television, any real truth is impossible.... The viewer does not see the event. He sees... an edited image of that event, one that gives an illusion of objectivity and truth... with television, reality becomes the image, "whether or not that image corresponds to any objective state of affairs— and we are not challenged to engage in this analysis."[11]

Simply replace the words "television" with "book" and "image" with "word" and you will see how the charges against images are equally chargeable against words. It's just simply not true that words and books are less distorting or illusory than images and multimedia. The medium is not necessarily the message, but the message often abuses the medium.

Objection 7:
Word Cultures Improve, Image Cultures Decline

Arthur Hunt claims that word-based movements like the Protestant Reformation, Puritanism and the founding American experiment emphasized literacy, which led to moral and civil achievement.[12] He contrasts these with the ancient pagan cultures that he claims were image-based, like ancient Egypt, Greece and Rome, which led to unrestrained chaos. He quotes a well-known anthropological maxim, "As language distinguishes man from animal, so writing distinguishes civilized man from the barbarian."[13]

While I would agree with the superiority of the three former cultures over the three latter, such oversimplification is certainly unwarranted. The success or failure of the cultures is based not on their being word-or image-centered but in the totality of their worldviews. On his criteria, one could argue that the absolutist nature of rationality-oriented, logocentric cultures fostered the inflexibility and intolerance that led to wars such as the Thirty Years' War,

---

[11] Mark Earley, "CNN's Snuff Film: Appalling Hypocrisy," *This Week's Viewpoint*, October 26, 2006, accessed February 5, 2008, at <www.crownvideo.com/viewpoint/index.cfm?Price=USprice>.

[12] Hunt, *Vanishing Word*, pp. 26-52.

[13] Ibid., p. 37.

which developed out of the Reformation. Under the wonderful logocentric American experiment, rationalistic doctors murder millions of preborn children a year by cutting them into pieces, burning their flesh off with salt and chemicals, and sucking their brains out with vacuums.

Meanwhile, ancient Greeks worshiped rationality and the word! Logocentrism is practically their invention. Or consider the Hebrew culture, ignored in Hunt's list. In this very book I've shown just how saturated in image and sensual experience their religion was. The difference was in the content of their sensate celebration, not in the form or style of it. The difference between sinful celebration and godly celebration, is not in using imagery or words, but in what deity the imagery and words are used for.

The idea that "writing distinguishes man from the barbarian" is another modern vestige of the Enlightenment lie that education is salvation. History shows in fact that writing has not always made men less barbaric, but it has made barbarians more effective in their barbarism, and enabled them to spread ignorance more widely. Writing, education and knowledge helped Nazis be more efficient in killing Jews with more effective machines. Writing helped Soviet Communists for eighty-nine years to more effectively propagandize their people into complete ignorance of reality.

The fact is, literacy can and does spread civilization. But it also spreads evil and barbarism as well. And it does so just as easily if not more so than imagery.

Objection 8:
Image Creates the Cult of Celebrity

Another complaint that Hunt raises against image-oriented culture is its tendency to worship celebrity. Because images become iconographic in nature through mass media, including the larger-than-life persona of entertainment, celebrity has raged in the twentieth century.[14]

Hunt unwittingly reveals later, however, that word-oriented culture suffers *from the same exact celebrity worship as do image-oriented ones*. He quotes a journalist's remarks, "Where we once deified the lifestyles of writers such as Hemingway and F. Scott Fitzgerald, we now fantasize about rock-and-roll gods, movie starlets or NBA superstuds. The notion of writer-as-culture-hero

---

[14]Ibid., pp. 173-76.

is dead and gone."[15] What is so ironic about this quote is that the lives of Hemingway and Fitzgerald were not in essence any different than rock gods and movie stars. They were easily as debauched and intellectually opposed to God as most Hollywood celebrities today. And just like Hollywood celebrities, they were exalted for their talent, not their character.

The truth is, from the beginning of creation, man has suffered the sin of idolatrous celebrity worship. Sometimes those celebrities are men of both words and images, like emperors or rulers; sometimes they are men of books and words, like Plato and Aristotle, who had entire schools following their every utterance; sometimes they are men of empirical sciences; sometimes they are men of image without substance like politicians and pretty people. But at the end of the day, the cult of celebrity is fueled in both image and word-oriented cultures.

Objection 9:
Image Cultivates Sensuality

A corollary closely linked to emotion is sensuality. As Hunt argues, images are seductive because they are physical. He claims an image-saturated society is deeply connected to pagan sensuality. The evidence of course is our own media-saturated pagan world filled with sexually explicit and violent exploitation from MTV rock videos to movies and magazines.[16]

In one sense, he is right. Much of our imagery is pagan in its sensuality, and this should cause alarm—just as alarm should be caused by the pagan-influenced, word-oriented academic journals, university departments, purveyors of scientism and modernist preachers. Alarm should be raised by the increase of *books* full of pagan ideas that reach the masses as well as the educational, political and media elite. Words can be just as sensually pagan as images.

The Marquis de Sade (1740-1814) wrote during the Enlightenment, the word-oriented culture that spawned modernity. And yet, the depraved sensuality in his *books of words* could make the publishers of modern pornographic images blush. He describes grotesque sexual fantasies of sado-masochism, rape, mutilation and murder that rival any modern cult horror film. And he did it in a logocentric era.

---

[15] Ibid., p. 195.
[16] Ibid., pp. 29-52.

So when all the objections are given and answered, one thing is consistently clear: All the dangers of images are equally dangers of words. In this book of words and images, I have tried to make the point that both are necessary to our understanding of God and his world, and that both should have an equal ultimacy in our views of interpretation of truth and reality. To the extent that we privilege word over image or image over word, is the extent to which we will distort our view of God and his world through the lie of modernism or the lie of postmodernism.

Our God is a God of both Reason and Imagination, both word and image. The spiritual Logos became incarnate flesh, and embraced the artistry of imagination in his teaching because he knew that the imagination can bring us into contact with truth in a way that reason cannot, and vise versa. So we too must embrace that paradigm if we wish to know him fully and properly express his image in us.

Amen.

• • • • •

If you liked this book, then please help me out by writing an honest review of it on Amazon. It's usually pretty easy. That is one of the best ways to say thank you to me as an author. It really does help my exposure and status as an author. Thanks! — *Brian Godawa*

• • • • •

More Books by Brian Godawa

See https://godawa.com/ for more information on other books by Brian Godawa. Check out his other series below:

Chronicles of the Nephilim

Chronicles of the Nephilim is a saga that charts the rise and fall of the Nephilim giants of Genesis 6 and their place in the evil plans of the fallen angelic Sons of God called, "The Watchers." The story starts in the days of Enoch and continues on through the Bible until the arrival of the Messiah: Jesus. The prequel to Chronicles of the Apocalypse.

ChroniclesOfTheNephilim.com

Chronicles of the Apocalypse

Chronicles of the Apocalypse is an origin story of the most controversial book of the Bible: Revelation. An historical conspiracy thriller trilogy in first century Rome set against the backdrop of explosive spiritual warfare of Satan and his demonic Watchers. ChroniclesOfTheApocalypse.com

Chronicles of the Watchers

Chronicles of the Watchers is a series that charts the influence of spiritual principalities and powers over the course of human history. The kingdoms of man in service to the gods of the nations at war. Completely based on ancient biblical, historical and mythological research.
ChroniclesOfTheWatchers.com

Book 2:
God Against the gods
Storytelling, Imagination & Apologetics in the Bible

By Brian Godawa

Brian Godawa

God Against the gods: Storytelling, Imagination And Apologetics In The Bible
1st Edition

Copyright © 2016, 2021 Brian Godawa
All rights reserved. No part of this book may be reproduced in any form or by any electronic or mechanical means, including information storage and retrieval systems, without prior written permission, except in the case of brief quotations in critical articles and reviews.

Warrior Poet Publishing
www.warriorpoetpublishing.com

Scripture quotations taken from *The Holy Bible: English Standard Version.* Wheaton: Standard Bible Society, 2001.

This book was previously released under the title: *Myth Became Fact: Storytelling, Apologetics and Imagination in the Bible*. A new chapter has been added. It is a compilation of various published articles and book appendices by Brian Godawa.

Special thanks to my editor, Don Enevoldsen.

Preface
Of Myth and the Bible

Whenever I consider that I have something important to say about faith, imagination, and/or apologetics, I usually discover that C.S. Lewis has already said it long before I could, and he has said it better than I will. True to form, his famous essay, *Myth Became Fact*, describes the heart of Christianity as a myth that is also a fact. He comforts the fearful modernist Christian whose faith in the Bible as a book of doctrine and abstract propositions is suddenly upset by the frightful reality of the interaction of holy writ with legend, pagan parallels, and mythology.

Rather than deny the ancient mythopoeic nature of God's Word as modern Evangelicals tend to do, Lewis embraced it as a reflection of God's preferred choice of concrete communication over abstraction (the worshipped discourse of the modernist). He understood myth to be the truth embedded into the creation by the Creator in such a way that even pagans would reflect some elements of that truth. Thus, when God Himself incarnates truth into history in the life, death, and resurrection of Jesus Christ, it is no surprise that it takes on mythopoeic dimensions reflected in previous pagan notions of dying and rising gods.

He concludes his essay with these memorable words:

> We must not be ashamed of the mythical radiance resting on our theology. We must not be nervous about "parallels" and "pagan Christs" — they ought to be there — it would be a stumbling block if they weren't. We must not, in false spirituality, withhold our imaginative welcome. If God chooses to be mythopoeic — and is not the sky itself a myth — shall we refuse to be mythopathic? For this is the marriage of heaven and earth: perfect myth and perfect fact: claiming not only our love and our obedience, but also our wonder and delight, addressed to the savage, the child, and the poet in

each one of us no less than to the moralist, the scholar, and the philosopher.[1]

A common reaction of many Christians to the word *myth* is often one of mistrust. In their minds, "myth" means "false," and since the Word of God can never be false, the category of myth is anathema in relation to the Bible.

But this is not an accurate assessment of the varied understandings of myth. Because of a modernist bias of anti-supernaturalism, some scholars define myth as "a necessary and universal form of expression within the early stage of man's intellectual development, in which unexplainable events were attributed to the direct intervention of the gods."[2] In some critical and liberal quarters of theology, this connotation has stuck to the meaning of myth and certainly warrants critique in light of its prejudicial definition that assumes a materialist universe without supernatural agents.

But a more specific and recent definition of myth is appropriate to our discussion. In this sense, myths are, as Northrop Frye has explained, "stories that tell a society what is important for it to know, whether about its gods, its history, its laws, or its structures."[3] In this sense, mythical stories, whether historically factual or fictional, do the same thing; they reveal true transcendent meaning. By this definition, calling the Bible mythical in some of its characteristics or imagery is not to jeopardize its historical claims. In fact, the Bible often claims to reveal the unseen transcendent meaning and purposes behind immanent historical events. Thus, Lewis' phrase, "myth became fact."

The problem comes when Christians seek to protect the Bible's reliability by demanding it be "historical" or "factually accurate" according to modern definitions of history writing and factual reporting or observation. They conclude that if the Bible is not accurate according to the "plain reading" of the text, then it cannot be relied upon to be truthful about the more important issues of God and salvation.

Let the reader be careful to note that I did not deny the historicity of the Bible, but I did make a distinction between *our modern notion* of what constitutes historical writing (historiography) and the ancient's notion of what constituted historical writing. For us to demand that the Biblical text be

---

[1] C.S. Lewis, *God in the Dock*, (Fount Publishing, 1998, 1970), 67.
[2] Brevard S. Childs, *A Study of Myth in Genesis 1-11*, (Dissertation, zur Erlangung der Doktorwurde der Theologischen Fakultat der Universitat Basel, 1955), 1-2.
[3] Robert A. Armour, *Gods and Myths of Ancient Egypt* (Cairo, Egypt and New York, NY: The American University in Cairo Press, 2001), 2.

scientifically or historically "accurate" *as we define those terms* is not a high view of Scripture, it is a low view of Scripture. It is in fact imposing our own prejudices upon the text by refusing to understand it within its context. This is called cultural imperialism and it is the height of hubris, or human pride.

One example of this kind of modern hubris in defining history can be found in the notion of genealogies. In the Bible, genealogies are often used as apologetic tools to prove chosen lineage. The modern notion of historical precision and chronological accuracy is not always a part of the Biblical understanding of genealogy that prioritizes theological truth over historical veracity. The genealogical formula of Genesis, "X is the son of Y" that once was interpreted as the "plain reading" of literal sons is now universally acknowledged to involve historical gaps which renders the term "son of" as often figurative and not literal. "X is the son of Y" often means, "X is a descendent of Y." This is not liberal denigration of the Bible, it is the Bible's own context of meaning when it comes to genealogies.

The most important genealogy to Christians is of course that of Jesus Christ, the Son of God and "Son of David." In Matthew chapter 1, Matthew details Christ's genealogy and concludes, "So all the generations from Abraham to David were fourteen generations, and from David to the deportation to Babylon fourteen generations, and from the deportation to Babylon to the Christ fourteen generations" (1:17). So Matthew uses Christ's genealogy as an apologetic by exegeting the symbolic number of 14 as being historically symmetrical in the lineage. There's only one problem: It's not historically accurate — at least by *our* definition of history. And it is the Bible itself that proves this, not liberal theology.

As Bible commentator Craig Blomberg explains,

> The actual number of generations in the three parts to the genealogy are thirteen, fourteen, and thirteen, respectively... When one compares the genealogy with Luke's account (Luke 3:23–37) and with various Old Testament narratives, it is clear that Matthew has omitted several names to achieve this literary symmetry.[4]

---

[4] Craig Blomberg, vol. 22, *Matthew, The New American Commentary*, 53 (Nashville: Broadman & Holman Publishers, 1992).

The Bible itself shows us that Biblical genealogies are not always historically accurate by our modern definitions of history. They are first and foremost theological in their interpretation and only secondarily are they historical. So to suggest that the way the Bible treats history sometimes includes figurative or mythopoeic dimensions that are not scientifically precise by our reckoning is not liberal subterfuge but Biblical fidelity. It is an unbiblical and humanistic belief to assume that the understanding of the Bible's approach to historical writing matches our understanding of historical writing. I hope to show in this book that there are quite a few more elements of mythopoeia and imagination that God uses that may make the modern Christian uncomfortable, but are clearly Biblical.

My approach in this book is to understand the Bible in its own ancient Near Eastern context, and thereby subordinate my own perspective to the perspective of the original writers and readers to whom the text was given. I seek to let the Bible define how it does history, fact, and imagination, and then I submit to that Biblical authority in how I seek to understand its meaning. The Bible is my authority, I am not the authority over the Bible.

To liberal theologians and critical scholars, this is antiquated fundamentalism, and to actual fundamentalists, it is syncretism, the attempt to blend pagan myths with the Bible. But the argument I make in this book is that the truth is neither of these bigoted hermeneutics, or prejudiced interpretations. I believe that God is doing something much more creative than fundamentalist believers and fundamentalist critics realize.

I believe that the Bible is God's Word and as such, it is breathed out of God through the writings of men inspired by the Holy Spirit. So, while the Biblical writers are very human and therefore very much creatures of their time and culture, there is also another author who is operating providentially behind the writing of the text to communicate transcendent truth, and that is the author and finisher of our faith, God Himself.

How He actually does this, I do not know, but the divine authorship does not reduce the human authorship to dictation or automatic writing. God uses the genre conventions and mindset of the ancient time period within which to communicate His transcendent truth.

This is what is called "accommodation" by theologians. In the same way that Jesus Christ is God incarnate within human flesh, so the Scriptures are God's message incarnate within human writings of the ancient Jewish world. A major part of that Jewish worldview was the special calling of a nation out of the nations of the earth to be His own people. God does separate Himself from the gods of the pagans, but at the same time, he utilizes much of the mythopoeic imagination that Israel shared with its pagan neighbors to communicate that separation.

One of the complaints of Christian apologists about the use of imagination and poetics in articulating or defending the faith is that it tends to lack the clarity of logical argumentation and rational discourse. The fuzziness and ambiguity of images, stories, metaphors and symbols tend to obscure or dilute the message of the Gospel. My book *Word Pictures: Knowing God Through Story and Imagination* deconstructs this rationalistic modernist fallacy as unbiblical. God uses so much imagery, symbolism, metaphor and poetic figurative language throughout the Scriptures (about 80% of the Bible) that one could even say he prefers it to abstract logical propositions (about 20% of the Bible).

Jesus is famous — or should I say *infamous* — for using parables to teach about the Kingdom of God instead of rational sermons of doctrinal exposition. Ironically, He quotes the Old Testament as explanation for why He used such fuzzy ambiguity in His parables:

> Matthew 13:10–17
> Then the disciples came and said to Him, "Why do you speak to them in parables?" And He answered them, "To you it has been given to know the secrets of the kingdom of heaven, but to them it has not been given. For to the one who has, more will be given, and he will have an abundance, but from the one who has not, even what he has will be taken away. This is why I speak to them in parables, because seeing they do not see, and hearing they do not hear, nor do they understand. Indeed, in their case the prophecy of Isaiah is fulfilled that says:
>
> "'You will indeed hear but never understand,
> and you will indeed see but never perceive."
> For this people's heart has grown dull,
> and with their ears they can barely hear,
> and their eyes they have closed,
> lest they should see with their eyes
> and hear with their ears

> and understand with their heart
> and turn, and I would heal them.'
>
> But blessed are your eyes, for they see, and your ears, for they hear. For truly, I say to you, many prophets and righteous people longed to see what you see, and did not see it, and to hear what you hear, and did not hear it."

The use of parables by Jesus had the two-fold purpose of revealing the truth only to those who "have ears to hear," and concealing from those who were unrepentant in rejecting the Gospel. One could say that Jesus engaged in an anti-apologetic apologetic. That is, He embedded the truth into imagination in order to avoid the inevitable confrontation of debaters who were more interested in arguing than in discerning truth. Only those who wanted truth would recognize it in the imaginative form the parables incarnated. A Master storyteller may have a deeper influence on culture than a Masters in Apologetics.

Now, I don't want to appear to be an anti-intellectual who scorns the use of traditional apologetics. I have aggressively argued for a proper place of rational argumentation in *Word Pictures*. My real goal is to uncover the *unreasonable exaltation* of modernist rational abstraction and empirical observation when it comes to articulation and defense of the Gospel.

But I also want to provide a positive case for the Biblical use of the equally important imagination and storytelling. And yes, that means I am writing a book that engages in rational argumentation for the Biblical use of imagination in theology and apologetics. I do this because I maintain an ultimate equivalency between reason and imagination when it comes to truth. If you want to read examples of actual application of imagination, watch the movies I've written and read my novel series *Chronicles of the Nephilim, Chronicles of the Watchers* and *Chronicles of the Apocalypse* (www.godawa.com). I am a both/and writer on this issue, not an either/or curmudgeon.

In the spirit of this both/and approach, I offer this volume to explore the following essays that address storytelling, imagination, and apologetics in the Bible:

In Chapter One, "Demonizing the Pagan Gods," I lay out the basic premise of this entire book, that God does in fact demonize his opponents and their beliefs, both human and divine, by showing the demonic reality behind their earthly façade. We wrestle not against flesh and blood, so our polemics should take that into account.

In Chapter Two, "Old Testament Storytelling Apologetics," I address two mythopoeic elements that Israel shared with other ancient Near Eastern peoples, the sea dragon of chaos, and the storm god. These are polemical concepts that are used by Biblical writers to show Yahweh as incomparably superior to the gods of Canaan.

In Chapter Three, "Biblical Creation and Storytelling," I tease out the genre of creation stories in the ancient Near East and the Bible, which express a primeval battle called *Chaoskampf*, as well as a symbol of covenant establishment that is defined in *both* comparison *and* contrast with surrounding pagan nations.

In Chapter Four, "The Universe in Ancient Imagination," I do a detailed study of the Biblical picture of the universe as being very similar to the ancient Mesopotamian one, and alien to our own. I explain how this shows God's real intent behind His description of the universe as one of theological meaning and not physical description. This is a case of God using common understanding in order to communicate His transcendent superiority through finite writers of His message.

In Chapter Five, "New Testament Storytelling Apologetics," I exegete Paul's sermon to the pagans on Mars Hill as an example of communicating the Gospel in terms of the Stoic narrative with a view toward subverting their worldview.

In Chapter Six, "Imagination in Prophecy and Apocalypse," I examine some of the mythopoeic imagery used by God to deliberately obscure His message to unbelievers while simultaneously "proving" to believers his claim about the true meaning and purpose behind history.

Chapter Seven, "An Apologetic of Biblical Horror," explores the otherwise offensive genre of horror writing to show how God Himself uses it as a powerful moral tool to communicate serious spiritual, moral, and social defilement in the context of repentance from sin and redemptive victory over evil.

While this is a collection of essays from assorted books and articles I have written, the unifying thread that connects them all is an underlying theme of Gods' use of storytelling and imagination as an apologetic tool in the Bible. My hope is that the Christian reader may gain inspiration from these insights to begin using more imagination in their own approach to communicating and defending the faith and glorifying God, since it is a severely underappreciated element of God's word.

Chapter 1
Demonizing the Pagan Gods

> This chapter expands upon some material from my scholarly book, "When Giants Were Upon the Earth."

In American political and religious discourse, the act of "demonizing" one's opponents is considered insulting, something that discredits one's arguments. It charges that the "demonizer" is the one at fault for casting "the other" or their ideas with dishonest exaggeration. It's based on the assumption that such extremes of evil do not exist in human beings or their ideas. It assumes that demons do not exist.

But what if demons do exist? What if someone or their ideas really are demonic or truly evil? Then demonization is not a moral fallacy, but a morally appropriate act of designation. In that case, we *ought* to demonize the truly demonic.

It might surprise those self-assured indoctrinated Americans to discover that God himself demonizes his opponents, the pagan gods of the ancient world and their ideas with them.

Demonic Ideas

To start with, the apostles in the New Testament vigorously affirm that some ideas are so evil, they qualify as "demonic." The apostle Paul calls the forbidding of marriage and the forced abstinence from certain foods for religious reasons "teaching of demons" and "deceitful spirits," or, as I prefer with this older English translation, "doctrines of devils" (1 Tim. 4:1).

The apostle James describes bitterness, jealousy, selfish ambition and boasting as being "demonic wisdom that does not come down from above, but is earthly and unspiritual." (James 3:13).

What these apostles are demonizing are not the explicitly spiritual teachings of necromancers, sorcerers and other spiritualists. They are not referring to the ontological reality of evil spirits, but rather to the moral behavior and religious teachings of people in their own fold! This is not a debate about whether one can lose their salvation. Paul was speaking of the Judaizers, those who claimed that in order to be a Christian, you must also follow the law of Torah. James was talking about those in the Christian congregation who were jockeying for power and causing division.

So much for the stigma of demonization. There are some ideas and behaviors that are so evil in their spiritual implications, they deserve to be called out as demonic.

The Gods as Demons

But that was only a warm-up. Because God also demonizes individuals and the pagan gods they worship – in both Old and New Testaments.

The Old Testament. A common understanding of absolute monotheism is that when the Bible refers to other gods it does not mean that the gods are real beings but merely *beliefs* in real beings that do not exist. For instance, when Deuteronomy 32:43 proclaims "rejoice with him, O heavens, bow down to him, all gods," this is a poetic way of saying "what you believe are gods are not gods at all because Yahweh is the only God that exists." What seems to support this interpretation is the fact that a few verses before this (v. 39), God says, "See now, that I, even I am he, and there is no god [elohim] beside me." Does this not clearly indicate that God is the only God [elohim] that really exists out of all the "gods" [elohim] that others believe in?

Not in its Biblical context it doesn't.

When the text is examined in its full context of the chapter and the rest of the Bible we discover a very different notion about God and gods. The phrase "I am, and there is none beside me" was an ancient Biblical slogan of incomparability of sovereignty, not exclusivity of existence. It was a way of saying that a certain authority was the most powerful *compared to* all other authorities. It did not mean that there were no other authorities that existed.

We see this sloganeering in two distinct passages, one of the ruling power of Babylon claiming proudly in her heart, "I am, and there is no one beside me" (Isa. 47:8), and the other of the city of Nineveh boasting in her heart, "I am, and there is no one else" (Zeph. 2:15). The powers of Babylon and Nineveh are obviously not saying that there are no other powers or cities that exist beside them, because they had to conquer other cities and rule over them. In the same way, Yahweh uses that colloquial phrase, not to deny the existence of other gods, but to express his incomparable sovereignty over them.[1]

In concert with this phrase is the key reference to gods early in Deuteronomy 32. Israel is chastised for falling away from Yahweh after he gave Israel the Promised Land:

> Deut. 32:17
> They sacrificed to demons not God, to gods they had never known, to new gods that had come recently, whom your fathers had never dreaded.

In this key text we learn that the idols or gods of the other nations that Israel worshipped were real beings that existed called "demons" (Hebrew: *shedim*). At the same time, they are called, "gods" and "not God," which indicates that they exist as real gods, but are not THE God of Israel.

Psalm 106 repeats this same exact theme of Israel worshipping the gods of other nations and making sacrifices to those gods that were in fact demonic.

> Psa. 106:34-37
> They did not destroy the peoples, as the LORD commanded them, but they mixed with the nations and learned to do as they did. They served their idols, which became a snare to them. They sacrificed their sons and their daughters to the demons.

One rendering of the Septuagint (LXX) version of Psalm 95:5-6 reaffirms this reality of national gods being demons whose deity was less than the Creator, "For great is the Lord, and praiseworthy exceedingly. More awesome he is than all the gods. For all the gods of the nations are demons, but the Lord made the heavens."[2] Another LXX verse, Isa. 65:11, speaks of Israel's

---

[1] Michael S. Heiser, "Monotheism, Polytheism, Monolatry, or Henotheism? Toward an Assessment of Divine Plurality in the Hebrew Bible" (2008). Faculty Publications and Presentations. Paper 277, p. 12-15,
http://digitalcommons.liberty.edu/cgi/viewcontent.cgi?article=1276&context=lts_fac_pubs&sei-redir=1#search=%22heiser+Monotheism,+Polytheism,+Monolatry,+or+Henotheism%22
accessed March 23, 2011.

[2] Randall Tan, David A. deSilva, and Logos Bible Software. *The Lexham Greek-English Interlinear Septuagint*. Logos Bible Software, 2009. Baruch 4:7 in the Apocrypha echoes this Scriptural theme as well when speaking of Israel's apostasy: "For you provoked him who made you, by sacrificing to demons and not to God."

idolatry: "But ye are they that have left me, and forget my holy mountain, and prepare a table for [a demon], and fill up the drink-offering to Fortune [a foreign goddess].[3]

In the Old Testament, Yahweh calls pagan gods what they really are: demons. He demonizes his opponents righteously. But this doesn't end with the Old Testament. The New Testament takes up the task as well.

The New Testament. In Revelation, the Apostle John defines the worship of gold and silver idols as being the worship of demons. The physical objects were certainly without deity as they could not "see or hear or walk," but the gods behind those objects were real beings with evil intent.

> Revelation 9:20
> The rest of mankind, who were not killed by these plagues, did not repent of the works of their hands nor give up worshiping demons and idols of gold and silver and bronze and stone and wood, which cannot see or hear or walk.

This is precisely the nuanced distinction that the Apostle Paul refers to when he addresses the issue of food sacrificed to idols—that is, physical images of deities on earth. He considers idols as having "no real existence," but then refers to other "gods" in the heavens or on earth *who do exist*, but are *not the same* as the One Creator God:

> 1 Cor. 8:4-6
> Therefore, as to the eating of food offered to idols, we know that "an idol has no real existence," and that "there is no God but one." For although there may be so-called gods in heaven or on earth—as indeed there are many "gods" and many "lords"—yet for us there is one God, the Father, from whom are all things and for whom we exist, and one Lord, Jesus Christ, through whom are all things and through whom we exist.

---

[3] Lancelot Charles Lee Brenton, *The Septuagint Version of the Old Testament: English Translation* (London: Samuel Bagster and Sons, 1870), Is 65:11. Randall Tan and David A. deSilva, Logos Bible Software, *The Lexham Greek-English Interlinear Septuagint* (Logos Bible Software, 2009), Is 65:11.

> 1 Cor. 10:18-20
> Consider the people of Israel: are not those who eat the sacrifices participants in the altar? What do I imply then? That food offered to idols is anything, or that <u>an idol is anything</u>? No, I imply that <u>what pagans sacrifice they offer to demons and not to God</u>. I do not want you to be participants with <u>demons</u>.

In 1 Corinthians, as in Revelation 9 quoted earlier, gods are not merely figments of imagination without existence in a world where the Trinity is the sole deity residing in the spiritual realm. Rather, physical idols (*images*) are "nothing," and "have no real existence" in that they are the representatives of the deities, not the deities themselves. But the deities behind those idols are real demonic beings; the gods of the nations who are not THE God, for they themselves were created by God and are therefore essentially incomparable to the God through whom we exist.

The terminology used by Paul in the first passage contrasting the many gods and lords with the one God and Lord of Christianity reflects the client-patron relationship that ANE cultures shared. As K.L. Noll explains in his text on ancient Canaan and Israel, "Lord" was the proper designation for a patron in a patron-client relationship. There may have been many gods, but for ancient Israel, there was only one Lord, and that was Yahweh."[4]

Gods of the Nations

Returning to Deuteronomy 32 and going back a few more verses in context, we read of a reality-changing incident that occurred at Babel:

> Deut. 32:8-9
> When the Most High gave to the nations their inheritance, when he divided mankind, he fixed the borders of the peoples according to the number of the sons of God. But the LORD's portion is his people, Jacob his allotted heritage.

The reference to the creation of nations through the division of mankind and fixing of the borders of nations is clearly a reference to the event of the

---

[4] K.L. Noll, *Canaan and Israel in Antiquity: An Introduction*, New York: NY; Shefffield Academic Press, 2001, p. 212.

Tower of Babel in Genesis 11 and the dispersion of the peoples into the 70 nations listed in Genesis 10.

But then there is a strange reference to those nations being "fixed" according to the number of the sons of God.[5] We'll explain in a moment that those sons of God are from the assembly of the divine council of God. But after that, the text says that God saved Jacob (God's own people) for his "allotment." Even though Jacob was not born until long after the Babel incident, this is an anachronistic way of referring to what would become God's people, because right after Babel, we read about God's calling of Abraham who was the grandfather of Jacob (Isa. 41:8; Rom. 11:26). So God allots nations and their geographic territory to these sons of God to rule over as their inheritance, but he allots the people of Jacob to himself, along with their geographical territory of Canaan (Gen. 17:8).

The idea of Yahweh "allotting" geographical territories to these sons of God who really existed and were worshipped as gods (idols) shows up again in several places in Deuteronomy:

> Deut. 4:19-20
> And beware lest you raise your eyes to heaven, and when you see the sun and the moon and the stars, all the host of heaven, you be drawn away and bow down to them and serve them, things that the LORD your <u>God has allotted to all the peoples</u> under the whole heaven.
>
> Deut. 29:26
> They went and served <u>other gods</u> and worshiped them, gods whom they have not known and whom <u>He had not allotted to them</u>.

"Host of heaven" was a term that referred to astronomical bodies that were also considered to be gods or members of the divine council.[6] The

---

[5] The astute reader will notice that some Bible translations read "according to the sons of Israel." The ESV reflects the latest consensus of scholarship that the Septuagint (LXX) and the Dead Sea Scrolls (DSS) segment of this verse is the earlier and more accurate reading than the later Masoretic Text (MT) of the same. See Heiser, Michael, "Does Deuteronomy 32:17 Assume or Deny the Reality of Other Gods?" (2008). Faculty Publications and Presentations. Paper 322, p 137-145. http://digitalcommons.liberty.edu/lts_fac_pubs/322/

[6] H. Niehr, "Host of Heaven," Toorn, K. van der, Bob Becking, and Pieter Willem van der Horst. *Dictionary of Deities and Demons in the Bible DDD*. 2nd extensively rev. ed. Leiden; Boston; Grand Rapids, Mich.: Brill; Eerdmans, 1999., 428-29; I. Zatelli, "Astrology and the Worship of the Stars in the Bible," *ZAW* 103 (1991): 86-99.

Encyclopedia Judaica notes that, "in many cultures the sky, the sun, the moon, and the known planets were conceived as personal gods. These gods were responsible for all or some aspects of existence. Prayers were addressed to them, offerings were made to them, and their opinions on important matters were sought through divination."[7]

But it was not merely the pagans who made this connection of heavenly physical bodies with heavenly spiritual powers. The Old Testament itself equates the sun, moon, and stars with the angelic "sons of God" who surround God's throne, calling them both the "host of heaven" (Deut. 4:19; 32:8-9).[8] Jewish commentator Jeffrey Tigay writes, "[These passages] seem to reflect a Biblical view that... as punishment for man's repeated spurning of His authority in primordial times (Gen. 3-11), God deprived mankind at large of true knowledge of Himself and ordained that it should worship idols and subordinate celestial beings."[9]

There is more than just a symbolic connection between the physical heavens and the spiritual heavens in the Bible. In some passages, the stars of heaven are linked *interchangeably* with angelic heavenly beings, also referred to as "holy ones" or "sons of God" (Psa. 89:5-7; Job 1:6).[10]

Daniel 10:10-21 speaks of these divine "host of heaven" allotted with authority over pagan nations as spiritual "princes" or rulers battling with the archangels Gabriel and Michael.

> Daniel 10:13, 20
>
> The <u>prince of the kingdom of Persia</u> withstood me twenty-one days, but <u>Michael, one of the chief princes</u>, came to help me... "But now I will return to fight against the <u>prince of Persia</u>; and when I go out, behold, the <u>prince of Greece</u> will come.

---

[7] "Astrology", *Encyclopaedia Judaica* Michael Berenbaum and Fred Skolnik, eds. 2nd ed. Detroit: Macmillan Reference USA, 2007, p. 8424.
[8] See also Deut 4:19; Deut 17:3; 2King 23:4-5; 1King 22:19; Neh 9:6.
[9] Jeffrey Tigay, *JPS Torah Commentary: Deuteronomy* (Philadelphia: The Jewish Publication Society, 1996): 435; as quoted in Michael S. Heiser, "Deuteronomy 32:8 and the Sons of God," *Bibliotheca Sacra* 158 (January-March 2001): 72; online: http://thedivinecouncil.com/. [Copyright © 2001 Dallas Theological Seminary;, online: http://thedivinecouncil.com/
[10] See also Job 38:4-7; Neh. 9:6; Psa 148:2-3, 1King 22:29 & 2King 21:5. In Isa 14:12-14 the king of Babylon is likened to the planet Venus (Morningstar) seeking to reign above the other stars of heaven, which are equivalent to the sons of God who surround God's throne on the "mount of assembly" or "divine council" (see Psa 89:5-7 and Psa 82).

In conclusion, the entire narrative of Deuteronomy 32 tells the story of God dispersing the nations at Babel and allotting the pagan nations to be ruled by "gods" who were demonic fallen divine beings. God then allots the people of Israel for himself, through Abraham, and their territory of Canaan. But God's people fall away from him and worship these other pagan gods and are judged for their apostasy.

We will now see that Yahweh will judge these gods as well.

Psalm 82

Bearing in mind this notion of Yahweh allotting gods over the Gentile nations while maintaining Canaan and Israel for himself, read this following important Psalm 82 where Yahweh now judges those gods for injustice and proclaims the Gospel that he will eventually take back the nations from those gods.

> Psa. 82:1-8
> God [elohim] has taken his place in the divine council;
> in the midst of the gods [elohim] he holds judgment:
> "How long will you judge unjustly
> and show partiality to the wicked? *Selah*
> Give justice to the weak and the fatherless;
> maintain the right of the afflicted and the destitute.
> Rescue the weak and the needy;
> deliver them from the hand of the wicked."
> They have neither knowledge nor understanding,
> they walk about in darkness;
> all the foundations of the earth are shaken.
> I said, "You are gods [elohim]
> sons of the Most High, all of you;
> nevertheless, like men you shall die,
> and fall like any prince."
> Arise, O God, judge the earth;
> for you shall inherit all the nations!

So from this text we see that God has a divine council that stands around him, and it consists of "gods" who are judging rulers over the nations and are also called *sons of the Most High* (synonymous with "sons of God"). Because they have not ruled justly, God will bring them low in judgment and take the nations away from them. Sound familiar? It's the same exact story as Deuteronomy 32:8-9 and Isaiah 24:21-22.

> Isaiah 24:21–22
> On that day the LORD will <u>punish the host of heaven, in heaven, and the kings of the earth, on the earth</u>. They will be gathered together as prisoners in a pit; they will be shut up in a prison, and after many days they will be punished.[11]

The idea that the Bible should talk about existent gods other than Yahweh is certainly uncomfortable for absolute monotheists. But our received definitions of monotheism are more often than not determined by our cultural traditions, many of which originate in theological controversies of other eras that create the baggage of non-Biblical agendas.

According to the Evangelical Protestant principle of *Sola Scriptura*, that the Bible alone is the final authority of doctrine, not tradition, believers are obligated to first find out what the Bible text says and then adjust their theology to be in line with Scripture, not the other way around. All too often we find individuals ignoring or redefining a Biblical text because it does not fit their preconceived notion of what the Bible *should* say, rather than what it actually says. The existence of other gods in Scripture is one of those issues.

In light of this theological fear, some try to reinterpret this reference of gods or sons of God as a poetic expression of human judges or rulers on earth metaphorically taking the place of God, the ultimate judge, by determining justice in his likeness and image. But there are three big reasons why this cannot be so: First, the terminology in the passage contradicts the notion of human judges and fails to connect that term ("sons of God") to human beings anywhere else in the Bible; Second, the Bible elsewhere explicitly reveals a divine council or assembly of supernatural sons of God that are judges over geographical allotments of nations that is more consistent with this passage; Third, a heavenly divine council of supernatural sons of God is more

---

[11] Interestingly, this passage of Isaiah is not clear about what judgment in history it is referring to. But the language earlier in the text is similar to Psalm 82 and to the Flood when it says, "For the windows of heaven are opened, and the foundations of the earth tremble. 19 The earth is utterly broken, the earth is split apart, the earth is violently shaken. 20 The earth staggers like a drunken man; it sways like a hut; its transgression lies heavy upon it, and it falls, and will not rise again." So this may be another passage that uses a Flood reference tied in with the Watchers and their punishment.

consistent with the ancient Near Eastern (ANE) worldview of the Biblical times that Israel shared with her neighbors.

What's in a Name

Another way in which God demonizes his opponents, the pagan gods, and their ideas is through name-calling. You read that right. I realize we think of name-calling as something immature children do on a playground. But there is a reason why that is so prevalent, not merely amongst children, but through all of human history. Because the act of naming something is an act of authority over the object named. It's how God created us.

If you want to understand the nature of something, look at its origin. The origin of naming rooted in authority comes from Genesis 2. God created the Garden and placed Adam in it to tend it and keep it (Gen. 2:8, 15). Then he created the animals over which he would give man dominion and rule to subdue (Gen. 1:26-28). One expression of that dominion, or authority, was in the act of naming.

God brought the animals he created to the man "to see what he would call them. And whatever the man called every living creature, that was its name" (Gen. 2:19).

Ancient Near Eastern Biblical scholar, John Walton explains,

> Names are not given randomly in the ancient world. A name may identify the essential nature of the creature, so that giving a name may be an act of assigning the function that creature will have.
>
> In Mesopotamia the assigning of function is referred to as the decreeing of destiny. Decreeing destiny by giving a name is an act of authority. In the ancient world, when a king conquered another country, the king he put on the throne was given a new name. In other cases, the giving of a name is an act of discernment in which the name is determined by the

circumstances. In either case, Adam's naming of the animals is his first step in subduing and ruling.[12]

The ancient world was patriarchal, that is, men were considered the authority over women in both society and marriage. While this may be offensive to the prejudices of our modern world, it was an organizing principle in the Bible. This is why the very next section of Genesis 2 shows Adam naming Eve, because he was the expressed authority over her. "She shall be called Woman, because she was taken out of Man" (Gen 2:23).

Since names were considered an incarnation of that person's essence or identity, or a change in their identity, God himself renames individuals for his purposes. We know that Abram's name which meant "exalted father" was changed to Abraham to mean "father of many nations" (Gen 17:5) based on the historical events of God's covenant with him. Later in the Bible, Jacob ("usurper") was changed to Israel ("struggles with God") as the ancestor of the people of God.

But God also renamed his enemies in the Bible. And often times, it was with mockery. Let's take a look at some of these demons.

Nimrod. Genesis 10:8-12 speaks of the mighty Nimrod, the first "warrior of name" after the Flood, who is credited with starting the kingdoms of Mesopotamia, including Babel, of the Tower of Babel infamy. The name of Nimrod is apparently a Hebrew play on words that demonized the leader, because Nimrod in Hebrew means "to revolt." One hardly thinks a person would make his name with such negative connotations, since such kings often considered themselves to be like the gods.

Scholars van der Toorn and van der Horst suggest that Nimrod was a deliberately distorted Hebrew version of Ninurta as the hunter god of Mesopotamia. They argue that the reign of Nimrod was most likely a symbolic synopsis of the history of Mesopotamia embodied in one character, a deity deliberately dethroned by the Jewish writer to a hunter king.

> The cities [of Nimrod] mentioned in Gen 10:9-12 are given in a more or less chronological sequence. The list reads as a condensed resume of Mesopotamian history. Akkad, though

---

[12] John H Walton, Zondervan *Illustrated Bible Backgrounds Commentary (Old Testament): Genesis, Exodus, Leviticus, Numbers, Deuteronomy, vol. 1* (Grand Rapids, MI: Zondervan, 2009), 31–32.

still in use as a cult-center in the first millennium, had its *floruit* under the Sargonic dynasty. Kalhu had its heyday in the first half of the first millennium BCE, some fifteen hundred years later. If Nimrod is not a god, he must at least have enjoyed a divine longevity, his reign embracing both cities.[13]

To top off God's "verbal bullying" of the villainous Nimrod, the infamous city he began, was also renamed. *Babylon*, meaning "gateway of the gods," was renamed by the writer of Genesis to *Babel*, meaning "confusion of tongues." How's that for a sarcastic swipe at man's positive self-image?

Nimrod's name is an example where God mocks a foreign deified "god-king" and his arrogant kingdom by renaming him as a mere rebel and hunter.

Cushan-rishathaim. In Judges 3:8-9, this king of Mesopotamia is mentioned with hostility toward Israel. Though he is not a deity, and he is most likely Naram-Sin (2367-2359 B.C.), he is renamed in the text with insulting degradation. This snarky rename means "doubly wicked son of Cush."[14] Sometimes name-calling is appropriate when it comes to truly evil people.

Jezebel. In 2 Kings, we read the story of this most ruthless and wicked queen of Israel. She was a royal pagan from Tyre whom King Ahab of Israel married as a treaty of appeasement. It didn't work out well for Israel, as her idolatry infected Israel and brought judgment, in both physical and verbal condemnation. Archaeological discoveries have revealed that her name in Tyre was actually Izebul, which meant, "Where is the Prince?" *Prince* meaning, Ba'al, the prince of gods in Canaan. In the Bible, Izebul is named Jezebel, which is a slurring wordplay on the Hebrew word for "dung" (*zebel*). 2 Kings 9:37 reduces that worldly powerful queen to pathos with a double entendre of caustic scorn: "And the corpse of Jezebel shall be as dung on the face of the field in the territory of Jezreel, so that no one can say, 'This is Jezebel.'"

But God does not merely jab kings and rulers with his verbal flame throwing, he also mocks the gods by renaming them.

Ba'alzebub. Jezebel, that wicked queen of dung, had introduced Ba'al worship into Israel in an unprecedented way that would haunt the people of God for generations. Ba'al was a high god in Canaan and he took on many

---

[13] K. van der Toorn and P. W. van der Horst, "Nimrod before and after the Bible," *Harvard Theological Review* 83 (1990): 1–29.

[14] Gerald E. Aardsma, Ph.D., *A New Approach to the Chronology of Biblical History from Abraham to Samuel* (Loda, IL: Aardsma Publishing, 2003, 2005), 76.

manifestations. In Ekron, his name was Ba'alzebul, which meant, "lord of the heavenly dwelling." The author of 2 Kings 1:2-6 renames Ba'alzebul as *Ba'alzebub*, which means the derogatory, "lord of the flies."[15] Ya gotta appreciate God's wicked sense of humor. Jesus carries on this tradition of mockery in the Gospels when he reduces that prince of gods to a prince of demons (Matt. 12:24 : Mark 3:22; Luke 11:15).

Ashtoreth. Ashtoreth is a goddess who shows up often in the Old Testament (1King 11:15, 33; 2King 23:13; 1Sam 31:10). The name refers to the infamous Ashtart (or Astarte) of Canaan. It is said that ignoring someone is the most vicious way to hurt them. False gods were bad enough to the ancient Hebrew, but female goddesses were so offensive that the Bible writers didn't use a word for goddess. They simply used their names. This may be because they believed that the demons behind the deities were of male gender, since angelic divine beings were all male. But it has long been noted that the name Ashtoreth was a deliberate diabolical distortion of Ashtart by using the vowels of the Hebrew word for "shame" (*bosheth*) between the consonants of Ashtart.[16]

Satyrs as Goat Demons

Another way of demonizing and mocking God's opponents was to use the pagan mythology against itself. That is, Biblical writers would quote or paraphrase pagan mythologies back to them, but in an undermining or ironic way. One of those examples is the references to satyrs in Biblical condemnation of false religion. Anyone familiar with ancient Greco-Roman religion has heard of Pan, the satyr deity of nature and shepherding. A satyr was a hybrid creature who had the upper body of a man, and the lower body and legs of a goat, accompanied by horns on his head as well. But these little nasties worshipped the chaos of unrestrained passion, in both sexual and consumptive behaviors. The notion of satyrs or goat deities finds a place in Canaanite lore, and therefore, in the Bible as well.

Take a look at these prophecies of Isaiah referencing the destruction of Edom and Babylon.

---

[15] "Baalzebub," *The International Standard Bible Encyclopedia, Revised.* (*ISBE*) Edited by Geoffrey W. Bromiley. Wm. B. Eerdmans, 1988.
[16] John Day, *Yahweh and the Gods and Goddesses of Canaan (The Library of Hebrew Bible/Old Testament Studies)* (Bloomsbury T&T Clark, 2002), 214.

Isaiah 34:11–15 (The destruction of Edom)
¹¹But the hawk and the porcupine shall possess it, the owl and the raven shall dwell in it… ¹³Thorns shall grow over its strongholds, nettles and thistles in its fortresses. It shall be the haunt of jackals, an abode for ostriches. ¹⁴And wild animals shall meet with hyenas; the wild goat (*seirim*) shall cry to his fellow.

Isaiah 13:21–22 (The destruction of Babylon)
²¹But wild animals will lie down there, and their houses will be full of howling creatures; there ostriches will dwell, and there wild goats (*seirim*) will dance. ²²Hyenas will cry in its towers, and jackals in the pleasant palaces; its time is close at hand and its days will not be prolonged.

The passages above speak of God's judgment upon the nations of Babylon and Edom (symbols of all that is against Israel and Yahweh). A cursory reading of the texts seem to indicate a common word picture of Yahweh destroying these nations so thoroughly that they end up a desert wasteland with wild animals and birds inhabiting them because the evil people will be no more.

Nothing about mythical monsters like satyrs there, right?

Wrong. Because the English translation of the Hebrew word *seirim* as "wild goats," obscures the full ancient meaning. If we look closer into the original Hebrew, we find a more expanded mythopoeic reference to pagan deities.

A look at the Septuagint (LXX) translation into Greek made by ancient Jews in the second century before Christ, reveals the hint of that different picture.

Isaiah 34:13-14 (LXX)
¹¹ and for a long time birds and hedgehogs, and ibises and ravens shall dwell in it: and the measuring line of desolation shall be cast over it, and satyrs shall dwell in it…¹³ And thorns shall spring up in their cities, and in her strong holds: and they shall be habitations of monsters, and a court for ostriches. ¹⁴ And devils shall meet with satyrs, and they shall cry one to

the other: <u>there shall satyrs rest,</u> having found for themselves *a place of* rest.[17]

Isaiah 13:21-22 (LXX)
But wild beasts shall rest there; and the houses shall be filled with howling; and <u>monsters</u> shall rest there, and devils shall dance there, [22] and <u>satyrs shall dwell there</u>.[18]

Wow, what a dramatic difference, huh? Of course, the LXX passages above are not in Greek, but are English translations, which adds a layer of complication that we will unravel shortly to reveal even more mythopoeic elements. But the point is made that ancient translators understood those words within their ancient context much differently than the modern bias of more recent interpreters.

The LXX translates the word for "satyrs" that appears in these Isaiah passages as *onokentaurois* or "donkey-centaurs," from which we get our word "centaur." The *Greek-English Lexicon of the Septuagint* defines this word as "donkey-centaur, mythic creature (a centaur resembling a donkey rather than a horse)."[19]

In Isaiah 34:14 of the ESV we read of "the wild goat crying to his fellow," and in 13:21, "there wild goats will dance." But the underlying Hebrew (*seirim*) is not about wild goats, but satyrs, that were prevalent in Canaanite religion. Scholar Judd Burton points out that Banias or Panias at the base of Mount Hermon in Bashan was a key worship site for the Greek goat-god Pan as early as the third century B.C. and earlier connections to the goat-idol Azazel.[20]

Satyrs were well known for their satyrical dance, the *Sikinnis*, consisting of music, lascivious dance, licentious poetry and sarcastic critique of culture.[21]

---

[17] Lancelot Charles Lee Brenton, *The Septuagint Version of the Old Testament: English Translation*, Is 34:13–14 (London: Samuel Bagster and Sons, 1870).

[18] Lancelot Charles Lee Brenton, *The Septuagint Version of the Old Testament: English Translation*, Is 13:21–22 (London: Samuel Bagster and Sons, 1870).

[19] Johan Lust, Erik Eynikel and Katrin Hauspie, *A Greek-English Lexicon of the Septuagint: Revised Edition* (Deutsche Bibelgesellschaft: Stuttgart, 2003).

[20] Judd H. Burton, *Interview With the Giant: Ethnohistorical Notes on the Nephilim* (Burton Beyond Press, 2009) 19-21. "Regardless of his [Azazel's] origins—in pre-Israelite practice he was surely a true demon, perhaps a satyr, who ruled in the wilderness." Jacob Milgrom, *A Continental Commentary: Leviticus: a Book of Ritual and Ethics* (Minneapolis, MN: Fortress Press, 2004), 169.

[21] Gaston Vuillier, trans. Joseph Grego, *A History Of Dancing From The Earliest Ages To Our Own Times* (New York, NY: D. Appleton and Co., 1848), 27-28.

This reflects the mockery of the "goats" dancing on the ruins of Edom and Babylon in Isaiah.

The Bible writers considered the satyr deities to be demons and thus called them "goat demons." So prevalent and influential were these pagan gods that Yahweh would have trouble with Israel worshipping them as idols.

> Leviticus 17:7
> 7 So they shall no more sacrifice their sacrifices to goat demons (*seirim*), after whom they whore. This shall be a statute forever for them throughout their generations.

> 2 Chronicles 11:15
> ¹Jeroboam] appointed his own priests for the high places and for the goat idols (*seirim*) and for the calves that he had made.

Not only did Israel fall into worshipping the *seirim* satyrs in Canaan, they were even committing spiritual adultery with them while in the wilderness! It is no wonder Yahweh considered them demons, a declaration reiterated in the Deuteronomy 32 worldview that after Israel would be brought into Canaan by the hand of God, she would betray Yahweh by turning aside to other gods, redefined as demons.

The New Testament reiteration of this demon interpretation is in the Apostle John's inspired reuse of the *same exact language* from Isaiah when pronouncing judgment upon first century Israel as a symbolic "Mystery Babylon."

> Revelation 18:2
> ²"Fallen, fallen is Babylon the great! She has become a dwelling place for demons, a haunt for every unclean spirit, a haunt for every unclean bird, a haunt for every unclean and detestable beast."[22]

Because of the exile under the Babylonians, Jews would use Babylon as the ultimate symbol of evil. So when John attacks his contemporaries in Israel for rejecting Messiah, he describes them as demonic Babylon worthy of the same judgment as that ultimate evil nation.

---

[22] Special thanks to Doug Van Dorn for this "revelation." Van Dorn, Douglas (2013-01-21). *Giants: Sons of the Gods* (K-ebook Locations 3922-3925). Waters of Creation. K-ebook Edition. In fact, his "Chapter 13: Chimeras" was helpful for more than one insight in this appendix.

Lilith

Another pagan deity subverted in the Old Testament narrative is Lilith, the she-demon. Regarding this monster, the *Dictionary of Deities and Demons in the Bible* says its Mesopotamian narrative reaches back to the third millennium B.C.

> Here we find Inanna who plants a tree later hoping to cut from its wood a throne and a bed for herself. But as the tree grows, a snake [Ningishzida] makes its nest at its roots, Anzu settled in the top and in the trunk the demon makes her lair... Of greater importance, however, is the sexual aspect of the—mainly—female demons lilitu and lili. Thus the texts refer to them as the ones who have no husband, or as the ones who stroll about searching for men in order to ensnare them.[23]

Lilith was also known as the demon who stole away newborn babies to suck their blood, eat their bone marrow and consume their flesh.[24] In Jewish legends, she was described as having long hair and wings, and claimed to have been the first wife of Adam who was banished because of Adam's unwillingness to accept her as his equal.[25]

Lilith the "night hag" makes her appearance in the Bible in Isaiah 34 that we already saw included the mythical and demonic satyr. In this chapter, prophetic judgment upon Edom involves turning it into a desert wasteland that is inhabited by all kinds of demons; ravens, jackals, hyenas, satyrs — and Lilith.

> Isaiah 34:13-14 (RSV)
> It shall be the haunt of jackals... And wild beasts shall meet with hyenas, the satyr shall cry to his fellow; yea, there shall the night hag [*Lilith*] alight, and find for herself a resting place.

> Isaiah 34:14–15 (NASB95)
> ¹⁴ Yes, the night monster (*Lilith*) will settle there And will find herself a resting place. ¹⁵ The tree snake (*qippoz*) will make

---

[23] "Lilith," *DDD*, 520.
[24] Handy, Lowell K. "Lilith (Deity)". In *The Anchor Yale Bible Dictionary*, edited by David Noel Freedman. New York: Doubleday, 1992, 324-325.
[25] Ginzberg, Louis; Szold, Henrietta (2011-01-13). *Legends of the Jews*, all four volumes in a single file, improved 1/13/2011 (K-ebook Locations 1016-1028). B&R Samizdat Express. K-ebook Edition.

its nest and lay *eggs* there, And it will hatch and gather *them* under its protection.

Notice how the text talks about the owl that nests and lays and hatches her young in its shadow. Lexicons such as the *Theological Wordbook of the Old Testament* and *Brown, Driver, Briggs Hebrew Lexicon* contest this Hebrew word for owl (*qippoz*) with more ancient interpretations of an "arrow snake."[26] If they are correct, then the poetry of the passage would be more complete as the NASB indicates.

The snake of verse 15 would match the Lilith myth (v. 14) with the snake in the roots making its nest. The correlation is too close to deny that this is another Biblical reference to a popular mythic creature that the Bible writers refer to in demonic terms.

A Demon by Any Other Name...

So we find that God himself demonizes his opponents. He renames evil people and their ideas with demonic name-calling, he mocks pagan myths and uses their own images against them, and he reveals that the pagan gods are actually demonic principalities and powers that rule with heavenly authority behind earthly authorities. He calls it like it is.

Perhaps we should take a lesson from the Living God and begin to break through the euphemisms of our modern culture that cover over reality with obscuring language. Perhaps we should call out the evil by demonizing it as God does in his holy Word. Perhaps we should demonize the stigma of "demonizing" because in fact, there really are demons that need to be called out and addressed for what they really are: evil.

---

[26] 2050a, קִפּוֹז *Theological Wordbook of the Old Testament*, ed. R. Laird Harris, Gleason L. Archer, Jr. and Bruce K. Waltke, electronic ed., 806 (Chicago: Moody Press, 1999).
קִפּוֹז Brown, Francis, Samuel Rolles Driver, and Charles Augustus Briggs. *Enhanced Brown-Driver-Briggs Hebrew and English Lexicon*. electronic ed. Oak Harbor, WA: Logos Research Systems, 2000.

Chapter 2
Old Testament Storytelling Apologetics[1]

The pantheon of gods assembles to battle the chaos monster to protect their territory and kingdom. When the waters of the heavens part, the sea dragon of chaos breaks through and leaves destruction in its wake. The pantheon fights the sea dragon and its monster allies until it is stopped in its tracks by the mighty storm god.

Those who are educated in ancient Near Eastern mythopoeia will recognize this storyline as the Canaanite epic of Baal and Leviathan or the Babylonian epic of Marduk and Tiamat the sea dragon. But what they may not know is that it is also the storyline of the 2012 Marvel blockbuster movie, *The Avengers*. The purpose of bringing up this point is to call attention to the modern relevancy of this ancient narrative before we descend into the turbulent sea of ancient mythological memes and motifs that are too quickly written off as petty scholarly obsession with obscure archaic minutia that fail to connect to our lives in the modern world. Leviathan vs. the Storm God is a tale we are still retelling today in cultures both religious and secular.

For many Christians, the word *apologetics* conjures a picture of defending the faith with philosophical arguments, archeological evidence, historical inquiry, and other rational and empirical forms of discourse. Apologetics also involves *polemics*, which are aggressive arguments against the opposition. Sometimes a good offense is the best defense. But what is often missed in some apologetic strategies is the Biblical use of imagination. This is illustrative of a distinct imbalance when one considers that the Bible is only about one-third propositional truth and about two-thirds imagination: image, metaphor, poetry, and story.[2]

With the discovery in the nineteenth and twentieth centuries of pagan religious texts from ancient Near Eastern (ANE) cultures such as Babylon,

---

[1] This chapter has been adapted from the article, "Old Testament Storytelling Apologetics" in the *Christian Research Journal* Vol. 34 / No. 03 / 2011.

[2] I discuss this fact and its ramifications in my book *Word Pictures: Knowing God through Story and Imagination* (Downers Grove, IL: InterVarsity Press, 2009).

Assyria, and Ugarit, Biblical scholarship has discovered many literary parallels between Scripture and the literature of ancient Israel's enemies. The Hebrews shared many words, images, concepts, metaphors, and narrative genres in common with their neighbors. And those Hebrew authors of Scripture sometimes incorporated similar literary imagination into their text.

With regard to these Biblical and ancient Near Eastern literary parallels, liberal scholarship tends to stress the similarities, downplay the differences, and construct a theory of the evolution of Israel's religion from polytheism to monotheism.[3] In other words, liberal scholarship is anthropocentric, or human-centered. Conservative scholarship tends to stress the differences, downplay the similarities, and interpret the evidence as indicative of the radical otherness of Israelite religion.[4] In other words, conservative scholarship is theocentric, or God-centered. In this way, both liberal and conservative hermeneutics err on opposite extremes.

The orthodox doctrine of the inspiration of Scripture states that it is composed of "God-breathed" human-written words (2 Tim. 3:16). Men wrote from God, moved by the Holy Spirit (2 Pet. 1:20–21). This is a "both/and" reality of humanly and heavenly authorship. While I affirm the heavenly side of God's Word, in this essay I will illustrate how the writers of the Old Testament both appropriated *and* subverted the story, imagery, and metaphor of their religious enemies as a polemic against those enemies' religion and deities. First, we will look at one of the princes of those pagan deities: Baal.

Baal in Canaan

In 1929, an archeological excavation at a mound in northern Syria called Ras Shamra unearthed the remains of a significant port city called Ugarit, whose developed culture reaches back as far as 3000 B.C..[5] Among the important finds were literary tablets that opened the door to a deeper understanding of ancient Near Eastern culture and the Bible. Those tablets included Syro-Canaanite religious texts of pagan deities mentioned in the Old Testament. One of those deities was Baal.

---

[3] A significant author of this view is Mark S. Smith, *The Origins of Biblical Monotheism: Israel's Polytheistic Background and the Ugaritic Texts* (Oxford: Oxford University, 2003).
[4] A significant author of this view is Gleason L. Archer, *A Survey of Old Testament Introduction* (Chicago: Moody Press, 2007).
[5] Avraham Negev, "Ugarit," *The Archaeological Encyclopedia of the Holy Land*, 3rd ed. (New York: Prentice Hall Press, 1996).

Though the Semitic noun *baal* means "lord" or "master," it was also used as the proper name of the Canaanite storm god.[6] In the Baal narrative cycle from Ugarit, El was the supreme "father of the gods," who lived on a cosmic mountain. A divine council of gods called "Sons of El" surrounded him, vying for position and power. When Sea is coronated by El and given a palace, Baal rises up and kills Sea, taking Sea's place as "most high" over the other gods (excepting El). A temple is built and a feast celebrated. Mot (Death) then insults Baal, who goes down to the underworld, only to be defeated by Mot. But Anat, Baal's violent sister, seeks Mot and cuts him up into pieces and brings Baal's body back up to earth where he is brought back to life, only to fight Mot to a stalemate.[7]

The Dictionary of Deities and Demons in the Bible explains of Baal:

> "His elevated position shows itself in his power over clouds, storm and lightning, and manifests itself in his thundering voice. As the god of wind and weather Baal dispenses dew, rain, and snow and the attendant fertility of the soil. Baal's rule guarantees the annual return of the vegetation; as the god disappears in the underworld and returns in the autumn, so the vegetation dies and resuscitates with him."[8]

Baal in the Bible

In the Bible, Baal is used both as the name of a specific deity[9] and as a generic term for multiple idols worshipped by apostate Israel.[10] It was also used in conjunction with city names and locations, such as Baal-Hermon and Baal-Zaphon, indicating manifestations of the one deity worshipped in a variety of different Canaanite situations.[11] Simply speaking, in Canaan, Baal was all over the place. He was the chief god of the land.

Upon entering Canaan, Yahweh gave specific instructions to the Israelites to destroy all the places where the Canaanites worshipped, along with their altars and images (Deut. 12:1–7). They were to "destroy the names"

---

[6] Karel van der Toorn, Bob Becking, and Pieter Willem van der Horst, *Dictionary of Deities and Demons in the Bible* (*DDD*), 2nd ext. rev. ed. (Grand Rapids: Eerdmans, 1999), 132.
[7] N. Wyatt, *Religious Texts from Ugarit*, 2nd ed., The Biblical Seminar, vol. 53 (London: Sheffield Academic Press, 2002), 36–39.
[8] "Baal," *DDD*, 134.
[9] Judg. 6; 1 Kgs. 18; 2 Kgs. 10.
[10] Judg. 2:13; 1 Sam. 12:10; Jer. 2:23.
[11] "Baal," *DDD*, 136.

of the foreign idols and replace them with Yahweh's name and habitation (vv. 3–4). God warned them, "Take care lest your heart be deceived, and you turn aside and serve other gods and worship them" (Deut. 11:16).

Yet, turning to other gods in worship is exactly what the Israelites did — over and over again. No sooner had the people settled in Canaan than they began to adopt Baal worship into their culture. The book of Judges describes this cycle of idolatry under successive leaders (Judg. 2:11; 3:7; 8:33). In the ninth century B.C., Elijah fought against rampant Baal worship throughout Israel (1 Kgs. 18). In the eighth century, Hosea decried the adulterous intimacy that both Judah and Israel had with Baal (Hos. 2:13, 16–17), and in the seventh century, Jeremiah battled with an infestation of it in Judah (Jer. 2:23; 32:35).

Baal worship was so cancerous throughout Israel's history that Yahweh would have to intervene periodically with dramatic displays of authority in order to stem the infection that polluted the congregation of the Lord. Gideon's miraculous deliverances from the Baal-loving Midianites (Judg. 6–8) and Elijah's encounter with the prophets of Baal (1 Kgs. 18) are just a couple examples of Yahweh's real-world polemic against Baal. If Baal is god, "let him contend for himself, because his altar is broken down" (Judg. 6) and "the God who answers by fire, He is God!" (1 Kgs. 18:24). I call that "power polemics." But physical battles and miraculous signs and wonders are not the only way God waged war against Baal in ancient Canaan. He also used story, image, and metaphor. He used subversive literary imagination.

Yahweh Vs. Baal

Literary subversion was common in the ancient world to effect the overthrow or overshadowing of one deity and worldview with another. For example, the high goddess Inanna, considered Queen of Heaven in ancient Sumeria, was replaced by her Babylonian counterpart, Ishtar. An important Sumerian text, *The Descent of Inanna into the Underworld*, was rewritten by the Babylonians as *the Descent of Ishtar into the Underworld* to accommodate their goddess Ishtar. The Babylonian creation epic, *Enuma Elish* tells the story of the Babylonian deity Marduk and his ascendancy to power in the Mesopotamian pantheon, giving mythical justification to the rise of Babylon as an ancient world power in the early eighteenth century B.C..[12] And then when King

---

[12] Alexander Heidel, trans., *The Babylonian Genesis* (Chicago: University of Chicago, 1942, 1951, 1963), 14.

Sennacherib of Assyria conquered Babylon around 689 B.C., Assyrian scribes rewrote the *Enuma Elish* and replaced the name of Marduk with Assur, their chief god.[13]

Picture this scenario: The Israelites have left Egypt where Yahweh literally mocked and defeated the gods of Egypt through the ten plagues (Exod. 12:12; Num. 33:4). Pharaoh claimed to be a god, who according to Egyptian texts was the "possessor of a strong arm" and a "strong hand."[14] So when Yahweh repeatedly hammers home the message that Israel will be delivered by Yahweh's "strong arm" and "strong hand," the polemical irony is not hard to spot. Yahweh used subversive literary imagery, which in effect said, "Pharaoh is not God, I am God." Nothing like an arm wrestling match to show who is stronger. Later, in the time of Ezekiel, God would liken Pharaoh to a dragon in the Nile that He would draw out with a hook in his jaws (Ezek. 29:1-5) — polemical metaphors abounding.

But now, God is leading Israel into the Promised Land, which is very different from where they came, with very different gods. "For the land that you are entering to take possession of it is not like the land of Egypt, from which you have come, where you sowed your seed and irrigated it, like a garden of vegetables. But the land that you are going over to possess is a land of hills and valleys, which drinks water by the rain from heaven" (Deut. 11:10–11). And the god of rain from heaven in this new land was believed to be the storm god, Baal.[15] Yahweh therefore would relate to the Israelites in new and different terms related to a new and different world.

A look at some Ugaritic texts will give us a literary description of the Baal that Israel faced in Canaan. A side-by-side sampling of those Ugaritic texts with Scripture illustrates a strong reflection of Canaanite echoes in the Biblical storytelling.

---

[13] C. Jouco Bleeker and Geo Widengren, eds., *Historia Religionum I: Religions of the Past* (Leiden, Netherlands: E. J. Brill, 1969), 134.

[14] John D. Currid, *Ancient Egypt and the Old Testament* (Grand Rapids: Baker; 1997), 83.

[15] Fred E. Woods, *Water and Storm Polemics against Baalism in the Deuteronomic History*, American University Studies, Series VII, Theology and Religion (New York: Peter Lange Publishing, 1994), 32–35.

UGARITIC TEXTS[16]	OLD TESTAMENT
Baal sits... in the midst of his divine mountain, Saphon, in the midst of the mountain of victory. Seven lightning-flashes, eight bundles of thunder, a tree-of-lightning in his right hand. His head is magnificent, His brow is dew-drenched. his feet are eloquent in wrath. (KTU 1.101:1–6)[17]	"Yahweh came from Sinai... At His right hand there was flashing lightning... There is none like the God of Jeshurun, Who rides the heavens to your help, And through the clouds in His majesty... And He drove out the enemy from before you, And said, 'Destroy!' So Israel dwells in security, The fountain of Jacob secluded, In a land of grain and new wine; His heavens also drop down dew." (Deut. 33:2, 26–28)
The season of his rains may Baal indeed appoint, the season of his storm-chariot. And the sound of his voice from the clouds, his hurling to the earth of lightning-flashes (KTU 1.4:5.5–9)	
At his holy voice the earth quaked; at the issue of his lips the mountains were afraid. The ancient mountains were afraid; the hills of the earth tottered. (KTU 1.4:7.30–35)	The voice of the LORD is over the waters; the God of glory thunders, the LORD, over many waters... The voice of the LORD breaks the cedars; the LORD breaks the cedars of Lebanon... The voice of the LORD flashes forth flames of fire [lightning]. The voice of the LORD shakes the wilderness...
now your foe, Baal, now your foe the Sea you must smite; now you must destroy your adversary! Take your everlasting kingdom,	And in His temple everything says, "Glory!" Yahweh sits enthroned over the flood; Yahweh is enthroned as King forever. (Psa. 29:3–11)

---

[16] The abbreviation *KTU* stands for "Keilalphabetische Texte aus Ugarit", the standard collection of this material from Ugarit.

[17] All these Ugaritic texts can be found in N. Wyatt, *Religious Texts from Ugarit*, 2nd ed., The Biblical Seminar, vol. 53 (London: Sheffield Academic Press, 2002).

your eternal dominion! (KTU 1.2:4.9–10) Then Baal returned to his house [temple]. 'Will either king or commoner establish for himself dominion in the earth? (KTU 1.4:7.30–35)

Like the usage of Yahweh's "strong arm" to poetically argue against the so-called "strong arm" of Pharaoh, so Yahweh inspires His authors to use water and storm language to reflect God's polemic against the so-called storm god Baal.

Comparing the texts yields identical words, memes, and metaphors that suggest God is engaging in polemics against Baal through scriptural imagery and storytelling. It is not Baal who rides his cloud chariot from his divine mountain Saphon, it is Yahweh who rides the clouds from His divine Mount Sinai (and later, Mount Zion). It is not Baal who hurls lightning flashes in wrath; it is Yahweh whose lightning flashes destroy His enemies. It is not Baal whose dew-drenched brow waters the land of Canaan; it is Yahweh who drops dew from heaven to Canaan. It is not Baal's voice that thunders and conquers the waters resulting in his everlasting temple enthronement, it is Yahweh whose voice thunders and conquers the waters resulting in His everlasting temple enthronement.

Psalm 29 (quoted in part above) is so replete with poetry in common with Canaanite poetry that many ANE scholars have concluded it is a Canaanite hymn to Baal that has been rewritten with the name Baal replaced by the name Yahweh.[18] God was not only *physically* dispossessing Canaan of its inhabitants, He was *literarily* dispossessing the Canaanite gods as well. Old Testament appropriation of Canaanite culture is a case of subversion, not syncretism — overthrowing cultural narratives as opposed to blending with them.

But this is only a glance at a single page of a book-load of resonances between Canaanite and Hebrew poetry. A closer look at comparing just two elements of the Baal cycle with Yahweh's story will yield a clearer picture of

---

[18] Aloysius Fitzgerald, "A Note on Psalm 29," *Bulletin of the American Schools of Oriental Research*, no. 215 (October 1974), 62. A more conservative interpretation claims a common Semitic poetic discourse.

the literary subversion of the Canaanite narrative that God and the human authors were employing. Those two elements are the epithet of "cloud-rider" and God's conflict with the dragon and the sea.

Mount Zaphon/Sapon

Another element of Baal's reign that was just touched upon is his mountain abode of Mount Saphon (*Zaphon* in Hebrew). As written above, a plethora of Ugaritic texts link Baal with his "divine mountain, Saphon" (KTU 1.101:1-9; 1.100:9; 1.3:3:29), that he is buried there (KTU 1.6:1:15–18), his sanctuary (KTU 1.3:3:30), and mountain of victory (KTU 1.101:1–4). Earlier Hurrian and Hittite traditions of Baal link Mount Zaphon with another mountain, Namni, both in the northern Syrian ranges.[19]

This linking of the two mountains is of particular importance because as the *Dictionary of Deities and Demons* in the Bible explains, the Psalmist asserts Yahweh's authority as creator and therefore owner of all the heavens and the earth by referring to the mountains of pagan mythology as under the lordship of Yahweh.

> Psalm 89:12
> The north (*zaphon*) and the south (*yamin*), you have created them; Tabor and Hermon joyously praise your name.

Tabor and Hermon are well known holy mountains within Canaanite and other mythology. But the deliberate linking of Zaphon and Yamin are most likely Hebrew references to the Saphon and Namni of Ugarit.

In Isaiah 14:13, Isaiah mocks the arrogance of the king of Babylon by likening him to another mythological figure, Athtar, who sought to take Baal's throne and failed "on the mountain of assembly on the summit of Zaphon."[20] In Psalm 48:1-2 Yahweh's holy mountain Zion replaces Mount Saphon as the divine mountain par excellence.[21]

---

[19] H. Niehr, "Zaphon", in *Dictionary of Deities and Demons in the Bible*, ed. Karel van der Toorn, Bob Becking and Pieter W. van der Horst, 2nd extensively rev. ed., 927 (Leiden; Boston; Köln; Grand Rapids, MI; Cambridge: Brill; Eerdmans, 1999).
[20] Michael Heiser, "The Mythological Provenance of Isaiah 14:12-15: A Reconsideration of the Ugaritic Material" Liberty University <http://digitalcommons.liberty.edu/lts fac pubs/280>
[21] H. Niehr, "Zaphon", in *Dictionary of Deities and Demons in the Bible*, ed. Karel van der Toorn, Bob Becking and Pieter W. van der Horst, 2nd extensively rev. ed., 929 (Leiden; Boston; Köln; Grand Rapids, MI; Cambridge: Brill; Eerdmans, 1999). Also see Job 26:7;

Cloud-Rider

In the Ugaritic text cited above, we are introduced to Baal as one who rides the heavens in his cloud-chariot dispensing judgment from the heights. "Charioteer (or 'Rider') of the Clouds" was a common epithet ascribed to Baal throughout the Ugaritic texts.[22] Here is another side-by-side comparison of Ugaritic and Biblical texts that illustrate that common motif.

UGARITIC TEXTS	OLD TESTAMENT
'Dry him up. O Valiant Baal! Dry him up, O Charioteer [Rider] of the Clouds! For our captive is Prince Yam [Sea], for our captive is Ruler Nahar [River]!' (KTU 1.2:4.8–9)	"[Yahweh] bowed the heavens also, and came down With thick darkness under His feet. "And He rode on a cherub and flew; And He appeared on the wings of the wind. "And He made darkness canopies around Him, A mass of waters, thick clouds of the sky. (2 Sam. 22:7–12)
What manner of enemy has arisen against Baal, of foe against the Charioteer of the Clouds? Surely I smote the Beloved of El, Yam [Sea]? Surely I exterminated Nahar [River], the mighty god? Surely I lifted up the dragon, I overpowered him? I smote the writhing serpent, Encircler-with-seven-heads! (KTU 1.3:3.38–41)	[Yahweh] makes the clouds His chariot; He walks upon the wings of the wind; (Psa. 104:3–4) Behold, the LORD is riding on a swift cloud and is about to come to Egypt; The idols of Egypt will tremble at His presence, (Isa. 19:1)

Yahweh is described here with the same exact moniker as Baal, in the same exact context as Baal — revealed in the storm and riding a cloud in judgment on other deities.

37:22; Ezek. 1:4 where the word "north" is used as a spiritual reference, more allusion to the divine mountain Saphon of Canaanite belief.
[22] KTU 1.2:4.8-9; 1.3:3.38–41; 1.3:4:4, 6, 26; 1.4:3:10, 18; 1.4:5:7, 60; 1.10:1:7; 1.10:3:21, 36; 1.19:1:43; 1.92:37, 39.

Baal the storm god is subverted by Yahweh, the God of storm.

The Dragon and the Sea

The second narrative element of the Canaanite Baal cycle that I want to address is God's conflict with the dragon and the sea. In ancient Near Eastern religious mythologies, the sea and the sea dragon were symbols of chaos that had to be overcome to bring order to the universe, or more exactly, the political world order of the myth's originating culture. Some scholars call this battle *Chaoskampf* — the divine struggle to create order out of chaos.[23] Creation accounts were often veiled polemics for the establishment of a king or kingdom's claim to sovereignty.[24] Richard Clifford quotes, "In Mesopotamia, Ugarit, and Israel the *Chaoskampf* appears not only in cosmological contexts but just as frequently — and this was fundamentally true right from the first — in political contexts. The repulsion and the destruction of the enemy, and thereby the maintenance of political order, always constitute one of the major dimensions of the battle against chaos."[25]

For example, the Sumerians had three stories where the gods Enki, Ninurta, and Inanna all destroy sea monsters in their pursuit of establishing order. The sea monster in two of those versions, according to Sumerian expert Samuel Noah Kramer, is "conceived as a large serpent which lived in the bottom of the 'great below' where the latter came in contact with the primeval waters."[26] In the Babylonian creation myth, *Enuma Elish*, Marduk battles the sea dragon goddess Tiamat, and splits her body into two parts, creating the heavens and the earth, the world order over which Babylon's deity Marduk ruled.

Another side-by-side comparison of those same Ugaritic passages that we considered above with *other* Old Testament passages reveals another common narrative: Yahweh, the charioteer of the clouds, metaphorically battles with Sea (Hebrew: *yam*) and River (Hebrew: *nahar*), just as Baal struggled with Yam and Nahar, which is also linked to victory over a sea dragon/serpent.

---

[23] Hermann Gunkel first suggested this theme in *Schöpfung und Chaos in Urzdt und Endzeit* (1895).
[24] Bruce R. Reichenbach, "Genesis 1 as a Theological-Political Narrative of Kingdom Establishment," *Bulletin for Biblical Research* 13, 1 (2003).
[25] Clifford, *Creation Accounts*, 8, n. 13.
[26] Samuel Noah Kramer, *Sumerian Mythology: A Study of Spiritual and Literary Achievement in the Third Millennium B.C.* (Philadelphia: University of Pennsylvania Press, 1944, 1961, 1972), 77–78.

UGARTIC TEXTS	OLD TESTAMENT
'Dry him up. O Valiant Baal! Dry him up, O Charioteer of the Clouds! For our captive is Prince Yam [Sea], for our captive is Ruler Nahar [River]!' (KTU 1.2:4.8–9)[27]	Did Yahweh rage against the rivers, Or was Your anger against the rivers (nahar), Or was Your wrath against the sea (yam), That You rode on Your horses, On Your chariots of salvation? (Hab. 3:8)
What manner of enemy has arisen against Baal, of foe against the Charioteer of the Clouds? Surely I smote the Beloved of El, Yam [Sea]? Surely I exterminated Nahar [River], the mighty god? Surely I lifted up the dragon, I overpowered him? I smote the writhing serpent, Encircler-with-seven-heads! (KTU 1.3:3.38–41)	In that day Yahweh will punish Leviathan the fleeing serpent, With His fierce and great and mighty sword, Even Leviathan the twisted serpent; And He will kill the dragon who lives in the sea. (Isa. 27:1) "You divided the sea by your might; you broke the heads of the sea monsters on the waters. You crushed the heads of Leviathan. (Psa. 74:13–14)

Baal fights Sea and River to establish his sovereignty. He wins by drinking up Sea and River, draining them dry, and thus establishing his supremacy over the pantheon and the Canaanite world order.[28] In the second passage, Baal's battle with Sea and River is retold in other words as a battle with a "dragon," the "writhing serpent" with seven heads.[29] Another Baal text calls this same dragon, "*Lotan*, the wriggling serpent."[30] The Hebrew equivalents of the Ugaritic words *tannin* (dragon) and *lotan* are *tanniyn* (dragon) and *liwyatan* (Leviathan) respectively.[31] Thus, the Canaanite

---

[27] "Charioteer of the Clouds" also appears in these texts: KTU 1.3:4:4, 6, 26; 1.4:3:10, 18; 1.4:5:7, 60; 1.10:1:7; 1.10:3:21, 36; 1.19:1:43; 1.92:37, 39.
[28] KTU 1.2:4:27–32.
[29] See KTU 1.5:1:1–35.
[30] KTU 1.5:1:1–4.
[31] Walter C. Kaiser, Jr., *The Ugaritic Pantheon* (dissertation) (Ann Arbor, MI: Brandeis University, 1973), 212.

narrative of Leviathan the sea dragon or serpent is undeniably employed in Old Testament Scriptures.[32] Notice the last Scripture in the chart that refers to Leviathan as having multiple heads *just like the Canaanite Leviathan.*

And notice as well the reference to the Red Sea event also associated with Leviathan in the Biblical text. In Psalm 74 above, God's parting of the waters is connected to the motif of the Mosaic covenant as the creation of a new world order in the same way that Baal's victory over the waters and the dragon are emblematic of his establishment of authority in the Canaanite pantheon. This covenant motif is described as a *chaoskampf* battle with the Sea and Leviathan (called *Rahab*) in several other significant Biblical references as well.[33]

Subverting Paganism

When it comes to comparative studies between the Bible and other ANE mythopoeia, confessing scholarship tends to operate under a faith commitment to overwrought supernaturalism. It paints a picture of Israel's mythopoeia as wholly other or completely alien to its surroundings, as if this is what is needed to secure religious authority behind the text. The evidence clearly contradicts such theories of "divine dictation" or modern notions of science and history. The humanity of Scriptural authorship does not negate providential divine authorship. But critical scholarship tends to operate under a faith commitment to anti-supernaturalism. Therefore it interprets common story motifs between Baal and Yahweh as evidence of evolutionary transformation of one religion into another — of polytheism into monotheism. They reduce the Bible to derivative "mythology" that plagiarizes or borrows from its pagan neighbors. The discerning reader need not fall for the cultural imperialism of either of these modernist narratives.

Common imagination springs from what John Walton calls a "common cognitive environment" of people in a shared space, time, or culture. Walton suggests, "Borrowing is not the issue [...] Likewise this need not concern whose ideas are derivative. There is simply common ground across the cognitive environment of the cultures of the ancient world."[34] The story of a

---

[32] See also Is. 51:9; Ezek. 32:2; Rev. 12:9, 16, 17.
[33] Ps. 89:9–10; Isa. 51:9–10; Job 26:12–13. Psa. 18, 29, 24, 29, 65, 74, 77, 89, 93, and 104 all reflect *chaoskampf*. See also Exod. 15, Job 9, 26, 38, and Isa. 51:14-16; 2 Sam. 22.
[34] John H. Walton, *Ancient Near Eastern Thought and the Old Testament: Introducing the Conceptual World of the Hebrew Bible* (Grand Rapids: Baker, 2006), 21.

Cloud-rider controlling the elements and battling the Sea and Leviathan to establish his sovereignty over other gods with a new world order is not a false "myth," it is a narrative shared between Israel and her pagan neighbors that Jewish authors appropriate, with divine approval of Yahweh, as a metaphor within their own discourse. And that discourse involves subversion, the replacement or overthrow of the opponent's worldview with one's own.

It is no different than what we do today, as we moderns use the current science narratives of string theory or multiverses to construct our worldview and spin our science fiction just as ancient man did with the Mesopotamian or Ptolemaic universe. And as writers well know, science fiction is a morality tale about where our current cultural values will lead us in the future. Or we see the narrative of atheistic evolution seek to reduce morality, altruism, and religion into categories of its own construction and control. Political opponents on all sides in the Media construct narratives to control public discourse. The real revelation is that subversion of narrative is not a special technique used only by activists and intellectuals. It is the very nature of most storytelling through history. We are all creatures of our times seeking to control the narrative of our times, just as the ancients did. And those who control the cultural narrative, control the culture.

Great fathers of the Christian Faith subverted their cultural narrative. Curtis Chang, in his book, *Engaging Unbelief*, examines the apologetic work of church fathers Augustine and Aquinas. Augustine lived within the Roman Empire whose cultural narrative was the history of the "Eternal City." So the Bishop of Hippo wrote his *City of God* to defend the Christian faith in terms of urban historical narrative saturated with references, motifs, and themes from classical Roman authors like Virgil and Marcus Varro. He subverted that "City of Man" by revealing the destructive pride lurking behind all human social construction. Aquinas, in his *Summa contra Gentiles*, appealed to the Aristotelian story of knowledge because he was addressing a Muslim culture steeped in Aristotle. But he subverted that cultural narrative by teasing out the ultimate insufficiency of human reason. Augustine and Aquinas changed their worlds through subversive literary metaphor.

Chang explains this rhetorical strategy as threefold: "1. Entering the challenger's story, 2. Retelling the story, 3. Capturing that retold tale with the gospel metanarrative." He writes that the challenge of each epoch in history is a contest in storytelling, a challenge to "overturn and supplant the inherited story of the epoch with its own metanarrative [...] The one who can tell the best story, in a very real sense, wins the epoch."[35]

The hostile "post-Christian" epoch in which we live requires enterprising believers to retell the narratives of our culture with bold fresh perspectives. Tolkien and Lewis are among the finest modern examples of subversive authors who entered into the genres and mythology of pagan worlds to harness them for Christian imagination. Tolkien's Middle Earth abounded with the mythical Norse characters of wizards, dwarves, elves, giants, and trolls all in the service of his Catholic worldview. Lewis's Narnia is saturated with a plethora of beasts from assorted pagan mythologies, deliberately subjugated to the Lordship of Aslan. As a professional filmmaker I would add to these examples Mel Gibson's *Apocalypto*, that subversively enters the narrative of indigenous pagan earth religion in order to reveal it as barbarism based on human sacrifice. Scott Derrickson's *The Exorcism of Emily Rose* subverts the materialist narrative by depicting the supernatural on trial. Horror is a genre in all the arts that tends to be considered pagan or destructive. Yet horror is another genre that the "Holy Book" uses to subvert the evil its authors fight against. Who can deny the power of epic horror fantasy in the books of Daniel and Revelation that seek to turn the fear of man into the fear of God?

The problem is that some of those who revere the Bible as their sacred text fear that engaging pagan thought forms or motifs will corrupt their narrative, dilute the truth, and drag the believer into apostasy. Hopefully, this exploration of how the Biblical authors subverted pagan narratives of the Storm God versus Leviathan the Sea Dragon will provide a boost of confidence that will help free the believing storyteller and reader from the religious shackles of fear of the imagination. For as the great artistic intellect Francis Schaeffer once wrote, "The Christian is the really free man — he is free to have imagination. The Christian is the one whose imagination should fly beyond the stars."[36]

I am a filmmaker, so I think in terms of movies. We need more storytellers to tell vampire stories with a Christian worldview (*The Addiction*); more zombie stories with a Christian worldview (*I Am Legend*); more demonic stories with Christian redemption (M. Night Shyamalan's *Devil*); more post-apocalyptic thrillers that honor God (*The Book of Eli*); more subversion of adultery (*Fatal Attraction*), fornication (*17 Again*), unbelief (*Paranormal Activity*), paganism

---

[35] Ibid., 27.
[36] Schaeffer, Francis. *Art and the Bible*. Downers Grove: InterVarsity Press, 1973, 91.

(*Apocalypto*), humanistic anti-supernaturalism (*The Last Exorcism*), and our "pro-Choice" culture of death (*The Island*).

I will end with a question and a charge. With two exceptions, why were all these movies that subversively incarnate the Christian worldview made by non-Christians instead of Christians? Rise up, O Christian apologists and subvert ye the world's imagination!

Chapter 3
Biblical Creation and Storytelling[1]

I am a professional storyteller. My interests lie in understanding the literary genres and cultural contexts of the Bible as it existed within an ancient Near Eastern worldview that included common metaphors, images, and concepts. As readers displaced from such an ancient world by time, space, and culture, we will misread the text through our own cultural prejudice if we do not seek to understand it through the eyes of its original writers and readers. Creation stories (cosmogonies) such as Genesis 1 are particularly vulnerable to this kind of interpretive violence.

Genesis 1 is an ancient cosmogony, a story of the origin of the universe. Its Semitic authorship is birthed within a varied cultural heritage of Babylonian, Egyptian and Canaanite environments. The orthodox Christian tradition claims that we have received the entire corpus of the Old Testament as "breathed out" by God through the writings and personalities of those human beings embedded within their cultures (2 Tim. 3:16; 1 Pet. 1:20-21). This doctrine of "dual authorship" between divinity and humanity is not a dictation theory or automatic writing, but rather a providential means of transmission of truth through incarnation of human literary convention.[2]

As an orthodox Christian, I affirm both the human and divine origin of the Bible with equal ultimacy. The differences between it and other ANE literature surely illustrate a divine antithesis, but the similarities between it and other ANE literature surely illustrate human synthesis that need not support the claim of untruth. God accommodates and uses human culture and conceptions to communicate His truth because we cannot comprehend God's kingdom outside of our finite paradigms of understanding. As John Calvin so aptly put it,

---

[1] This chapter has been adapted from the article "Biblical Creation and Storytelling: Cosmos, Combat, and Covenant" published at BioLogos Foundation.

[2] "The Chicago Statement on Biblical Inerrancy," Article VIII, 1978: "We affirm that God in His Work of inspiration utilized the distinctive personalities and literary styles of the writers whom He had chosen and prepared. We deny that God, in causing these writers to use the very words that He chose, overrode their personalities."

"[I]t shows an extraordinary degree of wickedness, that we yield less reverence to God speaking to us, because He condescends to our ignorance; and, therefore, when God prattles to us in Scripture in a rough and popular style, let us know that this is done on account of the love which He bears to us."[3]

In light of this "loving accommodation" that Calvin spoke of, The Chicago Statement on Biblical Inerrancy (1978) concluded, "Differences between literary conventions in Bible times and in ours must also be observed... Scripture is inerrant, not in the sense of being absolutely precise by modern standards, but in the sense of making good its claims and achieving that measure of focused truth at which its authors aimed."[4]

So, what is "the measure of focused truth" at which the Biblical authors aimed? If it was not absolute precision by modern standards, as these conservative scholars admit, then what kind of truth was it? Let's take a look at some of the ANE literary and storytelling features of Scripture to see just what kind of truth God's word intended when it comes to Biblical creation.

Creation as Cosmogony

The 18th century "Age of Enlightenment" established autonomous human reasoning as the primary source of authority and elevated "scientific" empirical observation over abstract philosophy and theology. One of the effects of this cultural revolution on the way we think today is a materialist prejudice, the belief that ultimate reality is material, not spiritual. Any appeal to teleology or purpose behind natural events became illegitimate because the dominant assumption was that we live in a closed system of natural causes. So when we as moderns approach cosmogony, or the story of the origin of the universe, we naturally assume any such story is about answering the question of where matter comes from (since this is ultimate reality to us). Our post-Enlightened scientific minds demand "objective" descriptions of material structure, natural laws that work upon matter, and taxonomic categories of material substances.

But this is not the way the ancient Near Eastern mind thought when approaching cosmogony. To interpret ancient pre-scientific cosmogonies through our post-Enlightened scientific materialist categories is to do violence

---

[3] John Calvin, *Commentary on the Gospel According to John*, 3:12.
[4] The Chicago Statement on Biblical Inerrancy (1978), Exposition: "Infallibility, Inerrancy, Interpretation."

to the text, an act of cultural imperialism. As John Walton argues, "People in the ancient world believed that something existed not by virtue of its material properties, but by virtue of its having a function in an ordered system."[5] And that ordered system was not a scientific system of matter and physics, but a human system of society and culture.

Walton explains that creation and existence in the ANE mindset involved three elements alien to modern notions of existence. He lays out examples from Mesopotamian and Egyptian creation myths in common with Genesis to illustrate that bringing something into existence was not about "making things" or manufacturing material substance but about *naming, separating, and assigning roles to things*.[6]

Naming

Consider these ANE creation activities of naming:

- The Egyptian Memphite Theology describes Ptah creating everything by pronouncing its name.[7]

- The Babylonian Enuma Elish begins with the heavens and earth as well as the deities "not yet named," whose existence comes from being so named.[8]

- The Hebrew Genesis shows Yahweh naming things and calling them "good," a word not of moral quality, but of orderly fittingness.[9]

This is not so much a denial of *creatio ex nihilo*, (creation out of nothing) as it is a cultural linguistic focus on purposes over properties. "Thus, the [Hebrew] text never uses *bara* [a special word used exclusively of divine

---

[5] John H. Walton, *The Lost World of Genesis One: Ancient Cosmology and the Origins Debate* (Downers Grove: IL, InterVarsity Press, 2009), 26.
[6] John H. Walton, *Ancient Near Eastern Thought and the Old Testament: Introducing the Conceptual World of the Hebrew Bible* (Grand Rapids, MI: Baker, 2006) 188-189.
[7] James B. Pritchard, ed., *Ancient Near Eastern Texts Relating to the Old Testament* (Princeton, NJ: Princeton University, 1950, 1955), 5.
[8] Alexander Heidel, trans., *The Babylonian Genesis* (Chicago, IL: University of Chicago, 1942, 1951, 1963), 18.
[9] Walton, *The Lost World*, 51.

activity] in a context in which materials are mentioned...that materials are not mentioned suggests that manufacture is not the issue."[10]

Separation

Consider these ANE creation activities of separation:

- Everything in the Egyptian universe came into existence through separation from something else. The limitless ocean above the sky (the god Nun) was separated from the waters under the earth (Tefnut) by Shu, the god of air.[11]

- In the Babylonian Enuma Elish, the victorious Marduk created the heavens and the earth by splitting the corpse of his vanquished foe Tiamat in two.[12]

- In Genesis, God separated the light from the darkness (1:4), the waters above from the waters below (1:6-7), the land from the waters below (1:9), male from female (2:21-24), and the Sabbath from other days (2:3).

Separation is differentiation or distinction between things. God separates a people for Himself (1 Sam. 12:22), and gives great detail in the Law from Sinai for cultic separations that reinforce a code of holiness. The separation of creation is a theological reinforcement of God's majority theme of holy otherness in Scripture.

Roles

Consider these ANE creation activities of assigning roles:

- The Egyptian Papyrus Insinger describes 18 creations of functions for things from the earth to wealth.[13]

---

[10] Walton, Ancient Near Eastern Thought, 183.
[11] Pritchard, Ancient Near Eastern Thought, 6.
[12] Heidel, Babylonian Genesis, 42.
[13] Walton, *The Lost World*, 32-33.

- The Babylonian Enuma Elish has Marduk creating sun, moon and constellations for their purposes, and specified stations for the gods.[14]

- Yahweh is described as creating the things-in-the-world of Genesis 1 by explaining their purposes: Light and dark to mark time (1:5); sun, moon, and stars to give light (1:16); and signs for seasons (1:14); plants and fruit for food (1:29); mankind to rule over animals and the creation (1:27-28).

Things-in-the-world were thought of in terms of their purpose for humankind not their material being. This stress on teleology (purpose) sheds light on the personification of nature into deities whose ANE stories become mythic explanations of cycles that are used instrumentally in religious cult.[15] Purpose can only come from persons, so pagan deities were immanent within nature. Though Yahweh was contrastingly transcendent He was nevertheless the person behind the purpose of the depersonalized nature. Thus, even Yahweh uses natural elements such as wind, lightning and thunderstorms as means of revealing His presence (theophany) and purposes.[16]

Interpreting the creation story of Genesis with an expectation of modern scientific discourse is hermeneutical violence. The notion of creation and existence in the Biblical ancient Near East was not one of physics, life sciences, material substance and structure, it was a story explaining the creation of the functions of the world through naming, separation and purpose. Purpose (teleology) is theological not empirical and does not therefore require any scientific theory, be it young earth creationism or theistic evolution.

---

[14] Heidel, *Babylonian Genesis*, 44-45.
[15] The Baal cycle tells the story of Baal, god of the storm, winds, and rain, being killed by Mot, the god of death. Baal's sister Anat, then defeats Mot and Baal is revived and the drought ends with the coming of rain. Michael David Coogan, trans. *Stories from Ancient Canaan* (Louisville, KY: Westminster Press), 84-85. In Egypt, a similar cycle of death and regeneration based on agriculture is found in such myths as Osiris. The "great god" Osiris is killed by his brother Seth, and "resurrected" as king by decree of the gods at the behest of Osiris's sister, Isis. Egyptians would worship Osiris as the god of agricultural fertility. Robert A. Armour, *Gods and Myths of Ancient Egypt* (Cairo, Egypt: American University in Cairo), 178-179.
[16] Ronald A. Simkins, *Creator and Creation: Nature in the Worldview of Ancient Israel* (Peabody, MA: Hendrickson, 1994, 2003) 145-146.

Creation as Combat

In his analysis of ancient creation accounts, Richard Clifford concludes that "many ancient cosmogonies are narratives and depend on plot and character for their movement; they must be read as drama rather than 'objective' description."[17] To the ancients, creation was not a historical chronology of material origins, but a drama of spiritual purposes. The essence of drama is conflict, and that conflict is reflected in Biblical creation, no less than in ANE accounts, through the text as theological-political polemic — images of combat.

One of the functions of ancient creation narratives is to literarily encode the religious and political overthrow of one culture by another. When a king or kingdom would rise to power in the ancient world, they would often displace the vassal culture's creation stories with their own stories of how their deities triumphed over others to create the world in which they now lived.

The Enuma Elish tells the story of the Babylonian deity Marduk, and his ascendancy to power in the Mesopotamian pantheon, giving mythical justification to the rise of Babylon as an ancient world power most likely in the First Babylonian Dynasty under Hammurabi (1792-1750 B.C.).[18] As the prologue of the Code of Hammurabi explains, "Anu, the majestic, King of the Anunnaki, and Bel, the Lord of Heaven and Earth, who established the fate of the land, had given to Marduk, the ruling son of Ea, dominion over mankind, and called Babylon by his great name; when they made it great upon the earth by founding therein an eternal kingdom, whose foundations are as firmly grounded as are those of heaven and earth."[19]

The Baal myth of Ugarit tells the story of the storm god "Baal the Conqueror," and his epiphany in becoming "Lord of the earth" in Canaan.[20] Chapter I of the text reads,

> "Let me tell you, Prince Baal,
> let me repeat, Rider on the Clouds:

---

[17] Richard J. Clifford, *Creation Accounts in the Ancient Near East and in the Bible*, Catholic Biblical Quarterly Monograph Series 26 (Washington D.C.: Catholic Biblical Association of America, 1994), 199.
[18] Heidel, *Babylonian Genesis*, 14.
[19] W.W. Davies, *The Codes of Hammurabi and Moses: With Copious Comments, Index, and Bible References* (Berkeley, CA: Apocryphile Press, 1905, 2006), 17.
[20] Coogan, *Stories from Ancient Canaan*, 75-115.

> Behold, your enemy, Baal,
> behold, you will kill your enemy,
> behold, you will annihilate your foes.
> You will take your eternal kingship,
> your dominion forever and ever."[21]

Genesis 1, according to scholar Bruce Reichenbach, was also written "as a theological-political document that describes how the Supreme Monarch establishes His kingdom and thereby justifies His claim to exclusive possession of everything in it."[22] If Moses wrote Genesis, it would make sense that he would appropriate the creation story genre as he learned it from the Egyptians. Respected Egyptian translator John Wilson wrote regarding the Egyptian creation genre. "Every important cult-center of Egypt asserted its primacy by the dogma that it was the site of creation."[23]

God was preparing Israel to displace the pagan Canaanites and their gods both physically and literarily, so He inspired this authorship of the creation account to express that ancient Near Eastern motif of justifying transcendent authority and land ownership with a creation story that argued their God created the Edenic garden ("Promised Land") upon which they laid claim.[24]

Genesis follows the literary structure of suzerain-vassal treaties that reflects the activity of ancient Near Eastern monarchs. "God says and it happens, names and it is His, sets His representative images throughout the land, sits and pronounces in council, establishes the cultic, and is the ultimate arbiter of what is good."[25] It is distinctly polemical for the Genesis account to describe the common male and female as God's representatives, created in His image, since this concept seems only to be applied to kings in ancient Mesopotamia.[26]

Genesis 1 is the poetic legitimation of Yahweh, the God of Israel, and His authority and power over all things, including the gods of Canaan, who are in fact, reduced to nothing. The literary act of replacing one identity with another

---

[21] Coogan, *Stories from Ancient Canaan*, 88.
[22] Bruce R. Reichenbach, "Genesis 1 as a Theological-Political Narrative of Kingdom Establishment," *Bulletin for Biblical Research* 13.1 (2003), p. 48.
[23] *The Ancient Near East an Anthology of Texts and Pictures.*, ed. James Bennett Pritchard, 8 (Princeton: Princeton University Press, 1958).
[24] Exod. 3:8; Num. 13:23-27.
[25] Reichenbach, "Genesis 1," 49.
[26] Edward Mason Curtis, *Man As The Image Of God In Genesis In The Light Of Ancient Near Eastern Parallels*, Dissertation (Philadelphia, PA: University of Pennsylvania).

by investing new meaning into commonly understood words, images, metaphors or motifs is called "subversion."

This subversion of pagan deities in the text is also achieved through the demythologizing of nature. Mesopotamian, Canaanite and Egyptian cosmogonies all personify nature through their various deities of sun, moon, stars, waters and the heavens. These gods are mere personifications of nature and are therefore subject to the cycles and seasons of nature.

Contrarily, in Genesis 1 we see a specific description of Yahweh as sovereign creator and sustainer of seasons and their signs for His purposes. Nature has no animistic personality. When describing the creation of sun and moon, the Hebrew text seems to avoid the names for sun (*shemesh*) and moon (*chodesh*), perhaps because these words were also the names of ancient Near Eastern gods. Instead, the writer simply calls them the "greater" and "lesser" lights, heavenly bodies.

When describing the surface of the deep over which the spirit of God hovered (Gen. 1:2), the author uses a word for the deep (*tehom*) with possible linguistic connections to ANE myths of a sea dragon, a symbol of the chaos out of which deity brings order.[27] While the Genesis account reflects a similar creation out of watery chaos, it nevertheless strips all animation from that watery chaos. It remains an inert lifeless state without personality, moldable in the hands of the Creator. Genesis subverts the ancient Near Eastern creation genre of literature by using common ANE narrative concepts and reinvesting them with new definitions and contexts.

Another way that Biblical creation reflects ancient Near Eastern culture, while subverting it is in its appropriation of what ANE scholars call the *Chaoskampf* motif, or the creation of order out of chaos through struggle. Hermann Gunkel first suggested in *Creation and Chaos* (1895) that some ancient Near Eastern creation myths contained a cosmic conflict between deity and sea, as well as sea dragons or serpents that expressed the creation of order out of chaos.[28] Gunkel argued that Genesis borrowed this idea from the Babylonian tale of Marduk battling the goddess Tiamat, serpent of chaos, whom he vanquished, and out of whose body he created the heavens and

---

[27] John Day, *God's Conflict with the Dragon and the Sea: Echoes of a Canaanite myth in the Old Testament* (Great Britain: Cambridge University Press, 1985), 5.
[28] Hermann Gunkel, Heinrich Zimmern; K. William Whitney Jr., trans., *Creation And Chaos in the Primeval Era And the Eschaton: A Religio-historical Study of Genesis 1 and Revelation 12* (Grand Rapids: MI: Eerdmans, 1895, 1921, 2006), xvi.

earth.[29] Later, John Day argued in light of the discovery of the Ugarit tablets in 1928, that Canaan, not Babylonia is the source of the combat motif in Genesis,[30] reflected in Yahweh's own complaint that Israel had become polluted by Canaanite culture.[31] In the Baal cycle, Baal battles Yam (Sea) and conquers it, along with "the dragon," "the twisting serpent," to be enthroned as chief deity of the Canaanite pantheon.[32]

While the image of struggle has already been noted as being polemically absent in Genesis 1, it is certainly alive and kicking in other creation passages throughout the Old Testament. Rather than speculating about who borrowed whose understanding of *Chaoskampf*, Walton suggests "borrowing is not the issue… Likewise this need not concern whose ideas are derivative. There is simply common ground across the cognitive environment of the cultures of the ancient world."[33] *Chaoskampf* is simply a common ancient Near Eastern motif

---

[29] "He cast down her carcass and stood upon it.
After he had slain Tiamat, the leader…
He split her open like a mussel into two parts;
Half of her he set in place and formed the sky…
And a great structure, its counterpart, he established, namely Esharra [earth]."
(Enuma Elish, Tablet IV, lines 104-105, 137-138, 144 from Heidel, *Babylonian Genesis*, 41-42)

[30] John Day, *God's Conflict with the Dragon*. Day argues that the Canaanite Baal cycle implies a connection with creation, since it is a ritual fertility festival (cyclical creation) falling on the New Year, traditionally understood as the date of creation. But his strongest appeal is the argument in reverse that the Canaanite myth makes a connection between creation and *Chaoskampf* because the Old Testament does so.

[31] "Then the word of the LORD came to me, saying, "Son of man, make known to Jerusalem her abominations and say, 'Thus says the Lord GOD to Jerusalem, "Your origin and your birth are from the land of the Canaanite, your father was an Amorite and your mother a Hittite."" (Ezek. 16:1-3)

[32] "Didn't I [Baal] demolish El's Darling, Sea?
didn't I finish off the divine river, Rabbim?
didn't I snare the Dragon?
I enveloped him,
I demolished the Twisting Serpent,
the seven-headed monster.
(Baal II from Coogan, *Stories from Ancient Canaan*, 92.)
"When you [Baal] killed Lotan, the Fleeing Serpent,
finished off the Twisting Serpent,
the seven-headed monster,
the heavens withered and drooped."
(Baal IV from Coogan, *Stories from Ancient Canaan*, 106.)
Most recently, David Tsumura has argued against any connection of such mythic struggle in the Biblical text in favor of mere poetic flair: David Toshio Tsumura, *Creation And Destruction: A Reappraisal of the Chaoskampf Theory in the Old Testament* (Winona Lake, IN: Eisenbrauns, 2006).

[33] Walton, *Ancient Near Eastern Thought*, 21.

shared between Israel and its pagan neighbors that Jewish authors appropriate, under divine authority of Yahweh, for their own discourse. For Biblical authors, creation and *Chaoskampf* language are intertwined to describe the action of Yahweh creating His world order out of chaos — alternately symbolized as Sea, Leviathan, Dragon and Rahab.

> Psa. 74:12-17
> You broke the heads of the sea monsters in the waters.
> You crushed the heads of Leviathan;...
> You have prepared the light and the sun.
> You have established all the boundaries of the earth;
>
> Was it not You who cut Rahab in pieces,
> Who pierced the dragon?
> Was it not You who dried up the sea,
> The waters of the great deep;
> [Y]ou have forgotten the LORD your Maker,
> Who stretched out the heavens
> And laid the foundations of the earth...
>
> Isa. 51:9-14
> "For I am the LORD your God, who stirs up the sea and its waves roar (the LORD of hosts is His name).
>
> Psa. 89:6-12
> You rule the swelling of the sea;
> When its waves rise, You still them.
> You Yourself crushed Rahab like one who is slain;
> You scattered Your enemies with Your mighty arm.
> The heavens are Yours, the earth also is Yours;
> The world and all it contains, You have founded them.
> The north and the south, You have created them;
>
> Isa. 27:1
> In that day the LORD will punish Leviathan the fleeing serpent,
> With His fierce and great and mighty sword,
> Even Leviathan the twisted serpent;
> And He will kill the dragon who lives in the sea.

So the language of *Chaoskampf* in battling the sea/dragon/Leviathan/Rahab is an image that Israel had in common with its ancient Near Eastern pagan neighbors to describe God's creation of the cosmos.[34] The controversial difference lies in God's transcendent control *over* creation versus Canaanite or Mesopotamian immanent struggle *within* creation. God doesn't battle with the beasts like Baal or Marduk does, he sovereignly controls them and destroys them for his own purposes. Creation of cosmos out of chaos is not a great effort for the one God Yahweh of the Hebrew Scriptures.

But exactly what kind of cosmos does Yahweh create in the Biblical text? It is not the cosmos of material substance and physics, but rather the cosmos of God's covenant.

Creation as Covenant

Chaoskampf and creation language are used as word pictures for God's covenant activity in the Bible. For God, describing the creation of the heavens and earth was a way of saying He has established His covenant with His people through exodus into the Promised Land,[35] reaffirming that covenant with the kingly line of David, and finalizing the covenant by bringing them out of exile. The reader should understand that the Scriptures listed above, exemplary of *Chaoskampf,* were deliberately abbreviated to make a further point in this section. I will now add the missing text in those passages in bold to reveal a deeper motif at play in the text — a motif not of creation as mere material manufacturing, but of creation as covenantal formation. God redeeming His people and establishing His covenant with them is poetically likened to the suppression of the dragon of chaos and the creation of the cosmos.

> Psa. 74:12-17
> Yet God is my king from of old,
> Who works deeds of deliverance in the midst of the earth.
> You divided the sea by Your strength;
> [A reference to the Exodus deliverance of the covenant at Sinai]
> You broke the heads of the sea monsters in the waters.

---

[34] See also Isa. 27:1; Psa. 77:16-18; Job 26:7-13.
[35] John Owen, *Works*, 16 vols. (London: The Banner of Truth Trust, 1965-1968), Vol. 9 134.

You crushed the heads of Leviathan…
You have prepared the light and the sun.
You have established all the boundaries of the earth;
Was it not You who cut Rahab in pieces,
Who pierced the dragon?
Was it not You who dried up the sea,
The waters of the great deep;
Who made the depths of the sea a pathway
For the redeemed to cross over?...
[Y]ou have forgotten the LORD your Maker,
Who stretched out the heavens
And laid the foundations of the earth…

Isa. 51:9-16
"For I am the LORD your God, who stirs up the sea and its waves roar (the LORD of hosts is His name). "I have put My words in your mouth and have covered you with the shadow of My hand, to establish the heavens, to found the earth, and to say to Zion, 'You are My people.'"
[a reaffirmation of the Sinai covenant through Moses]

Psa. 89:6-12,19-29
You rule the swelling of the sea;
When its waves rise, You still them.
You Yourself crushed Rahab like one who is slain;
You scattered Your enemies with Your mighty arm.
The heavens are Yours, the earth also is Yours;
The world and all it contains, You have founded them.
The north and the south, You have created them…
"I have found David My servant;
With My holy oil I have anointed him,
With whom My hand will be established;
And in My name his horn will be exalted.
"I shall also set his hand on the sea
And his right hand on the rivers…
"My lovingkindness I will keep for him forever,
And My covenant shall be confirmed to him.

> "So I will establish his descendants forever
> And his throne as the days of heaven.
>
> Isa. 27:1, 6-13
> In that day the LORD will punish Leviathan the fleeing
> serpent,
> With His fierce and great and mighty sword,
> Even Leviathan the twisted serpent;
> And He will kill the dragon who lives in the sea…
> In the days to come Jacob will take root,
> Israel will blossom and sprout,
> And they will fill the whole world with fruit.
>
> It will come about also in that day that a great trumpet will be
> blown, and those who were perishing in the land of Assyria
> and who were scattered in the land of Egypt will come and
> worship the LORD in the holy mountain at Jerusalem.
> [the future consummation of the Mosaic and Davidic
> covenant in the New Covenant of Messiah]

In these texts, and others,[36] God does not merely appeal to His power of material creation as justification for the authority of His covenant, but more importantly He uses the creation of the heavens and earth, involving subjugation of the sea and dragon, as poetic descriptions of God's covenant with His people, rooted in the Exodus story. The creation of the covenant is the creation of the heavens and the earth. The covenant is a cosmos — not a material one centered in astronomical location and abstract impersonal forces as modern worldview demands, but a theological one, centered in the sacred space of land, temple, and cult as ancient Near Eastern worldview demands.[37]

As Ronald Simkins observes of other ANE creation texts:

> "According to the *Enuma Elish*, for example, Marduk chose
> Babylon to be the special place of his temple and organized
> the rest of the creation around it. In the [Sumerian] *Creation
> of the Pickax* humans sprout from the ground at Uzumua, and

---

[36] See also Psa. 77:16-20; 136:1-22.
[37] N.T. Wright, *The New Testament and the People of God* (Minneapolis, MN: Fortress Press, 1992), 306-307.

Duranki is the place at which heaven and earth were originally attached. In the Egyptian creation myths, the land of Egypt is the hillock that first emerged out of the primeval ocean Nun...Each place is a symbolic geographical expression of the structure of creation...The ideas of creation and the experiences of sacred space are mutually dependent."[38]

This "covenant as creation" word picture is reiterated in a negative way when God judges nations and cultures. If creation of covenant involved establishing the foundations of the heavens and the earth, then covenantal judgment involves "decreation" imagery of the destruction or "shaking" of heavens and earth. Haggai conveys this decreation polemic against the nations:

> Hag. 2:20-22
> "Then the word of the Lord came a second time to Haggai... saying, "Speak to Zerubbabel governor of Judah, saying, 'I am going to shake the heavens and the earth.' I will overthrow the thrones of kingdoms and destroy the power of the kingdoms of the nations".

Jeremiah calls the destruction of Jerusalem in 587 B.C. a return of the heavens and earth to the "formless and void" (*tohu wabohu*) of Genesis 1:2 without man or beast yet created[39]:

> Jer. 4:23-27
> "I looked on the earth, and behold, it was formless and void; And to the heavens, and they had no light. I looked on the mountains, and behold, they were quaking, And all the hills moved to and fro. I looked, and behold, there was no man, And all the birds of the heavens had fled. I looked, and behold, the fruitful land was a wilderness".

Isaiah proclaims the "good news" of a New Covenant in Messiah (Isa. 61) as a "new heavens and a new earth" (Isa. 65).[40] Covenant is understood as

---

[38] Simkins, *Creator and Creation*, 133.
[39] David Chilton, *The Days of Vengeance: An Exposition of the Book of Revelation* (Ft. Worth, TX: Dominion Press, 1987-1990), 541.
[40] John Calvin, *Commentary on the Book of the Prophet Isaiah*, Trans William Pringle (Grand Rapids, MI: Eerdmans, 1948), 4:397-398.

creation of a heaven and earth, so important covenantal events, such as judgment on a people or creation of a new covenant, are understood as shaking that heaven and earth or a return to a pre-creation state of the universe.

The New Covenant kingdom as a "new heavens and earth" is picked up in the New Testament with the same language of shaking and removing of the previous heavens and earth:

> Heb. 12:26-28
> "Yet once more I will shake not only the earth, but also the heaven." And this expression, "Yet once more," denotes the removing of those things which can be shaken, as of created things, in order that those things which cannot be shaken may remain. *Therefore, since we receive a kingdom which cannot be shaken* [emphasis added]..."

The replacement of the Old Covenant of Moses with the New Covenant of Christ is here described as God "shaking" and "removing" the old heavens and earth.[41] To the ancient Jew, the covenants of God with His people are the very "cosmos" of their existence and meaning. So important covenantal events are described in cosmic terms, and the purpose of creation language is theological not natural or "scientific."

The inauguration of the New Covenant through the incarnation of Christ is reaffirmed in Revelation as a new heaven and earth cosmos coming out of heaven to eliminate chaos (the sea) and bring a new sacred space of holy city and temple fulfilled in Christ[42]:

> Rev. 21:1-3
> "Then I saw a new heaven and a new earth; for the first heaven and the first earth passed away, and there is no longer any sea. And I saw the holy city, new Jerusalem, coming down out of heaven from God, made ready as a bride adorned for her husband. And I heard a loud voice from the throne, saying, "Behold, the tabernacle of God is among men,

---

[41] Kenneth L. Gentry, Jr., *He Shall Have Dominion: A Postmillennial Eschatology* (Draper, VA: Apologetics Group Media, 1992, 2009), 259.

[42] Kenneth L. Gentry, Jr., *Navigating the Book of Revelation: Special Studies on Important Issues* (Fountain Inn, SC: GoodBirth Ministries, 2009), 167-174;

and He will dwell among them, and they shall be His people, and God Himself will be among them"[43]

Conclusion

A *merism* is a phrase of joined opposites that indicate a totality. The Hebrew for "heavens and earth" has long been accepted as a merism of the ordered cosmos.[44] Whereas the modern scientific mind conceives of "cosmos" as a physical system of materials and their properties, the ancient Near Eastern mind of the Hebrew conceived of "cosmos" as the covenantal order of God. Everything had its place and purpose in God's plan for His people in their land. The idea of the earth as a spherical globe and the heavens as a vast expanse of light years was alien to their thinking. As noted expert on Biblical apocalyptics, Milton Terry wrote, "In these opening chapters of Genesis we are not to look for historic narrative, nor contributions to natural science, but to recognize a symbolic apocalypse of God's relation to the world and to man."[45]

John Sailhamer makes the connection between covenant and creation in arguing that God's preparation of the Edenic Garden in Genesis is a parallel to His preparation of the Promised Land in Deuteronomy, because in fact, they are the same exact location!; "Heavens and earth" is not about a globe and solar systems, but about a more localized "sky and land"; "Formless and void" (*tohu wabohu*) is better translated "wilderness and uninhabitable," a term applied to the Promised Land without God's blessing (Jer. 4:23); "working" and "keeping" (*abad* and *shamar*) the Garden of God's presence (Gen. 2:15) is more suitably translated as "worshipping and obeying" in a parallel of the Tabernacle of God.[46] Sailhamer concludes that the covenant on Sinai is

---

[43] That this passage depicts the inauguration of the New Covenant with the incarnation of Christ rather than a future event at Christ's "Second Coming," is evident in a couple of observations. First, the reference to God dwelling with tabernacle among men is well understood as a theological expression of the incarnation in John 1:14 "And the Word became flesh, and dwelt (*tabernacled*) among us." Secondly, a heavenly Jerusalem coming down from above is previewed in the Hebrews 12:18-24 description of the New Covenant as the "heavenly Jerusalem," in comparison with the Old Covenant of an earthly Jerusalem; and that New Covenant is reiterated by the apostle Paul in Galatians 4:24-26 as the "Jerusalem from above." Also, the body of Christ is the bride of Christ, which constitutes the new temple of God (Eph 2:19-22).
[44] Bruce Waltke, *Genesis: A Commentary* (Grand Rapids, MI: Zondervan, 2001), 59.
[45] Milton Terry, *Biblical Apocalyptics: A Study of the Most Notable Revelations of God and of Christ* (Grand Rapids, MI: Baker Books, 1898, 1988), 49.
[46] John Sailhamer, *Genesis Unbound: A Provocative New Look at the Creation Account* (Sisters, OR: Multnomah, 1996), 47-59, 61-66, 75-76.

grounded in the events of creation. "The writer of the Pentateuch wrote Genesis 1 primarily because he wanted his readers to understand something about God and the nature of the covenant He made with Israel on Mt. Sinai… Thus, the theme of the Sinai Covenant — God's good gift of the promised land — lies at the center of the author's account of creation."[47]

The Bible is covenantal storytelling in theme and structure. The purpose of the exalted prose of Genesis 1 seems to be covenantal justification of Yahweh's ownership of everything, specifically the Promised Land He was about to forcibly take from the Canaanites and give to Israel. *Chaoskampf* poetry of subduing the Sea and the twisting serpent or dragon Leviathan/Rahab is metaphorically united with creation language. That creation language is often used to narrate the covenantal order of Israel while decreation language is used to narrate covenantal disorder. The localized ancient Near Eastern mindset of the text of Genesis revealing purpose through naming, separating, and giving function does not comport with a modern post-Enlightenment scientific mindset of astrophysics and material substance and properties. One can only conclude that the attempt to find a concordance between Genesis 1 and any kind of scientific theory, be it young-earth or old-earth, 24 hour days or long ages, fiat creation or evolutionary adaptation is an act of interpretive violence against the text that comes from a culturally imposing modern hubris.

---

[47] Sailhamer, *Genesis Unbound*, 87-88.

Chapter 4
The Universe in Ancient Imagination[1]

Cosmography is a technical term that means a theory that describes and maps the main features of the heavens and the earth. A cosmography or "cosmic geography" can be a complex picture of the universe that includes elements like astronomy, geology, and geography; and those elements can include theological implications as well. Throughout history, all civilizations and peoples operate under the assumption of a cosmography or picture of the universe. We are most familiar with the historical change that science went through from a Ptolemaic cosmography of the earth at the center of the universe (geocentrism) to a Copernican cosmography of the sun at the center of a galaxy (heliocentrism).

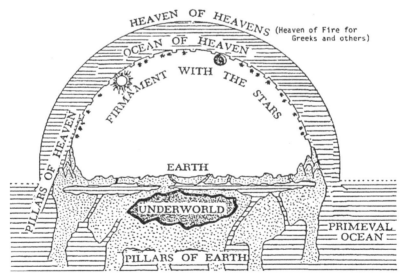

This antique drawing represents the Mesopotamian picture of the universe used in this story.

---

[1] This chapter has been adapted from "Appendix D: Mesopotamian Cosmic Geography in the Bible" in my novel *Noah Primeval*.

Some mythologies maintained that the earth was a flat disc on the back of a giant turtle; animistic cultures believe that spirits inhabit natural objects and cause them to behave in certain ways; modern westerners believe in a space-time continuum where everything is relative to its frame of reference in relation to the speed of light. Ancients tended to believe that the gods caused the weather; moderns tend to believe that impersonal physical processes cause weather. All these different beliefs are elements of a cosmography or picture of what the universe is really like and how it operates. Even though "pre-scientific" cultures like the ancient Jews did not have the same notions of science that we moderns have, they still observed the world around them and made interpretations as to the structure and operations of the universe.

A common ancient understanding of this cosmos is expressed in the visions of 1 Enoch. In this Second Temple Jewish writing, codified around the third to fourth century B.C., and most likely written much earlier, Enoch is taken on a journey through heaven and hell and describes the cosmic workings as they understood them in that day. Here is just a short glimpse into the elaborate construction of this ANE author:

> 1 Enoch 18:1-5
> And I saw the storerooms of all the winds and saw how with them he has embroidered all creation as well as the foundations of the earth. I saw the cornerstone of the earth; I saw the four winds which bear the earth as well as the firmament of heaven. I saw how the winds ride the heights of heaven and stand between heaven and earth: These are the very pillars of heaven. I saw the winds which turn the heaven and cause the star to set — the sun as well as all the stars. I saw the souls carried by the clouds. I saw the path of the angels in the ultimate end of the earth, and the firmament of the heaven above.[2]

I am not a scientist, I am a professional storyteller, and so my interest in Biblical cosmography comes from my study of imagery, metaphor, and story. But a picture of the cosmos certainly has a bearing on scientific notions of the way the universe is and operates. Imagination and science are not completely

---

[2] James H. Charlesworth, *The Old Testament Pseudepigrapha: Volume 1*, 1 En 18 (New York; London: Yale University Press, 1983).

unconnected. I am also a Christian who believes that the Bible is the Word of God. But does this mean that the Bible will have a cosmography that agrees with modern western science? I used to believe it did. I used to believe that if the Bible was scientifically "wrong" in anyway, then it could not be the Word of God, since God would never communicate false information to us. That would make God a liar.

This led to the corollary that whatever modern science discovered could not contradict the Bible. This is called "scientific concordism," and it is the attempt to bring our knowledge of natural revelation *in accord* with our interpretation of special revelation. So, if we now know that the earth is a sphere and that the universe is expanding, then Scripture would not contradict that truth. What's more, I might even be able to find a verse that would have that truth hidden in it. Behold, I thought I found it: "It is He who sits above the circle of the earth...who stretches out the heavens like a curtain" (Isa. 40:22). In this scientific concordist paradigm, the Bible contains veiled scientific truths before their time in a gnostic hiddeness that is uncovered by modern initiates into such mysteries.

Unfortunately, this paradigm would lead to much cognitive dissonance for me as I tortured the text to fit whatever scientific theory I was trying to support at the time. First, I accepted Genesis as literally explaining material creation chronology and relegated evolutionary scientists to dishonest manipulators of facts.[3] Then I tried to find dinosaurs in the Bible by interpreting the Leviathan or Behemoth as references to ichthyosaurs and sauropods.[4] Then I tried to make six literal days and young chronology of Creation in Genesis square symbolically with the seriously old age of the earth.[5] Then I tried to creatively

---

[3] I never believed they were all lying, but many were certainly blinded by their worldview bias. I still believe that some scientists do in fact lie, cheat, and manipulate facts and studies just as in every other discipline because they are human like everyone else and can be just as driven by political and personal agenda as everyone else. A good book that documents this is *Betrayers Of The Truth: Fraud And Deceit In The Halls Of Science* By Nicholas Wade William Broad (Ebury Press, 1983); Michael Fumento is a science journalist who reports on current scientific fraud and its widespread economic and political effects at www.fumento.com.
[4] *Scientific Creationism* by Henry M. Morris (Master Books, 1974, 1985) is an example of this viewpoint.
[5] *Creation and Time: A Biblical and Scientific Perspective on the Creation-Date Controversy* by Hugh Ross (NavPress, 1994) is an example of this viewpoint.

reconcile the billions of years of the Big Bang with 24-hour earth-bound solar days though gravity-warped space-time.[6]

I also thought that the best interpretation of the Bible was the "plain reading" of the text. That is, any interpretation that would turn the meaning into unwarranted figurative, symbolic, allegorical or metaphorical language would be disingenuous hermeneutics. I didn't mean obvious figurative and allegorical language like parables of talking brambles and trees (Judg. 9:7-15) or clearly poetic expressions of singing mountains and clapping trees (Isa. 55:12). I meant that when the Bible talked about the physical order and events in heaven and earth it would mean just what it said since the Creator of the cosmos would know best what was actually happening.

But something started to seriously challenge these assumptions. First, as I studied the ancient Hebrew culture and its surrounding Near Eastern background, I began to see how very different a "plain reading" of a text was to them than a "plain reading" was to me.[7] The ancient Hebrew mind was steeped in different symbols, ideas, and language than I was. If I read a phrase like "sun, moon and stars," my western cultural understanding, which is deeply affected by a post-Galileo, post-Enlightened, materialist science would tend to read such references in terms of the physical bodies of matter, gas, and gravity spread out over vast light years of space-time. When ancient Israelites used that phrase, they would have pictures in their minds of markers and signs (Gen. 1:14), and more personal objects like pagan gods (Deut. 4:19), heavenly beings (1 Kgs. 22:19), symbolic influential leaders (Gen. 37:9), or the fall of governing powers (Isa. 13:10).[8]

An ancient Jew hearing the words *leviathan* and *sea* conjured up notions of a disordered world without Yahweh's rule, and Yahweh's covenant creation out of chaos.[9] Whereas for me, hearing those words makes me think of a monster

---

[6] *Genesis and the Big Bang: The Discovery Of Harmony Between Modern Science And The Bible* by Gerald Schroeder (Bantam, 1990) is an example of this viewpoint.

[7] The seminal book that opened the door for me to a better understanding of this ANE cultural context of the Bible was John H. Walton, *Ancient Near Eastern Thought and the Old Testament: Introducing the Conceptual World of the Hebrew Bible* (Grand Rapids, MI: Baker, 2006).

[8] "The worship of the host of heaven [was] often set in parallelism to the worship of foreign gods (Deut. 17:3; 2 Kgs. 17:16; 21:3; 23:4–5; Jer. 19:13; Zeph. 1:4–5)." K. van der Toorn, Bob Becking and Pieter Willem van der Horst, *Dictionary of Deities and Demons in the Bible DDD*, 2nd extensively rev. ed., 429 (Leiden; Boston; Grand Rapids, Mich.: Brill; Eerdmans, 1999), 429.

[9] Brian Godawa, "Biblical Creation and Storytelling: Cosmogony, Combat and Covenant," The BioLogos Foundation, http://biologos.org/uploads/projects/godawa_scholarly_paper.pdf.

fish swimming in the ocean — or maybe *Moby Dick*, a symbol of man's hubris — but primarily the physical material being of those objects. It is easier to see now that my plain reading of the text through my modern western worldview could completely miss the plain meaning that the Scripture would have to an ancient Israelite. My so-called act of "plain reading" was ironically an imposition of my own cultural bias onto the text removed by thousands of years, thousands of miles, and thousands of cultural motifs.[10] We must seek the "plain reading" *of the ancient authors and their audience*, and in this way we can be "diligent to present yourself approved to God as a workman who does not need to be ashamed, accurately handling the word of truth" (2 Tim. 2:15).

Something else had always haunted me like a nagging pebble in the shoe of my mind, and that was the Galileo affair. There was a time (the 17th century) when brilliant godly Christian theologians and scientists that I greatly respect considered the new heliocentric theory as being against the plain teaching of the Bible. They believed the Bible could not be wrong about the way the cosmos operated without jeopardizing its authority as the Word of God. They asserted that the Bible plainly says *in clear and unambiguous language* that the earth does not move (Psa. 93:1; 104:5) and that the sun goes around the earth (Josh. 10:13; Eccl. 1:5).[11] These were brilliant men and not the ignorant anti-scientific bigots that they are still portrayed to be by critics with an axe to grind. They eventually accepted the theory as the evidence came in to back it up. But the point was that they learned a principle that has far reaching implications in Bible interpretation (hermeneutics): *Sometimes science can correct our interpretation of the Bible.*

There it is, I said it. A statement that draws the ire of Evangelicals who automatically accuse you of being a "liberal" and of not believing the Bible. But the fact of history is that science *has* corrected that very Evangelical tradition of interpreting of the Bible. I really hated to admit this too, because I believe that the Bible is my ultimate authority on the truth of God, so if science could correct the Bible, then would that not make science a higher authority than the Bible? Only if you assume that your *interpretation of the Bible* is exactly what

---

[10] Othmar Keel's *The Symbolism of the Biblical World* (Eisenbrauns) is an encyclopedia of imagery and motifs that Israel shared with her ANE neighbors that are quite alien to our thinking.

[11] In *John Calvin's Commentary on the Book of Psalms*, Psa. 93:1, Psa. 104:5-6 he affirms the Ptolemaic notion in Scripture. See "Calvin and the Astronomical Revolution" Matthew F. Dowd, University of Notre Dame:
http://www.nd.edu/~mdowd1/postings/CalvinAstroRev.html accessed March 21, 2011

God is trying to communicate to you. But our *interpretation* of God's intent and meaning is not always the same thing as God's *actual* intent and meaning. So revising our understanding of the meaning of God's Word does not make God's Word wrong, but rather it makes our *interpretation* of God's Word wrong *by showing us that we are expecting of the Scriptures something that the Scriptures are not offering us.*

The implications of this principle forced me to re-evaluate my own understanding of just what the Bible is saying when it comes to science and cosmography. Because of my modern western scientific bias, I could easily misinterpret something as literal that was intended to be figurative, such as stars falling from the sky and the sun and moon losing their light (Isa. 13:10; Ezek. 32:7; Matt. 24:29).[12] But I also realized something just as important: My modern western scientific bias could also guide me to misinterpret something as figurative that the Bible intended to be literal! If I read about the "floodgates of heaven" for rain (Gen. 7:11), or the earth set upon a foundation of pillars (Psa. 75:3) or of Sheol being below the earth (Num. 13:32-33), I automatically think of these as poetic metaphors because modern science has revealed that none of these things are "literally" or physically there. But the ancient Israelite did not know these scientific facts that I know now, so what did these images mean to them?

The Bible also contains a picture of the universe that its stories inhabit. It uses cosmic geographical language in common with other ancient Near Eastern cultures that shared its situated time and location. Believers in today's world use the language of Relativity when we write, even in our non-scientific discourse; because Einstein has affected the way they see the universe. Christians before the 17th century used Ptolemaic language because they too were children of their time. It should be no surprise to anyone that believers in ancient Israel would use the language of ANE cosmography because it was the mental construct within which they lived and thought.[13]

---

[12] N.T. Wright, *Jesus and the Victory of God* (Minneapolis: Fortress, 1996), p. 320-367. For more biblical examples of this collapsing universe and earth shattering hyperbole used of the fall of worldly powers see Jer. 4:23-30; Amos 8:9; Isa. 24:1-23; 40:3-5; Nah. 1:4-6. For an excellent book about the nature of this apocalyptic imagery and symbolism in the Bible, a must-buy book is *Last Days Madness*, by Gary DeMar, Powder Springs, GA: American Vision, 1999.

[13] The book that opened my mind to the Mesopotamian cosmography in the Bible was *Evolutionary Creation: A Christian Approach to Evolution* by Denis O. Lamoureux, Eugene; OR, Wipf & Stock, 2008. I owe much of the material in this essay to Mr. Lamoureux's meticulous research on the ancient science in the Bible.

The Three-Tiered Universe

Othmar Keel, leading expert on ANE art has argued that there was no singular technical physical description of the cosmos in the ancient Near East, but rather patterns of thinking, similarity of images, and repetition of motifs.[14] But a common simplification of these images and motifs is expressed in the three-tiered universe of the heavens, the earth, and the underworld.

Wayne Horowitz has chronicled Mesopotamian texts that illustrate this multi-leveled universe among the successive civilizations of Sumer, Akkad, Babylonia, and Assyria. The heavens above were subdivided into "the heaven of Anu (or chief god)" at the very top, the "middle heavens" below him and the sky. In the middle was the earth's surface, and below that was the third level that was further divided into the waters of the abyss and the underworld.[15] The generalized version of this was "heaven, earth, and under the earth."

Let's take a look at the Scriptures that appear to reinforce this three-tiered universe so different from our modern understanding of physical expanding galaxies of warped space-time, where the notion of heaven and hell are without physical location. Though the focus of this essay will be on Old Testament context, I want to start with the New Testament to make the point that their cosmography did not necessarily change with the change of Old to New Covenants.

> Phil. 2:10
> That at the name of Jesus every knee should bow, <u>in heaven</u>, and <u>on earth</u>, and <u>under the earth</u>.

> Rev. 5:3, 13
> And no one <u>in heaven, or on earth, or under the earth</u>, was able to open the scroll, or to look into it… And every creature <u>in heaven and on the earth and under the earth</u> and in the sea, and all that is in them, saying,
> "To Him who sits on the throne and to the Lamb be blessing and honor and glory and might forever & ever!"

---

[14] Othmar Keel, *The Symbolism of the Biblical World*, Winona Lake; IN: Eisenbrauns, 1972, 1997, 16-59.
[15] Wayne Horowitz, *Mesopotamian Cosmic Geography*, Winona Lake; IN: Eisenbrauns, 1998, xii-xiii.

> Exod. 20:4
> "You shall not make for yourself a carved image, or any likeness of anything that is in <u>heaven above,</u> or that is <u>in the earth beneath</u>, or that is in the <u>water under the earth</u>.

> Matt. 11:23
> Jesus said, "Capernaum, will you be <u>exalted to heaven</u>? You will be <u>brought down to Hades</u>. [the underworld].

Both apostles Paul and John were writing about the totality of creation being subject to the authority of Jesus on His throne. So this word picture of "heaven, earth, and under the earth" was used as the description of the total known universe — which they conceived of spatially as heaven above, the earth below, and the underworld below the earth. And not only did the inspired human authors write of the universe in this three-tiered fashion but so did God Himself, the author and finisher of our faith, when giving the commandments on Sinai.

One may naturally wonder if this notion of "heaven above" may merely be a symbolic or figurative expression for the exalted spiritual nature of heaven. Since we cannot see where heaven is, God would use physical analogies to express spiritual truths. This explanation would be easier to stomach if the three-tiered notion were not so rooted in a cosmic geography that clearly was their understanding of the universe (as proven below). A figurative expression would also jeopardize the doctrine of the ascension of Jesus into heaven which also affirms the spatial location of heaven above and the earth below, in very literal terms.

> Acts 1:9-11
> He was lifted up, and a cloud took Him out of their sight. And while they were gazing <u>into heaven</u> as he went, behold, two men stood by them in white robes, and said, "Men of Galilee, why do you stand looking <u>into heaven</u>? This Jesus, who was <u>taken up from you into heaven</u>, will come in the same way as you saw Him go <u>into heaven</u>."

> John 3:13
> No one has <u>ascended into heaven</u> except He who <u>descended from heaven</u>, the Son of Man.

John 6:62
Then what if you were to see the <u>Son of Man ascending</u> to where He was before?

John 20:17
Jesus said to her, "Do not cling to me, for I have not yet <u>ascended to the Father</u>; but go to my brothers and say to them, 'I am <u>ascending to my Father</u> and your Father, to my God and your God.'"

Eph. 4:8-10
Therefore it says, "When <u>He ascended on high</u> He led a host of captives, and He gave gifts to men." (In saying, "<u>He ascended</u>," what does it mean but that <u>He had also descended into the lower regions, the earth</u>? He who <u>descended is the one who also ascended far above all the heavens</u>, that He might fill all things.)

The location of heaven being above us may be figurative to our modern cosmology, but it was not figurative to the Biblical writers. To suggest that they understood it figuratively would be to impose our own modern cultural bias on the Bible. That is what we call *cultural imperialism*. It marks the inability to see outside of one's own perception and understand others.

Now let's take a closer look at each of these tiers or domains of the cosmos through the eyes of Scripture in their ANE context.

Flat Earth Surrounded by Waters

I want to start with the earth because the Scriptures start with the earth. That is, the Bible is geocentric in its picture of a flat earth founded on immovable pillars at the center of the universe. Over a hundred years ago, a Babylonian map of the world was discovered that dated back to approximately the ninth century B.C. As seen below, this map was unique from other Mesopotamian maps because it was not merely local but international in its scale, and contained features that appeared to indicate cosmological interpretation. That map and a translated interpretation are reproduced below.[16]

---

[16] Photo is public domain (Courtesy of the British Museum). Illustration is my own based on Horowitz, *Mesopotamian Cosmic Geography*, 21. See also pages 25-27.

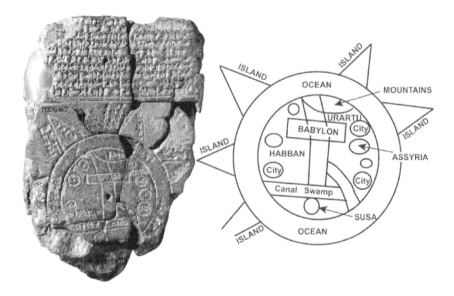

The geography of the Babylonian map portrayed a flat disc of earth with Babylon in the center and extending out to the known regions of its empire, whose perimeters were surrounded by cosmic waters and islands out in those waters. Of the earliest Sumerian and Akkadian texts with geographical information, only the Babylonian map of the world and another text, *The Sargon Geography,* describe the earth's surface, and they both picture a central circular flat continent surrounded by cosmic waters, often referred to as "the circle of the earth."[17] Other texts like the Akkadian *Epic of Gilgamesh,* and Egyptian and Sumerian works share in common with the Babylonian map the notion of mountains at the edge of the earth beyond which is the cosmic sea and the unknown, and from which come "the circle of the four winds" that blow upon the four corners of the earth (a reference to compass points).[18]

The Biblical picture of the earth is remarkably similar to this Mesopotamian cosmic geography. When Daniel had his dream *from God in Babylon,* of a tree "in the middle of the earth" whose height reached so high that "it was visible to the end of the whole earth," (Dan. 4:10) it reflected this very Babylonian map of the culture that educated Daniel. One cannot see the end of the whole earth on a globe, but one can do so on a circular continent embodying the known world of Babylon as the center of the earth.

---

[17] Horowitz, *Mesopotamian Cosmic Geography*, 320, 334. This interpretation continued to maintain influence even into the Greek period of the 6th century B.C. (41).
[18] Horowitz, *Mesopotamian Cosmic Geography*, 195-97, 334.

"The ends of the earth" is a common phrase, occurring over fifty times throughout the Scriptures that means more than just "remote lands," but rather includes the notion of the very physical end of the whole earth all around before the cosmic waters that hem it in. Here are just a few of the verses that indicate this circular land mass bounded by seas as the entire earth:

> Isa. 41:9
> You whom I took from the ends of the earth, and called from its farthest corners…

> Psa. 65:5
> O God of our salvation, the hope of all the ends of the earth and of the farthest seas…

> Zech. 9:10
> His rule shall be from sea to sea, and from the River to the ends of the earth.

> Mark 13:27
> And then He will send out the angels and gather His elect from the four winds, from the ends of the earth to the ends of heaven.

> Acts 13:47
> 'I have made you a light for the Gentiles, that you may bring salvation to the ends of the earth.'

> Job 28:24
> For He looks to the ends of the earth and sees everything under the heavens.

Remember that Mesopotamian phrase, "circle of the earth" that meant a flat disc terra firma? Well, it's in the Bible, too. "It is He who sits above the circle of the earth, and its inhabitants are like grasshoppers" (Isa. 40:22). Some have tried to say that the Hebrew word for "circle" could mean *sphere*, but it does not. The Hebrew word used here (*ḥûg*) could however refer to a vaulted dome that covers the visible circular horizon, which would be more accurate to say, "above the vault of the earth."[19] If Isaiah had wanted to say the earth was a sphere he would have used another word that he used in a previous chapter (22:18) for a ball, but he did not.[20]

Two further Scriptures use this "circle of the earth" in reference to God's original creation of the land out of the waters and extend it outward to include the circumferential ocean with its own mysterious boundary:

> Prov. 8:27, 29
> When He established the heavens, I was there; when He drew a circle on the face of the deep… when He assigned to the sea its limit, so that the waters might not transgress His command, when He marked out the foundations of the earth.

> Job 26:10
> He has inscribed a circle on the face of the waters at the boundary between light and darkness [where the sun rises and sets].

Even when the Old Testament writers are deliberately using metaphors for the earth, they use metaphors for a flat earth spread out like a flat blanket.

> Job 38:13
> Take hold of the skirts of the earth, and the wicked be shaken out of it.

> Job 38:18
> Have you comprehended the expanse of the earth?

> Psa. 136:6
> To Him who spreads out the earth above the waters.

> Isa. 44:24
> "I am the LORD, who spread out the earth by myself."

---

[19] "*ḥûg*" Harris, R. Laird, Robert Laird Harris, Gleason Leonard Archer, and Bruce K. Waltke. *Theological Wordbook of the Old Testament*. electronic ed. Chicago: Moody Press, 1999, p 266-67.

[20] Even the Septuagint (LXX) does not translate the Hebrew word into the Greek word for sphere. "Isaiah 40:22," Tan, Randall, David A. deSilva, and Logos Bible Software. *The Lexham Greek-English Interlinear Septuagint*. Logos Bible Software, 2009.

Geocentricity

In the Bible, the earth is not merely a flat disk surrounded by cosmic waters under the heavens; it is also the center of the universe. To the ANE mindset, including that of the Hebrews, the earth did not move (except for earthquakes) and the sun revolved around that immovable earth. They did not know that the earth was spinning one thousand miles an hour and flying through space at 65,000 miles an hour. Evidently, God did not consider it important enough to correct this primitive inaccurate understanding. Here are the passages that caused such trouble with Christians who took the text too literally because it did not seem to be figurative to them:

> Psa. 19:4-6
> Their voice goes out through all the earth,
> and their words to the end of the world.
> In them He has set a tent for the sun,
> which comes out like a bridegroom leaving His chamber,
> and, like a strong man, runs its course with joy.
> Its rising is from the end of the heavens,
> and its circuit to the end of them.

> Psa. 50:1
> The Mighty One, God, the LORD, speaks and summons the earth from the rising of the sun to its setting.

> Eccl. 1:5
> The sun rises, and the sun goes down,
> and hastens to the place where it rises.

> Josh. 10:13
> And the sun stood still, and the moon stopped,
> until the nation took vengeance on their enemies…
> The sun stopped in the midst of heaven and did not hurry to set for about a whole day.

> Matt. 5:45
> Jesus said, "For He makes His sun rise on the evil and on the good."

Before the Copernican Revolution, Christians took the "plain reading" of the text to mean that the sun clearly goes around the stationary earth. Two objections are often raised when considering these passages. First, that they use phenomenal language. That is, they describe simply what the viewer observes and makes no cosmological claims beyond simply description of what one sees. We even use these terms of the sun rising and setting today and we know the earth moves around the sun. Fair enough. The only problem is that the ancient writers were pre-scientific and did not know the earth went around the sun, so when they said the sun was moving from one end of the heavens to the other they believed reality was exactly as they observed it. They had absolutely no reason to believe in a "phenomenal distinction" between their observation and reality.[21]

The second objection is that some of the language is obvious metaphor. David painted the sun as a bridegroom coming out of his chamber or of being summoned by God and responding like a human. This is called anthropomorphism and is obviously poetic. But the problem here is that the metaphors still reinforce the sun doing all the moving around a stationary immobile earth.

> 1 Chr. 16:30
> Tremble before Him, all the earth;
> yes, the world is established; it shall never be moved.

> Psa. 93:1
> Yes, the world is established; it shall never be moved.

> Psa. 96:10
> Yes, the world is established; it shall never be moved;

Understandably, these texts have been thought to indicate that the Bible is explicitly saying the earth does not move. But the case is not so strong for these examples because the Hebrew word used in these passages for "the world" is not the word for *earth* (*erets*), but the word that is sometimes used for the inhabited world (*tebel*). So it is possible that these verses are talking about the "the world order" as does the poetry of 2 Sam. 22:16.

---

[21] "The Firmament And The Water Above: Part I: The Meaning Of Raqia In Gen 1:6-8," Paul H. Seely, *The Westminster Theological Journal* 53 (1991) 227-40.

But the problem that then arises is that the broader chapter context of these verses describe the earth's physical aspects such as oceans, trees, and in the case of 1 Chron. 16:30, even the "earth" (*erets*) in redundant context with the "world" (*tebel*), which would seem to indicate that "world" may indeed refer to the physical earth.

Lastly, *world* can be interchangeable with *earth* as it is in 1 Sam. 2:8, "For the pillars of the earth are the LORD'S, And He set the world on them."

And this adds a new element to the conversation of a stationary earth: *A foundation of pillars*.

Pillars of the Earth

The notion of an immovable earth is not a mere description of observational experience by earth dwellers; it is based upon another cosmographical notion that the earth is on a foundation of pillars that hold it firmly in place.

> Psa. 104:5
> He set the earth on its foundations, so that it should never be moved.

> Job 38:4
> "Where were you when I laid the foundation of the earth? Tell Me, if you have understanding, Who set its measurements, since you know? Or who stretched the line on it? "On what were its bases sunk? Or who laid its cornerstone,

> 2 Sam. 22:16
> "Then the channels of the sea were seen; the foundations of the world were laid bare, at the rebuke of the LORD, At the blast of the breath of His nostrils.

> 1 Sam. 2:8
> For the pillars of the earth are the LORD's, and on them, He has set the world.

> Psa. 75:3
> "When the earth totters, and all its inhabitants,
> it is I who keep steady its pillars.

Zech. 12:1
Thus declares the LORD who stretches out the heavens, <u>and founded the earth.</u>

Ancient man such as the Babylonians believed that mountains and important ziggurat temples had foundations that went below the earth into the abyss (*apsu*) or the underworld.[22] But even if one would argue that the notion of foundations and pillars of the earth are only intended to be symbolic, they are still symbolic *of a stationary earth that does not move.*

Some have pointed out the single verse that seems to mitigate this notion of a solid foundation of pillars, Job 26:6-7: "Sheol is naked before God, and Abaddon has no covering. He stretches out the north over the void and <u>hangs the earth on nothing</u>." They suggest that this is a revelation of the earth in space before ancient man even knew about the spatial location of the earth in a galaxy. But the reason I do not believe this is because of the context of the verse.

Within chapter 26 Job affirms the three-tiered universe of waters of the Abyss below him (v. 5) and under that Sheol (v. 6), with pillars holding up the heavens (v. 11). Later in the same book, God Himself speaks about the earth laid on foundations (38:4), sinking its bases and cornerstone like a building (38:5-6). Ancient peoples believed the earth was on top of some other object like the back of a turtle, and that it was too heavy to float on the waters. So in context, Job 26 appears to be saying that the earth is over the waters of the abyss and Sheol, on its foundations, but there is nothing under *those pillars* but God Himself holding it all up. This is not the suggestion of a planet hanging in space, but rather the negative claim of an earth that is *not* on the back of a turtle or other ancient object.

Sheol Below

Before we ascend to the heavens, let's take a look at the Underworld below the earth. The Underworld was a common location of extensive stories about gods and departed souls of men journeying to the depths of the earth through special gates of some kind into a geographic location that might also be accessed through cracks in the earth above.[23] Entire Mesopotamian stories engage the location of the subterranean netherworld in their narrative such as

---

[22] Horowitz, *Mesopotamian Cosmic Geography*, 98, 124, 308-12, 336-37.
[23] Horowitz, *Mesopotamian Cosmic Geography*, p 348-362

The Descent of Inanna, The Descent of Ishtar, Nergal and Ereshkigal, and many others.

Sheol was the Hebrew word for the underworld.[24] Though the Bible does not contain any narratives of experiences in Sheol, it was nevertheless described as the abode of the dead that was below the earth. Though Sheol was sometimes used interchangeably with "Abaddon" as the place of destruction of the body (Prov. 15:11; 27:20),[25] and "the grave" (*qibrah*) as a reference to the state of being dead and buried in the earth (Psa. 88:11; Isa. 14:9-11) it was also considered to be *physically* located beneath the earth in the same way as other ANE worldviews.

When the sons of Korah are swallowed up by the earth for their rebellion against God, Numbers chapter 16 says that "they went down alive into Sheol, and the earth closed over them, and they perished from the midst of the assembly (v. 33)." People would not "fall alive" into death or the grave and then perish if Sheol was not a location. But they would die after they fall down into a location (Sheol) and the earth closes over them in that order.

The divine being (*elohim*), known as the departed spirit of Samuel, "came up out of the earth" for the witch of Endor's necromancy with Saul (1 Sam. 28:13). This was not a reference to a body coming out of a grave, but a spirit of the dead coming from a location beneath the earth.

When Isaiah writes about Sheol in Isaiah 14, he combines the notion of the physical location of the dead body in the earth (v. 11) with the location beneath the earth of the spirits of the dead (v. 9). It's really a both/and proposition.

Here is a list of some verses that speak of Sheol geographically as a spiritual underworld in contrast with heaven as a spatially located spiritual overworld.

> Amos 9:2
> "If they dig into Sheol, from there shall my hand take them; if they climb up to heaven, from there I will bring them down.
>
> Job 11:8
> It is higher than heaven—what can you do? Deeper than Sheol—what can you know?

---

[24] "Sheol," *DDD*, p 768.
[25] "Abaddon," *DDD*, p 1.

Psa. 16:10
For you will not abandon <u>my soul</u> to Sheol, or let your holy one <u>see corruption</u>.

Psa. 139:8
If I <u>ascend to heaven</u>, you are there! If I make my <u>bed in Sheol</u>, you are there!

Isa. 7:11
"Ask a sign of the LORD your God; let it be <u>deep as Sheol</u> or <u>high as heaven</u>."

These are not mere references to the body in the grave, but to locations of the spiritual soul as well. Sheol is a combined term that describes both the grave for the body and the underworld location of the departed souls of the dead.

In the New Testament, the word *Hades* is used for the underworld, which was the Greek equivalent of Sheol.[26] Jesus Himself used the term Hades as the location of damned spirits in contrast with heaven as the location of redeemed spirits when He talked of Capernaum rejecting miracles, "And you, Capernaum, will you be <u>exalted to heaven</u>? You will be <u>brought down to Hades</u> (Matt. 11:23)." Hades was also the location of departed spirits in His parable of Lazarus and the rich man in Hades (Luke 16:19-31).

In Greek mythology, Tartarus was another term for a location beneath the "roots of the earth" and beneath the waters where the warring giants called "Titans" were bound in chains because of their rebellion against the gods.[27] Peter uses a derivative of that very Greek word Tartarus to describe a similar location and scenario of angels being bound during the time of Noah and the warring Titans called "Nephilim."[28]

---

[26] "Hades," *DDD*, p 382.
[27] "They then conducted them [the Titans] under the highways of the earth as far below the ground as the ground is below the sky, and tied them with cruel chains. So far down below the ground is gloomy Tartarus...Tartarus is surrounded by a bronze moat...above which the roots of earth and barren sea are planted. In that gloomy underground region the Titans were imprisoned by the decree of Zeus." Norman Brown, Trans. *Theogony: Hesiod*. New York: Bobbs-Merrill Co., 1953, p 73-4.
[28] 1.25 ταρταρόω [*tartaroo*] Louw, Johannes P., and Eugene Albert Nida. *Greek-English Lexicon of the New Testament : Based on Semantic Domains*. electronic ed. of the 2nd edition. New York: United Bible societies, 1996. Bauckham, Richard J. Vol. 50, *Word Biblical Commentary : 2 Peter, Jude*. Word Biblical Commentary. Dallas: Word, Incorporated, 2002, p 248-249.

2 Pet. 2:4-5
For if God did not spare <u>angels</u> when they sinned, but <u>cast them into hell [tartaroo] and committed them to chains</u> of gloomy darkness to be kept until the judgment; if He did not spare the ancient world, but preserved Noah.

The Watery Abyss

In Mesopotamian cosmography, the Abyss (*Apsu* in Akkadian) was a cosmic subterranean lake or body of water that was between the earth and the underworld (Sheol), and was the source of the waters above such as oceans, rivers, and springs or fountains.[29] In *The Epic of Gilgamesh*, Utnapishtim, the Babylonian Noah, tells his fellow citizens that he is building his boat and will abandon the earth of Enlil to join Ea in the waters of the Abyss that would soon fill the land.[30] Even bitumen pools used to make pitch were thought to rise up from the "underground waters," or the Abyss.[31]

Similarly, in the Bible the earth also rests on the seas or "the deep" (*tehom*) that produces the springs and waters from its subterranean waters below the earth.

Psa. 24:1-2
The world, and those who dwell therein, for He has <u>founded it upon the seas</u>, and established it upon the rivers.

Psa. 136:6
To Him who spread out the earth <u>above the waters</u>.

Gen. 49: 25
The Almighty who will bless you with blessings of heaven above, Blessings of <u>the deep that crouches beneath.</u>

---

[29] Horowitz, *Mesopotamian Cosmic Geography*, p 334-348.
[30] *The Epic of Gilgamesh* XI:40-44. *The Ancient Near East an Anthology of Texts and Pictures*. Edited by James Bennett Pritchard. Princeton: Princeton University Press, 1958, p 93.
[31] Horowitz, *Mesopotamian Cosmic Geography*, p 337.

> Exod. 20:4
> You shall not make for yourself a carved image, or any likeness of anything that is in heaven above, or that is in the earth beneath, or that is in the water under the earth.

Leviathan is even said to dwell in the Abyss in Job 41:24 (LXX)[32]. When God brings the flood, part of the waters are from "the fountains of the great deep" bursting open (Gen. 7:11; 8:2).

The Firmament

If we move upward in the registers of cosmography, we find another ancient paradigm of the heavens covering the earth like a solid dome or vault with the sun, moon, and stars embedded in the firmament yet still somehow able to go around the earth. Reformed scholar Paul Seely has done key research on this notion.[33]

> Gen. 1:6-8
> And God said, "Let there be an expanse [firmament] in the midst of the waters, and let it separate the waters from the waters." And God made the expanse [firmament] and separated the waters that were under the expanse [firmament] from the waters that were above the expanse [firmament]. And it was so. And God called the expanse [firmament] Heaven.

I used to think, what is that all about? Waters below separated from waters above by the sky? Some try to explain those waters above as a water canopy above the earth that came down at Noah's flood. But that doesn't make sense Biblically because birds are said to "fly over the face of the firmament" (Gen. 1:20) with the same Hebrew grammar as God's Spirit hovering "over the face of the waters" (Gen. 1:2). The firmament cannot be

---

[32] "[Leviathan] regards the netherworld [Tartauros] of the deep [Abyss] like a prisoner. He regards the deep [Abyss] as a walk." Job 41:34, Tan, Randall, David A. deSilva, and Logos Bible Software. *The Lexham Greek-English Interlinear Septuagint.* Logos Bible Software, 2009.

[33] "The Firmament And The Water Above: Part I: The Meaning Of Raqia In Gen 1:6-8," Paul H. Seely, *The Westminster Theological Journal* 53 (1991) 227-40.
http://faculty.gordon.edu/hu/bi/ted_hildebrandt/OTeSources/01-Genesis/Text/Articles-Books/Seely-Firmament-WTJ.pdf

the "water canopy" because the firmament is not the waters, *but the object that is separating and holding back the waters*. If the firmament is an "expanse" or the sky itself, then the birds would be flying *within* the firmament, not *over the face of* the firmament as the text states. So the firmament cannot be a water canopy and it cannot be the sky itself.

The T.K.O. of the canopy theory is the fact that according to the Bible those "waters above" and the firmament that holds them back were still considered in place during the time of King David long after the flood:

> Psa. 104:2-3
> Stretching out the heavens like a tent. He lays the beams of His chambers on the waters;

> Psa. 148:4
> Praise Him, you highest heavens, and you waters above the heavens!

Seely shows how modern scientific bias has guided the translators to render the word for "firmament" (*raqia*) as "expanse." *Raqia* in the Bible consistently means a solid material such as a metal that is hammered out by a craftsman (Exod. 39:3; Isa. 40:19). And when *raqia* is used elsewhere in the Bible for the heavens, it clearly refers to a solid crystalline material, sometimes even metal!

> Job 37:18
> Can you, like Him, <u>spread out</u> [*raqia*] the skies, <u>hard as a cast metal mirror</u>?

> Exod. 24:10
> And they saw the God of Israel. There was under His feet as it were a <u>pavement [*raqia*] of sapphire stone, like the very heaven</u> for clearness.

> Ezek. 1:22-23
> Over the heads of the living creatures there was the likeness of an <u>expanse [*raqia*], shining like awe-inspiring crystal, spread out above</u> their heads. And <u>under the expanse [*raqia*]</u> their wings were stretched out straight.

> Prov. 8:27-28
> When He established the heavens... when He made firm the skies above.

> Job 22:14
> He walks on the <u>vault of heaven</u>.

> Amos 9:6
> [God] builds His upper chambers in the heavens and founds His vault upon the earth.

Not only did the ancient translators of the Septuagint (LXX) translate *raqia* into the Latin equivalent for a hard firm solid surface (*firmamentum*), but also the Jews of the Second Temple period consistently understood the word *raqia* to mean a solid surface that covered the earth like a dome. Consider these examples of 2nd Temple literature:

> 3 Bar. 3:6-8
> And the Lord appeared to them and confused their speech, when they had built the tower... And they took a gimlet, and sought to <u>pierce the heaven</u>, saying, <u>Let us see (whether) the heaven is made of clay, or of brass, or of iron</u>.

> 2 Apoc. Bar. 21:4
> 'O you that have made the earth, hear me, that have <u>fixed the firmament</u> by the word, and have <u>made firm the height of the heaven.</u>

> Josephus, Antiquities 1:30 (1.1.1.30)
> On the second day, he placed the heaven over the whole world... He also placed <u>a crystalline [firmament] round it.</u>

The Talmud describes rabbis debating over which remains fixed and which revolves, the constellations or the solid sky (Pesachim 94b),[34] as well as how to calculate the thickness of the firmament scientifically (Pesab. 49a) and Biblically (Genesis Rabbah 4.5.2).[35] While the Talmud is not the definitive

---

[34] Quoted in The Science in Torah: the Scientific Knowledge of the Talmudic Sages By Leo Levi, page 90-91.
[35] Seely, "The Firmament," p 236.

interpretation of the Bible, it certainly illustrates how ancient Jews of that time period understood the term, which can be helpful in learning the Hebrew cultural context.

When the Scriptures talk poetically of this vault of heaven it uses the same terminology of stretching out the solid surface of the heavens over the earth *as it does of stretching out an ancient desert tent over the flat ground* (Isa. 54:2; Jer. 10:20) — not like an expanding Einsteinian time-space atmosphere.

> Psa. 19:4
> He has set <u>a tent</u> for the sun.
>
> Psa. 104:2
> Stretching out the heavens like <u>a tent</u>.
>
> Isa. 45:12
> It was my hands that stretched out the heavens,
>
> Isa. 51:13
> The LORD... who <u>stretched out the heavens</u> and laid the foundations of the earth.
>
> Jer. 10:12
> It is He who <u>established the world</u> by His wisdom, and by His understanding <u>stretched out the heavens</u>.
>
> Jer. 51:15
> It is He who <u>established the world</u> by His wisdom, and by His understanding <u>stretched out the heavens</u>.

Keeping this tent-like vault over the earth in mind, when God prophesies about the physical destruction He will bring upon a nation, He uses the symbolism of rolling up that firmament like the tent He originally stretched out (or a scroll), along with the shaking of the pillars of the earth and the pillars of heaven which results in the stars falling from the heavens because they were embedded within it.

> Isa. 34:4
> All the host of heaven shall rot away, and <u>the skies roll up like a scroll</u>. All their host <u>shall fall, as leaves fall</u> from the vine.

Rev. 6:13-14
[An earthquake occurs] and the stars of the sky fell to the earth as the fig tree sheds its winter fruit when shaken by a gale. The sky vanished like a scroll that is being rolled up, and every mountain and island was removed from its place.

Matt. 24:29
"The stars will fall from heaven, and the powers of the heavens will be shaken."

Job 26:11
"The <u>pillars of heaven tremble</u>, and are astounded at His rebuke.

2 Sam. 22:8
Then the earth reeled and rocked; the foundations of the heavens trembled and quaked.

Isa. 13:13
Therefore I shall make <u>the heavens tremble</u>, and <u>the earth will be shaken</u> out of its place at the wrath of the LORD of hosts.

Joel 2:10
The earth quakes before them, <u>the heavens tremble</u>.

Waters Above the Heavens

Now on to the highest point of the Mesopotamian cosmography, the "highest heavens," or "heaven of heavens," where God has established His temple and throne (Deut. 26:15; Psa. 11:4; 33:13; 103:19). But God's throne also happens to be in the midst of a sea of waters that reside there. These are the waters that are above the firmament, that the firmament holds back from falling to earth (Gen. 1:6-8).

Psa. 148:4
Praise Him, you highest heavens, and you <u>waters above the heavens</u>!

Psa. 104:2-3
Stretching out the heavens like a tent. He lays the <u>beams of His chambers on the waters</u>.

Psa. 29:3, 10
The voice of the <u>LORD is over the waters</u>... the LORD, <u>over many waters</u>... The LORD sits <u>enthroned over the flood</u> [not a reference to the flood of Noah, but to these floodwaters above the heavens][36] the LORD sits enthroned as king forever.

Jer. 10:13
When He utters His voice, there is a tumult of <u>waters in the heavens</u>,

Ezek. 28:2
"I sit in the seat of the gods, in the heart of the seas."

The solid firmament that holds back the heavenly waters has "windows of the heavens" ("floodgates" in the NASB) that let the water through to flood the earth in Noah's day.

Gen. 7:11
All the fountains of the great deep burst forth, and the <u>windows of the heavens</u> were opened.

Gen. 8:2
The fountains of the deep and the <u>windows of the heavens</u> were closed, and the rain from the heavens was restrained.

Isa. 24:18
For the <u>windows of heaven</u> are opened, and the foundations of the earth tremble.

---

[36] Robert G. Bratcher, and William David Reyburn. *A Translator's Handbook on the Book of Psalms*. Helps for translators. New York: United Bible Societies, 1991, p 280. Psalm 29 takes place in heaven amidst God's heavenly host around his throne.

Summary of Mesopotamian Cosmography in Scriptures

The sheer volume of passages throughout both Testaments illustrating the parallels with Mesopotamian cosmography seems to prove a deeply rooted ancient pre-scientific worldview that permeates the Scriptures, and this worldview is not coincident with modern science. Here is a summary listing of its elements (extra-biblical 2nd Temple literature in parentheses):

Three-Tiered Universe
Gen. 28:12, 17; Exod. 20:4; Rev. 5:3, 13; Phil. 2:10; Luke 16:19-31; (2 Esdr. 4:7).

God's Throne on Waters Above the Heavens
Gen. 7:11; 8:2; Deut. 26:15; Psa. 11:4; 33:13; 103:19; 104:2; 29:3, 10; 104:2-3; 148:4; Jer. 10:12-13; Ezek 28:2; (2 Esdr. 4:7-8).

Floodgates in the Heavens
Gen. 7:11; 8:2; Isa. 24:11.

Solid Firmament Vault over the Earth
Gen. 1:6-8, 20; Job 37:18; Exod. 24:10; Job 22:14; Ezek. 1:22-26; Psa. 19:4-6; 104:2; Isa. 40:22; Prov. 8:27-28; Isa. 45:12; 51:13-14; Jer. 10:12; 51:15; Isa. 34:4; Amos 9:7; Rev. 6:13-14; (3 Baruch 3:6-8; 2 Apoc. Baruch 21:4; 2 Enoch 3:3; Pesachim 94b; Peab. 49a; Gen. Rabbah 4.5.2; Josephus *Antiquities* 1:30).

Stars Embedded in the Firmament
Matt. 24:29; Isa. 34:4; Rev. 6:13; Dan. 8:10; (Sibyl. 5:514).

Flat Disc Earth Surrounded by Circumferential Sea
Prov. 8:27-29; Job 26:10-11; Psa. 19:6; 72:8; Zech. 9:10; Isa. 40:22; Rev. 7:1; 20:8; Isa. 11:12; Ezek. 7:2; Dan. 4:10-11, 32-33; Matt. 4:8; Isa. 13:5; 41:8-9; Matt. 12:42; Job 37:3; Matt. 24:31; Job 38:12-13; Psa. 136:6; Isa. 42:4; 44:24; Job 11:9; 38:18.

Geocentricity
Psa. 19:4-6; 50:1; Eccl. 1:5; Josh. 10:13; Matt. 5:45.

Immovable Earth
1 Chr. 16:30; Psa. 75:3; 93:1; 96:10; 104:5.

Pillars under the Earth
Psa. 75:3; 104:5; Job 38:4-6; 26:6; 1 Sam. 2:8; 22:16; Zech. 12:1; Prov. 8:29; (Targum Job 26:7).

Pillars under the Heavens
Job 26:11; 2 Sam. 22:8; Isa. 13:13; Joel 2:10.

Watery Abyss Below the Earth
Gen. 49:25; Psa. 24:1-2; 136:6; Dan. 33:13.

Sheol Below the Earth
Num. 16:31-33; 1 Sam. 28:13-15; Isa. 14:9-11; Amos 9:2; Matt. 1:23; Luke 10:15; 16:23; Rev. 20:14; 2 Pet. 2:4-5 (with 1 Pet. 3:18-20).

So, What's Wrong With the Bible?

The cosmic geography of the ancient Near East as revealed in Scripture consists of a three-tiered universe with God on a heavenly throne above a heavenly sea, underneath which is a solid vaulted dome with the sun, moon, and stars connected to it, covering the flat disc earth, founded immovably firm on pillars, surrounded by a circular sea, on top of a watery abyss, beneath which is the underworld of Sheol.

Some well-intentioned Evangelicals seek to maintain their particular definition of Biblical inerrancy by denying that the Bible contains this ancient Near Eastern cosmography. They try to explain it away as phenomenal language or poetic license. Phenomenal language is the act of describing what one sees subjectively from one's perspective without further claiming objective reality. So when the writer says the sun stood still, or that the sun rises and sets within the solid dome of heaven, he is only describing his observation, not cosmic reality. The claim of observation from a personal frame of reference is certainly true as far as it goes. Of course the observer describes what they are observing. But the distinction between appearance and reality is an imposition of our alien modern understanding onto theirs. As Seely explains,

> It is precisely because ancient peoples were scientifically naive that they did not distinguish between the appearance of the sky and their scientific concept of the sky. They had no reason to doubt what their eyes told them was true, namely, that the stars above them were fixed in a solid dome and that the sky literally touched the earth at the horizon. So, they equated appearance with reality and concluded that the sky must be a solid physical part of the universe just as much as the earth itself.[37]

If the ancients did not know the earth was a sphere in space, they could not know that their observations of a flat earth were anything other than what they observed. It would be easy enough to relegate one or two examples of Scripture to the notion of phenomenal language, but when dozens of those phenomenal descriptions reflect the same complex integrated picture of the universe that Israel's neighbors shared, and when that picture included many elements that were *not* phenomenally observable, such as the Abyss, Sheol, or the pillars of earth and heaven, it strains credulity to suggest these were merely phenomenal descriptions intentionally unrelated to reality. If it walks like an ancient Near Eastern duck and talks like an ancient Near Eastern duck, then chances are they thought it was an ancient Near Eastern duck, not just the "appearance" of one having no reality.

It would also be a mistake to claim that there is a single monolithic Mesopotamian cosmography.[38] There are varieties of stories with overlapping imagery, and some contradictory notions. But there are certainly enough commonalities to affirm a generic yet mysterious picture of the universe. And that picture in Scripture undeniably includes poetic language. The Hebrew culture was imaginative. They integrated poetry into everything, including their observational descriptions of nature. Thus a hymn of creation such as Psalm 19 tells of the heavens declaring God's glory as if using speech, and then describes the operations of the sun in terms of a bridegroom in his chamber or a man running a race. Metaphor is inescapable and ubiquitous.

---

[37] Seely, "The Firmament," p 228.
[38] Horowitz, *Mesopotamian Cosmic Geography*.

And herein lies a potential solution for the dilemma of the scientific inaccuracy of the Mesopotamian cosmic geography in Scripture: *The Israelite culture, being pre-scientific, thought more in terms of function and purpose than material structure.* Even if their picture of the heavens and earth as a three-tiered geocentric cosmology, was scientifically "false," from our modern perspective, it nevertheless still accurately describes the teleological purpose and meaning of creation that they were intending to communicate.

Othmar Keel, one of the leading scholars on Ancient Near Eastern art has argued that even though modern depictions of the ancient worldview like the illustration of the three-tiered universe above are helpful, they are fundamentally flawed because they depict a "profane, lifeless, virtually closed mechanical system," which reflects our own modern bias. To the ancient Near East "rather, the world was an entity open at every side. The powers which determine the world are of more interest to the ancient Near East than the structure of the cosmic system. A wide variety of diverse, uncoordinated notions regarding the cosmic structure were advanced from various points of departure."[39]

John Walton has written recently of this ANE concern with powers over structure in direct relation to the creation story of Genesis. He argues that in the ancient world existence was understood more in terms of function within a god-created *purposeful order* than in terms of material status within a natural physical structure.[40] This is not to say that the physical world was denied or ignored, but rather that the priority and interests were different from our own. We should therefore be careful in judging their purpose-driven cosmography too strictly in light of our own material-driven cosmography. And in this sense, modern material descriptions of reality are just as "false" as the ancient pictures because they do not include the immaterial aspect of reality: Meaning and purpose.

Biblical writers did not *teach* their cosmography as scientific doctrine revealed by God about the way the physical universe was materially structured, they *assumed* the popular cosmography to teach their doctrine about God's purposes and intent. To critique the cosmic model carrying the message is to miss the meaning altogether, which is the message. God's

---

[39] Othmar Keel, *The Symbolism of the Biblical World*, Winona Lake; IN: Eisenbrauns, 1972, 1997, 56-57.
[40] John H. Walton, *The Lost World of Genesis One: Ancient Cosmology and the Origins Debate* (Downers Grove: IL, InterVarsity Press, 2009), 23-36.

throne may not be physically above us in waters held back by a solid firmament, but He truly does rule "over" us and is king and sustainer of creation in whatever model man uses to depict that creation. The phrase "every created thing which is in heaven and on the earth and under the earth" (Rev. 5:13) is equivalent in meaning to the modern concept of every particle and wave in every dimension of the Big Bang space-time continuum, as well as every person dead or alive in heaven or hell.

The geocentric picture in Scripture is a depiction through man's ancient perspective of God's purpose and humankind's significance. For a modern heliocentrist to attack that picture as falsifying the theology would be cultural imperialism of the worst kind. Reducing significance to physical location is simply a prejudice of material priority over spiritual purpose.

One of the humorous ironies of this debate is that if the history of science is any judge, a thousand years from now, scientists will no doubt consider our current paradigm with which we judge the ancients to be itself fatally flawed. This is not to reduce reality to relativism, but rather to illustrate that all claims of empirical knowledge contain an inescapable element of human fallibility and finitude. A well-meaning "concordist" Christian who believes that the Bible was revealing scientific truths before their time must ask themselves just which "scientific truths" do they think it is, the Ptolemaic universe that Christians believed before Galileo, the Newtonian clockwork universe that Christians believed in the 17th century, the Einsteinian relative universe that Christians believe in the present, or the future unknown picture of the universe yet to be posited? As soon as they tie their faith to one paradigm, when that paradigm is overthrown they will have to change their interpretation again, or give up their Faith. Scientific paradigms by definition are man-centered because they describe our finite perceptions, not necessarily ultimate reality. A proper response should be a bit more humility and a bit less hubris regarding the use of our own scientific models as standards in judging theological meaning or purpose.

On the other hand, the skeptic who says that the Bible is scientifically false and therefore unreliable myth reducible to mere human construction assumes the same criteria of judgment as the Evangelical Christian who says that the Bible must be scientifically accurate or it is not the Word of God. They both assume the fallacy that precision of physical description verifies the accuracy of transcendent meaning or interpretation. The worldview that most accurately depicts material structure is the one that knows true meaning. The proposition that a scientifically "false" description can communicate spiritual truth or meaning becomes an outrageous truth claim. But is it really so outrageous?

If a young child asks where babies come from, who is right: The father who says, "from mommy's tummy," the scientist who says, "no, from your mother and father," or the pastor who says, "from God."[41] Answer: They are all right and all wrong, depending on the frame of reference (my Einstein bias). The father is scientifically imprecise in his structural definition. The baby actually comes from the uterus. But for a young child, the father must alter his language to accommodate the child's own context and understanding or the child will simply not understand. But the truth claim is still true enough despite the lack of scientific precision. Though the scientist is more precise, he too must adapt his description to the child and suffers the falsity of attributing creative powers to the humans whose genetics are not determined by their choices. Lastly, the pastor is imprecise in that the baby does not come *directly* from God to the world, as his statement may imply, but is mediated through human behavior and genetics. But he is right in that ultimately, God is the origin of all created things and certainly in terms of meaning, God gives that baby its meaning of existence.

Knowledge of the material world is simply not the only form of legitimate knowledge. So now, imagine the foolishness of that scientist spending his time and energy trying to discredit loving fathers and pastors for using imprecise descriptions of biology in their answer to the child. As the child grows into a young adult, she will become more precise or accurate in her understanding of just exactly where babies come from in a scientific sense, but that knowledge has no bearing on the enduring truth that babies come from mommy's tummy and from God. God remains the transcendent origin of that baby as well as its provider of significance and meaning, something science simply cannot discover in material processes alone.

So, now our modern cosmography/cosmology is more precise than the Mesopotamian cosmography assumed by the Biblical writers, but that does not discredit the intent of the Scriptural picture which is to give glory to God for His sovereign origin and control of creation. Even in today's modern world I can still affirm with full truthfulness that…

Psa. 19:1-6
The heavens declare the glory of God,
and the sky above proclaims His handiwork.
Day to day pours out speech,
and night to night reveals knowledge.
There is no speech, nor are there words,
whose voice is not heard.
Their voice goes out through all the earth,
and their words to the end of the world.
In them He has set a tent for the sun,
which comes out like a bridegroom leaving his chamber,
and, like a strong man, runs its course with joy.
Its rising is from the end of the heavens,
and its circuit to the end of them,
and there is nothing hidden from its heat.

Rev. 5:13
And every created thing which is in heaven and on the earth and under the earth and on the sea, and all things in them, I heard saying, "To Him who sits on the throne, and to the Lamb, be blessing and honor and glory and dominion forever and ever."

Chapter 5
New Testament Storytelling Apologetics[1]

In Acts 17:16–34, the apostle Paul presents and defends the Gospel to the pagans of his day at the Areopagus in Athens. The Areopagus (from the Greek *Areios pagos*, meaning "Hill of Ares") was named after the Greek god Ares; when the Roman god Mars was linked with Ares, the spot also became known as Mars' Hill.[2] Athens, especially this hill, was the primary location where the Greek and Roman poets, the cultural leaders of the ancient world, met to exchange ideas (v. 21). The poets would espouse philosophy through didactical tracts, oration, and poems and plays for the populace, just as the popular artists of today propagate pagan worldviews through music, television, and feature films from the Hollywood hill.

Paul's Areopagus discourse has been used to justify opposing theories of apologetics by Christian cross-cultural evangelists, theologians, and apologists alike. It has been interpreted as being a Hellenistic (i.e., culturally Greek) sermon (Martin Dibelius) as well as being entirely antithetical to Hellenism (Cornelius Van Til, F. F. Bruce). Dibelius concludes, "The point at issue is whether it is the Old Testament view of history or the philosophical — particularly the Stoic — view of the world that prevails in the speech on the Areopagus. The difference of opinion that we find among the commentators seems to offer little prospect of a definite solution."[3]

One thing most differing viewpoints have in common is their emphasis on Paul's discourse as rational debate or empirical proof. What they all seem to

---

[1] This chapter is almost exactly the same as Chapter 6 of the other book in this box set, *The Imagination of God*. Both have been adapted from the article, "Storytelling as Subversive Apologetics: A New View from the Hill in Acts 17" in *the Christian Research Journal* Vol. 30/No. 02/2007.

[2] See *Wikipedia, the Free Encyclopedia*, s.v. "Areopagus," the Wikimedia Foundation, Inc., http://en.wikipedia.org/wiki/Areopagus. See also *The Columbia Encyclopedia*, 6th ed. (New York: Columbia University Press, 2001–05), s. vv. "Mars, in Roman Religion and Mythology," "Mars' Hill," http://www.bartleby.com/65/ma/Mars-god.html, and http://www.bartleby.com/65/ma/MarsHill.html.

[3] Martin Dibelius and K. C. Hanson, *The Book of Acts: Form, Style, and Theology* (Minneapolis: Augsburg Fortress Publishers, 2004), 98.

miss is the narrative structure of his presentation. Perhaps it is this narrative structure that contains the solution to Dibelius' dilemma. An examination of that structure reveals that Paul does not so much engage in dialectic as he does *retell the pagan story* within a Christian framework.

First, our examination must put Paul's presentation in context. He is brought to the Areopagus, which was not merely the name of a location, but also the name of the administrative and judicial body that met there, the highest court in Athens. The Areopagus formally examined and charged violators of the Roman law against "illicit" new religions.[4] Though the context suggests an open public interaction and not a formal trial, Luke, the narrator, attempts to cast Paul in Athenian narrative metaphor to Socrates, someone with whom the Athenians would be both familiar and uncomfortable. It was Socrates who Xenophon said was condemned and executed for being "guilty of rejecting the gods acknowledged by the state and of bringing in new divinities."[5] Luke uses a similar phrase to describe Paul when he conveys the accusation from some of the philosophers against Paul in verse 18: "He seems to be a proclaimer of strange deities."[6] Luke depicts Paul from the start as a heroically defiant Socrates, a philosopher of truth against the mob.

Exploring Paul's Story

Paul's sermon clearly contains Biblical truths that are found in both Old and New Testaments: God as transcendent creator and sustainer, His providential control of reality, Christ's resurrection, and the final judgment. It is highly significant to note, however, that throughout the entire discourse Paul did not quote a single Scripture to these unbelievers. Paul certainly was not ashamed of the Gospel and regularly quoted Scriptural references when he considered it appropriate (Acts 17:13; 21:17–21; 23:5; 26:22–23; 28:23–28); therefore, his avoidance of Scripture in this instance is instructive of how to preach and defend the gospel to pagans. Quoting chapter and verse may work with those who are already disposed toward God or the Bible, but Paul appears to consider it inappropriate to do so with those who are hostile or opposed to the faith. Witherington adds, "Arguments are only persuasive if they work within

---

[4] Robert L. Gallagher and Paul Hertig, *Mission in Acts: Ancient Narratives in Contemporary Context* (Maryknoll, NY: Orbis Books, 2004), 224–25.
[5] Xenophon, *Memorabilia*, chap. 1. See also Plato, *Apology* 24B-C; *Euthyphro* 1C; 2B; 3B.
[6] All Scripture quotations are from the New American Standard Bible.

the plausibility structure existing in the minds of the hearers."[7] Paul, rather than quoting the Bible like an alien proof-text of propositional doctrines, addresses them using the narrative of the Stoic worldview.

Stoic Narrative

Missions scholars Robert Gallagher and Paul Hertig explain that the facts of Paul's speech mimic the major points of Stoic beliefs. They quote the ancient Roman academic Cicero who outlines these Stoic beliefs: "First, they prove that gods exist; next they explain their nature; then they show that the world is governed by them; and lastly that they care for the fortunes of mankind."[8] The correspondence of these themes with what Paul has to say about God shows that he approaches this topic in the standard way that would have been expected by his audience. He thus establishes his credibility as one who should claim their attention.

Paul enters into the discourse of his listeners; he plays according to the rules of the community he is trying to reach. An examination of each point he makes in his oration will reveal that the identification he is making with their culture is not merely with their structural procedures of argument, but with the narrative of the Stoic worldview. He is retelling the Stoic story through a Christian metanarrative.[9]

> **Verse 22**
> "Men of Athens, I observe that you are very religious in all respects."

Paul begins his address with the Athenian rhetorical convention, "Men of Athens," noted by such luminary Greeks as Aristotle and Demosthenes.[10] He then affirms their religiosity, which also had been acknowledged by the famous Athenian dramatist Sophocles: "Athens is held of states, the most devout"; and

---

[7] Ben Witherington III, *The Acts of the Apostles: A Socio-Rhetorical Commentary* (Grand Rapids: Eerdmans, 1998), 530.
[8] Cicero, *On The Nature of the Gods* 2.4, quoted in Gallagher and Hertig, 230.
[9] Although the text reveals that both Epicureans and Stoics were there (Acts 17:17–18), it appears that Paul chooses Stoicism to identify with, perhaps because of its closer affinity with the elements of his intended message.
[10] Aristotle, *Pan. Or.* 1, Demosthenes, *Exordia* 54, quoted in Witherington, 520.

the Greek geographer Pausanias: "Athenians more than others venerate the gods."[11]

Verse 23
"I also found an altar with this inscription, 'TO AN UNKNOWN GOD.' Therefore what you worship in ignorance, this I proclaim to you."

This "Unknown God" inscription may have been the Athenian attempt to hedge their bets against any god they may have missed paying homage to out of ignorance.[12] Paul quoted the ambiguous text as a point of departure for reflections on true worship, which was the same conventional technique Pseudo-Heraclitus used in his *Fourth Epistle*.[13]

Verse 24
"The God who made the world and all things in it, since He is Lord of heaven and earth, does not dwell in temples made with hands."

The Greeks had many sacred temples throughout the ancient world as houses for their gods. The Stoics and other cultural critics, however, considered such attempts at housing the transcendent incorporeal nature of deity to be laughable. Zeno, the founder of Stoicism, was known to have taught that "temples are not to be built to the gods."[14] Euripides, the celebrated Athenian tragedian, foreshadowed Paul's own words with the rhetorical question, "What house fashioned by builders could contain the divine form within enclosed walls?"[15] The Hebrew tradition also carried such repudiation of a physical dwelling place for God (1 Kgs. 8:27) but the context of Paul's speech rings particularly sympathetic to the Stoics residing in the midst of the sacred hill of the Athenian Acropolis, populated by a multitude of temples such

---

[11] Sophocles, *Oedipus Tyrannus*, 260; Pausanias, *Description of Greece*, 1.17.1, quoted in Charles H. Talbert, *Reading Acts: A Literary and Theological Commentary on the Acts of the Apostles* (Macon, GA: Smyth and Helwys Publishing, 2001), 153.
[12] Dibelius and Hanson, 103.
[13] Talbert, 153.
[14] Explained of Zeno by Plutarch in his *Moralia*, 1034B, quoted in Juhana Torkki, "The Dramatic Account of Paul's Encounter with Philosophy: An Analysis of Acts 17:16–34 with Regard to Contemporary Philosophical Debates" (academic dissertation, Helsinki: Helsinki University Printing House, 2004), 105.
[15] Euripides, frag. 968, quoted in F. F. Bruce, *Paul, Apostle of the Heart Set Free* (Cumbria, UK: Paternoster Press Ltd., 2000), 240.

as the Parthenon, the Erechtheion, the Temple of Nike, and the Athenia Polias.

> **Verse 25**
> "Nor is He served by human hands, as though He needed anything, since He Himself gives to all people life and breath and all things,"

The idea that God does not need humankind, but that humankind needs God as its creator and sustainer is common enough in Hebrew thought (Psa. 50:9–12), but as Dibelius points out:

> The use of the word "serve" is, however, almost unknown in the Greek translation of the Bible, but quite familiar in original Greek (pagan) texts, and in the context with which we are acquainted. The deity is too great to need my "service," we read in the famous chapter of Xenophon's *Memorabilia*, which contains the teleological proof of God.[16]

Seneca wrote, "God seeks no servants; He Himself serves mankind," which is also reflected in Euripides' claim that "God has need of nothing."[17] Paul is striking a familiar chord with the Athenian and Stoic narratives.

> **Verse 26a**
> "and He made from one every nation of mankind,"

Cicero noted that the "universal brotherhood of mankind"[18] was a common theme in Stoicism — although when Stoics spoke of "man" they tended to exclude the barbarians surrounding them.[19] Nevertheless, as Seneca observed, "Nature produced us related to one another, since she created us from the same source and to the same end."[20]

What is striking in Paul's dialogue is that he neglects to mention Adam as the "one" from which we are created, something he readily did when writing to the Romans (Rom. 5:12–21). The Athenians would certainly not be thinking

---

[16] Dibelius and Hanson, 105–6.
[17] Seneca, *Epistle* 95.47; Euripides, *Hercules* 1345–46, quoted in Talbert, 155.
[18] Cicero, *On Duties*, 3.6.28, quoted in Lee, 88.
[19] Bruce, 241.
[20] Seneca, *Epistle* 95.52, quoted in Michelle V. Lee, *Paul, the Stoics, and the Body of Christ* (Cambridge, UK: Cambridge University Press, 2006), 84.

of the Hebrew Adam when they heard that reference to "one." The "one" they would be thinking of would be the gods themselves. Seneca wrote, "All persons, if they are traced back to their origins, are descendents of the gods," and Dio Chrysostom affirmed, "It is from the gods that the race of men is sprung."[21] Paul may have been deliberately ambiguous by not distinguishing his definition of "one" from theirs, in order to maintain consistency with the Stoic Greek narrative without revealing his hand. He is undermining Stoicism with the Christian worldview, which will be confirmed conclusively in a climactic plot twist at the end of his narrative.

Verse 26b
"to live on all the face of the earth, having determined their appointed times [seasons] and the boundaries of their habitation,"

Christians may read this and immediately consider it an expression of God's providential sovereignty over history, as in Genesis 1, where God determines the times and seasons, or in Deuteronomy 32:8 where He separates the sons of men and establishes their "boundaries." Paul's Athenian audience, however, would refer to their own intellectual heritage on hearing these words. As Juhana Torkki points out, "The idea of God's kinship to humans is unique in the New Testament writings but common in Stoicism. The Stoic [philosopher] Epictetus devoted a whole essay to the subject."[22] Epictetus writes, "How else could things happen so regularly, by God's command as it were? When he tells plants to bloom, they bloom, when he tells them to bear fruit, they bear it…Is God [Zeus] then, not capable of overseeing everything and being present with everything and maintaining a certain distribution with everything?"[23]

Cicero, in one of his *Tusculan Disputations*, writes that seasons and zones of habitation are evidence of God's existence.[24] Paul continues, with every sentence Luke narrates, to engage Stoic thought by retelling its narrative.

---

[21] Seneca, *Epistle* 44.1; Dio Chrysostom, *Oration* 30.26, quoted in Talbert, 156.
[22] Torkki, 87.
[23] Epictetus *Discourse* 1.14, quoted in A. A. Long, *Epictetus: A Stoic and Socratic Guide to Life* (Oxford, UK: Oxford University Press, 2002), 25–26.
[24] Cicero *Tusculan Disputations* 1.28.68–69, quoted in Talbert, 156.

Verse 27
> "that they would seek God, if perhaps they might grope for Him and find Him, though He is not far from each one of us;"

This image, as one commentator explains, "carries the sense of 'a blind person or the fumbling of a person in the darkness of night,'" as can be found in the writings of Aristophanes and Plato.[25] Christian apologist Greg Bahnsen suggests that it may even be a Homeric literary allusion to the Cyclops blindly groping for Odysseus and his men.[26] In any case, the image is not a positive one. F. F. Bruce affirms the Hellenistic affinities of this section by quoting the Stoic Dio Chrysostom, "primaeval men are described as 'not settled separately by themselves far away from the divine being or outside him, but…sharing his nature.'"[27] Seneca, true to Stoic form, wrote, "God is near you, He is with you, He is within you."[28]

This idea of humanity blindly groping around for what is, in fact, very near it is also a part of scriptural themes (Deut. 28:29), but with a distinct difference. To the Stoic, God's nearness was a pantheistic nearness. They believed everything was a part of God and God was a part of everything, something Paul would vehemently deny (Rom. 1) but, interestingly enough, does not at this point. He is still maintaining a surface connection with the Stoics by affirming the immanence of God without explicitly qualifying it.

Verse 28
> "for in Him we live and move and exist, as even some of your own poets have said, 'For we also are His offspring.'"

Paul thus far implicitly has followed the Stoic narrative without qualifying the differences between it and his full narrative. He would certainly be attacked by modern Christian apologist watchdogs for being heretical since he does not qualify his word usage with endless distinctions from the pagans.

He now, however, becomes more explicit in identifying with these pagans. He favorably quotes some of their own poets to affirm even more

---

[25] Aristophanes *Ec.* 315, *Pax* 691; Plato *Phaedo* 99b, quoted in Witherington, 528–29.
[26] Greg Bahnsen, *Always Ready: Directions for Defending the Faith*, ed. Robert Booth (Atlanta: American Vision, 1996), 260–61.
[27] Dio Chrysostom *Olympic Oration* 12:28, quoted in F. F. Bruce, *The Book of the Acts,* New International Commentary on the New Testament, rev. ed. (Grand Rapids: Eerdmans, 1988), 339.
[28] Seneca *Epistle* 41.1-2, quoted in Talbert, 156.

identity with them. "In Him we live and move and exist" is a line from Epimenides's well-known *Cretica*:

> They fashioned a tomb for thee, 'O holy and high one' But thou art not dead; 'thou livest and abidest for ever', *For in thee we live and move and have our being* (emphasis added).[29]

The second line that Paul quotes, "we also are His offspring," is from Epimenides's fellow-countryman Aratus, in his *Phaenomena*:

> Let us begin with Zeus, Never, O men, let us leave him Unmentioned. All the ways are full of Zeus…And all the market-places of human beings. The sea is full Of him; so are the harbors. In every way we have all to do with Zeus, *For we are truly his offspring* (emphasis added).[30]

Aratus was most likely rephrasing Cleanthe's poem *Hymn to Zeus,* which not only refers to men as God's children, but to Zeus as the sovereign controller of all — in whom men live and move:

> Almighty Zeus, nature's first Cause, governing all things by law. It is the right of mortals to address thee, For we *who live and creep upon the earth are all thy children* (emphasis added).[31]

These are the same elements of Paul's discourse in Acts 17:24-29.

The Stoics themselves had redefined Zeus to be the impersonal pantheistic force, also called the "logos," as opposed to a personal deity in the pantheon of Greek gods. This *logos* was still not anything like the personal God of the Scriptures. What is disturbing about this section is that Paul does not qualify the pagan quotations that originally were directed to Zeus. He doesn't clarify by explaining that Zeus is not the God he is talking about. He simply quotes these hymns of praise to Zeus as if they are in agreement with the Christian Gospel. The question arises, why does he not distinguish his Gospel narrative from theirs?

---

[29] Bruce, *The Book of the Acts* 338–39.
[30] Ibid.
[31] C. Loring Brace, *Unknown God or Inspiration Among Pre-Christian Races* (1890; repr., Whitefish, MT: Kessinger Publishing, 2003), 123.

The answer is found in the idea of subversion. Paul is subverting their concept of God by using common terms with a different definition that he does not reveal immediately, but that eventually undermines their entire narrative. He begins with their conventional understanding of God but steers them eventually to his own.

In quoting pagan references to Zeus, Paul was not affirming paganism but was referencing pagan imagery, poems, and plays to make a point of connection with them as fellow humans. The *imago dei* (image of God) in pagans reflects distorted truth, but a kind of truth nonetheless. Paul then recasts and transforms that connection with pagan immanence in support of Christian immanence through the doctrine of transcendence (17:24, 27), the resurrection, and final judgment (17:30–31), but he saves that twist for the end of his sermon.

Verse 29
"We ought not to think that the Divine Nature is like gold or silver or stone, an image formed by the art and thought of man."

Another belief of Stoicism was that the divine nature that permeated all things was not reducible to mere artifacts of humanity's creation. As Epictetus argued, "You are a 'fragment of God'; you have within you a part of Him… Do you suppose that I am speaking of some external God, made of silver or gold? It is within yourself that you bear Him."[32] Zeno taught, "Men shall neither build temples nor make idols." Dio Chrysostom wrote, "The living can only be represented by something that is living."[33] Once again, Paul is not ignoring the Biblical mocking of "idols of silver and gold" as in Psalm 115:4, but is certainly addressing the issue in a language his hearers would understand, the language of the Stoic narrative.

Verse 30
"Therefore having overlooked the times of ignorance,"

For the Stoics, ignorance was an important doctrine. It represented the loss of knowledge that humanity formerly possessed, knowledge of their

---

[32] Epictetus, *Discourses* 2.8.11–12, quoted in Gallagher, 232.
[33] Clement of Alexandria, *Miscellanies* 5.76; Dio Chrysostom, *Oration* 12.83, quoted in Talbert, 156.

pantheistic unity with the *logos*. Dio Chrysostom asks in his *Discourses*, "How, then, could they have remained ignorant and conceived no inkling…[that] they were filled with the divine nature?"[34] Epictetus echoes the same sentiment in one of his *Discourses*, which is quoted in part above: "You are a 'fragment of God'; you have within you a part of Him. Why then are you ignorant of your own kinship?"[35]

Contrarily, Pauline "ignorance" was a willing, responsible ignorance, a hardness of heart that came from sinful violation of God's commands (Eph. 4:17–19). But, yet again, Paul does not articulate this distinction. He instead makes an ambiguous reference to a generic "ignorance" that the Stoics most naturally would interpret in their own terms. As Talbert describes, "In all of this, he has sought the common ground. There is nothing he has said yet that would appear ridiculous to his philosophic audience."[36]

> **Verses 30–31**
> "God is now declaring to men that all people everywhere should repent, because He has fixed a day in which He will judge the world in righteousness through a Man whom He has appointed, having furnished proof to all men by raising Him from the dead."

Here is where the subversion of Paul's storytelling rears its head, like the mind-blowing twist of a movie thriller. Everything is not as it seems. Paul the storyteller gets his pagan audience to nod their heads in agreement, only to be thrown for a loop at the end. Repentance, judgment, and the resurrection, all antithetical to the Stoic narrative, form the conclusion of Paul's narrative.

Witherington concludes of this Areopagus speech, "What has happened is that Greek notions have been taken up and given new meaning by placing them in a Jewish-Christian monotheistic context. Apologetics by means of defense and attack is being done, using Greek thought to make monotheistic points. The call for repentance at the end shows where the argument has been going all along — it is not an exercise in diplomacy or compromise but ultimately a call for conversion."[37]

---

[34] Dio Chrysostom, *Discourses* 12.27; cf. 12.12, 16, 21, quoted in Gallagher, 229.
[35] Epictetus, *Discourses* 2.8.11–14, quoted in Gallagher, 229.
[36] Talbert, 156.
[37] Witherington, 524.

The Stoics believed in a "great conflagration" of fire where the universe would end in the same kind of fire out of which it was created.[38] This was not the fire of damnation, however, as in Christian doctrine. It was rather the cyclical recurrence of what scientific theorists today would call the "oscillating universe." Everything would collapse into fire, and then be recreated again out of that fire and relive the same cycle and development of history over and over again. Paul's call of final, linear, once-for-all judgment by a single man was certainly one of the factors, then, that caused some of these interested philosophers to scorn him (v. 32).

Note again, however, that even here, Paul never gives the name of Jesus. He alludes to Him and *implies* His identity, which seems to maintain a sense of mystery about the narrative. Modern day evangelists would surely criticize Paul for never naming the name of Jesus. Is that not the power of the Gospel? According to Paul, a mere name was not a magical formula or thermometer of orthodoxy. Did everyone know that he was talking about Jesus? At times, silence can be louder than words, and implication can be more alluring than explication.

The other factor sure to provoke the ire of the cosmopolitan Athenian culture-shapers was the proclamation of the resurrection of Jesus. The poet and dramatist Aeschylus wrote what became a prominent Stoic slogan: "When the dust has soaked up a man's blood, once he is dead there is no resurrection."[39] Paul's explicit reference to the resurrection was certainly a part of the twist he used in his subversive storytelling to get the Athenians to listen to what they otherwise might ignore.

Secular Sources

A couple of important observations are in line regarding Paul's reference to pagan poetry and non-Christian mythology. First, it points out that, as an orthodox Pharisee who stressed the separation of holiness, he did not consider it unholy to expose himself to the godless media and art forms (books, plays, and poetry) of his day. He did not merely familiarize himself with them, he *studied* them — well enough to be able to quote them and even utilize their narrative. Paul primarily quoted Scripture in his writings, but he also quoted sinners favorably when appropriate.

---

[38] Ibid., 526.
[39] Aeschylus, *Eumenides* 647, quoted in Bruce, *Paul, Apostle of the Heart Set Free*, 247.

Second, this appropriation of pagan cultural images and thought forms by Biblical writers reflects more than a mere quoting of popular sayings or shallow cultural reference. It illustrates a redemptive interaction with those thought forms, a certain amount of involvement in, and affirmation of, the prevailing culture, in service to the Gospel. A simple comparison of Paul's sermon in Acts 17 with Cleanthes's *Hymn to Zeus,* a well-known summary of Stoic doctrine, illustrates an almost point-by-point correspondence of narratives.[40] Paul's preaching in Acts 17 is not a shallow usage of mere phrases, but a deep structural identification with Stoic narrative and images that "align with" the gospel. The list of convergences can be summarized thus:

ACTS 17	STOIC NARRATIVE
v. 24–25	The incorporeal nature of God
v. 25	God's self-sufficiency
v. 26	"Oneness" or brotherhood of mankind
v. 26	Providence over seasons and habitations
v. 27	Humanity's blind groping
v. 27–28	Pantheism /Immanence
v. 28	Zeus/Logos
v. 28	Humans as God's offspring
v. 29	Divine nature, not gold or silver
v. 23, 30	Wisdom vs. ignorance
v. 30–31	Justice

Lastly, this incident is not the only place where subversion occurs in the Bible. *The Dictionary of New Testament Background* cites more than 100 New Testament passages that reflect "Examples of Convergence between Pagan and Early Christian Texts." Citations, images and word pictures are quoted, adapted, or appropriated from such pagans as Aeschylus, Sophocles, Plutarch, Tacitus, Xenophon, Aristotle, Seneca, and other Hellenistic cultural sources. The sheer volume of such Biblical reference suggests an interactive

---

[40] See Cleanthes, "Hymn to Zeus" (trans. M. A. C. Ellery, 1976), Department of Classics, Monmouth College, http://www.utexas.edu/courses/citylife/readings/cleanthes_hymn.html.

intercourse of Scriptural writings with culture rather than absolute separation or shallow manipulation of that culture.[41]

Subversion Vs. Syncretism

Some Christians may react with fear that this kind of redemptive interaction with culture is syncretism, an attempt to fuse two incompatible systems of thought. Subversion, however, is not syncretism. Subversion is what Paul engaged in.

In subversion, the narrative, images, and symbols of one system are discreetly redefined or altered in the new system. Paul quotes a poem to Zeus, but covertly intends a different deity. He superficially affirms the immanence of the Stoic "Universal Reason" that controls and determines all nature and men, yet he describes this universal all-powerful deity as personal rather than as abstract law. He agrees with the Stoics that men are ignorant of God and His justice, but then affirms that God proved that He will judge the world through Christ by raising Christ from the dead — two doctrines the Stoics were vehemently against. He affirms the unity of humanity and the immanence of God in all things, but contradicts Stoic pantheism and redefines that immanence by affirming God's transcendence and the Creator/creature distinction. Paul did not reveal these stark differences between the Gospel and the Stoic narrative until the end of his talk. He was subverting paganism, not syncretizing Christianity with it.

Subversive Story Strategy

By casting his presentation of the Gospel in terms that Stoics could identify with and by undermining their narrative with alterations, Paul is strategically subverting through story. Author Curtis Chang, in his book *Engaging Unbelief*, explains this rhetorical strategy as three-fold: "1. Entering the challenger's story, 2. Retelling the story, 3. Capturing that retold tale with the gospel metanarrative."[42] He explains that the claim that we observe evidence objectively and apply reason neutrally to prove our worldview is an artifact of

---

[41] J.D. Charles, "Examples of Convergence between Pagan and Early Christian Texts," *The Dictionary of New Testament Background* (InterVarsity Christian Fellowship/USA, 2000). Electronic text hypertexted and prepared by OakTree Software, Inc. Version 1.0.

[42] Curtis Chang, *Engaging Unbelief: A Captivating Strategy from Augustine to Aquinas* (Downers Grove, IL: InterVarsity Press, 2000), 26.

Enlightenment mythology. The truth is that each epoch of thought in history, whether Medieval, Enlightenment, or Postmodern, is a contest in storytelling. "The one who can tell the best story, in a very real sense, wins the epoch."[43]

Chang affirms the inescapability of story and image through history even in philosophical argumentation: "Strikingly, many of the classic philosophical arguments from different traditions seem to take the form of a story: from Plato's scene of the man bound to the chair in the cave to Hobbes's elaborate drama of the 'state of nature,' to John Rawls's 'choosing game.'"[44] Stories may come in many different genres, but we cannot escape them.

Many Christian apologists and theologians have tended to focus on the doctrinal content of Paul's Areopagus speech at the expense of the narrative structure that carries the message. There is certainly more proclamation in this passage than rational argument.

The progression of events from creation to fall to redemption that characterize Paul's narrative reflects the beginning, middle, and end of linear Western storytelling. God is Lord, He created all things and created all people from one (creation), then determined the seasons and boundaries. People then became blind and were found groping in the darkness post-Eden, ignorant of their very identity as His children (fall). Then God raised a man from the dead and will judge the world in the future through that same man. Through repentance, people can escape their ignorance and separation from God (redemption). Creation, fall, redemption; beginning, middle, end; Genesis, Covenant, Eschaton are elements of narrative that communicate worldview.

Does this retelling of stories simply reduce persuasion to a relativistic "stand-off" between opposing stories with no criteria for discerning which is true? Scholar N. T. Wright suggests that the way to handle the clash of competing stories is to tell yet another story, one that encompasses and explains the stories of one's opposition, yet contains an explanation for the anomalies or contradictions within those stories:

> There is no such thing as "neutral" or "objective" proof; only the claim that the story we are now telling about the world as a whole makes more sense, in its outline and detail, than other potential or actual stories that may be on offer.

---

[43] Ibid, 29.
[44] Ibid, 30.

> Simplicity of outline, elegance in handling the details within it, the inclusion of all the parts of the story, and the ability of the story to make sense beyond its immediate subject-matter: these are what count.[45]

While a significant number of Christian apologists would consider Wright's claim as neglectful of Paul's appeal to evidence elsewhere (v. 31), it is certainly instructive of the opposite neglect that many have had for the legitimate operations of story or narrative coherence in persuasion.

Paul tells the story of mankind in Acts 17, a story that encompasses and includes images and elements of the Stoic story, but solves the problems of that system within a more coherent and meaningful story that conveys Christianity. He studies and engages in the Stoic story, retells that story, and captures it with the gospel metanarrative. Paul subverts Stoic paganism with the Christian worldview.

Samples of Subversion

In the first paragraph of this chapter, I mentioned the entertainment of Hollywood as a strong analogy with the influence of the Greek poets. I would like to conclude with an example of a Hollywood movie that uses subversive storytelling in a way similar to Paul on the Areopagus. *The Exorcism of Emily Rose*, written and directed by Scott Derrickson, uses the power of story to subvert the modernist mindset that believes all spiritual beliefs are superstitious misunderstandings of scientific phenomena. *Emily Rose* is based on an allegedly true story of a Roman Catholic priest on trial for criminal negligence in the death of a college girl named Emily Rose. Emily comes to the priest because she believes she is demon possessed. In the midst of a laborious exorcism ritual, she dies from self-inflicted wounds, and the priest goes to trial. The setting of a court is strikingly reminiscent of Paul's standing in the Areopagus, speaking to the "modernist" lawyers and rhetoricians of his day.

Erin Bruner, a female attorney, defends the priest by seeking to prove the "possibility" of demon possession in court. The prosecutor mocks her through the trial, referring to her spiritual arguments as superstition unworthy of legal procedure in a modern scientific world. He then seeks to prove that Emily had

---

[45] N. T. Wright, *The New Testament and the People of God* (Minneapolis: Augsburg Fortress Press, 1992), 42.

epilepsy, which required drugs, not "voodoo," resulting in the priest's blood guiltiness. The movie presents both sides of the argument in court so equally that legal or rational certainty is impossible. The privilege of seeing Emily's experience of demon possession outside that court of law leaves the viewer with a strong sense that the empirical prejudice of modern science has been undermined. Supernatural evil, and by extension, supernatural good (God) are real. Derrickson uses the story to subvert the stranglehold of modernity on the Western mind, and the inadequacy of rationalism and the scientific method in discovering everything there is to know about truth.

Other examples of subversion in Hollywood movies are: *The Island*, which uses a science-fiction action chase film to subvert the utilitarian murderous ethos of our "pro-choice" culture; *The Wicker Man,* a subversion of Wicca and pagan earth worship; and *Apocalypto*, a subversion of the "noble savage" myth of the indigenous native Americans.

The traditional approach to Christian apologetics is the detailed accumulation of rational arguments and empirical evidence for the existence of God, the reliability of the Bible, and the miraculous resurrection of Jesus Christ. The conventional image of a Christian apologist is one who studies apologetics or philosophy at a university, one who wields logical arguments for the existence of God and manuscript evidence for the reliability of the Bible, or one who engages in debates about evolution or Islam. These remain valid and important endeavors, but in a postmodern world focused on narrative discourse we need also to take a lesson from the apostle Paul and expand our avenues for evangelism and defending the faith. We need more Christian apologists writing revisionist biographies of godless deities such as Darwin, Marx, and Freud; writing for and subverting pagan TV sitcoms; bringing a Christian worldview interpretation to their journalism in secular magazines and news reporting; making horror films that undermine the idol of modernity; writing, singing, and playing subversive industrial music, rock music, and rap music. We need to be actively, sacredly subverting the secular stories of the culture, and restoring their fragmented narratives for Christ. If it was good enough for the apostle Paul on top of Mars' Hill then, it's certainly good enough for those of us in the shade of the Hollywood hills now.

Chapter 6
Imagination in Prophecy and Apocalypse[1]

Creation and Decreation

> Rev. 6:12–14
> When he opened the sixth seal, I looked, and behold, there was a great earthquake, and the sun became black as sackcloth, the full moon became like blood, and the stars of the sky fell to the earth as the fig tree sheds its winter fruit when shaken by a gale. The sky vanished like a scroll that is being rolled up, and every mountain and island was removed from its place.

As argued in a previous chapter of this book, the non-concordist view of science and Scripture argues that Biblical texts about creation were never intended to concord with modern scientific theories. Thus, Genesis 1 is not cryptically describing the Big Bang or instant fiat, a young earth or old earth, special creation or evolutionary creation. It is not "literal" language describing the physics of the universe, it is "literary" genre describing God's sovereignty over creation and most likely His covenantal relationship with His people.

But the argument against literalism of language of the creation of the heavens and the earth is also applicable to the language of the destruction of the heavens and the earth, or what the Bible calls, "the last days," "the end of the age," "the end of days," or "the Day of the Lord." Christians often refer to this as "the end times," but the technical theological term is *eschatology*, which means "the study of end things."

Regarding the end times, the modern Evangelical popular imagination has been deeply influenced and at times dominated by a theological construct that is best reflected in the 1970s bestselling *The Late Great Planet Earth* by Hal Lindsey and the newer bestselling fictional phenomenon *Left Behind* by Tim LaHaye and Jerry Jenkins.

---

[1] This chapter has been adapted from the article, "The Collapsing Universe in the Bible: Literal Science or Poetic Metaphor?" published at BioLogos Foundation.

This view believes that the Bible foretells an as-yet future scenario on the earth of a rapture of Christians, followed by the rise of an "Anti-Christ," a world dictator who initiates a Great Tribulation on the earth, requires a "Mark of the Beast," and assembles global forces for a battle of Armageddon against Israel, resulting in the Second Coming of Christ who replaces the universe with a new heavens and earth to rule forever. The technical theological term for this view is *futurism*, the belief that prophecies about the end times are yet to be fulfilled in the future.[2]

In this chapter, I will address the hermeneutic or interpretive approach used by this futurist perspective and apply it to the particular aspect of creation language, or in this case, decreation language — the collapsing universe and the destruction of the heavens and the earth.

In short, the language of cosmic catastrophe often interpreted literally as referring to the end of the space-time universe is actually used by Biblical authors to figuratively express the cosmic significance of the covenantal relationship between God and humanity.

The tendency of modern literalism is to interpret descriptions of signs in the heavens and earth as being quite literal events of the heavens and earth shaking, stars falling from the sky, the moon turning blood red, and the sky rolling up like a scroll. The problem with this hermeneutic is that it assumes the priority of modernity over the ancient world. Rather than seeking to understand the origins of symbols and images used by the writers within their ancient context, this literalism often suggests the writer was seeing events that would occur in our modern day but did not understand them, so he used his ancient "primitive" language to describe it.

So for instance when the apostle John saw modern day tools of war in his revelation, such as battle helicopters, he did not know what they were so he described them in ancient terms that he did understand such as locusts with the sting of scorpions, breastplates of iron, a crown of gold and human faces, whose chopper blades made the "noise of many chariots with horses rushing into battle" (Rev. 9:3-9).

I was taught this modernist interpretation and lived by it for many years. When I read about Jesus explaining the "end of the age" I would assume He

---

[2] The *Left Behind* series is a particular version of futurism called Dispensational Premillennialism. For a more in depth presentation of these varieties of eschatology see Bock, Darrell L. ed., *Three Views on the Millennium and Beyond*. Grand Rapids, MI: Zondervan, 1999.

meant the "end of the space-time universe" because that's the kind of language I, a post-Enlightened modern scientific mind, would use to describe such an event. When He spoke of the moon turning blood red and the sun being darkened, I assumed such events were easy miracles for God, so if you considered them figurative, you were falling down the slippery slope of neo-orthodoxy. When Jesus said stars would fall from the sky, you had better bet stars would literally fall from the sky (a primitive description of meteors[3]) or else you're a liberal who doesn't believe in the literal accuracy of the Bible.

But all that changed when I sought to understand the prophetic discourse on its own terms within its ancient cultural context instead of from my own cultural bias. I now propose that the ancient writers did understand what they were seeing, but were using mythopoeic symbols and images they were culturally steeped in, symbols and images with a history of usage from the Old Testament, *their* cultural context — not mine.

In this essay, I will argue that the decreation language of a collapsing universe with falling stars and signs in the heavens was actually symbolic discourse about world-changing events and powers related to the end of the old covenant and the coming of the new covenant as God's "new world order." In this interpretation, predictions of the collapsing universe were figuratively fulfilled in the historic past of the first century. The technical theological term for this view is *preterism*, the belief that prophecies about the end times have been fulfilled in the past.[4]

Sun, Moon and Stars

First, let's take a look at the usage of sun, moon and stars in the Old Testament. In the ancient Near East, there is often a conceptual equivalency or link between stars, heavenly bodies, and deities.[5] The Encyclopedia Judaica notes that, "in many cultures the sky, the sun, the moon, and the known planets were conceived as personal gods. These gods were

---

[3] Interestingly, as soon as the interpreter thinks falling stars are meteors, he has just engaged in figurative speculation, which is not literal.
[4] An example of orthodox scholars who hold to this view are Sproul, R.C. *The Last Days According to Jesus*. Grand Rapids, MI: Baker, 1998; and Gentry, Kenneth L. Jr. *Navigating the Book of Revelation*. Fountain Inn: SC, Goodbirth Ministries, 2009.
[5] I. Zatelli, "Constellations." Toorn, K. van der, Bob Becking, and Pieter Willem van der Horst. *Dictionary of Deities and Demons in the Bible*. 2nd extensively rev. ed. Leiden; Boston; Grand Rapids, Mich.: Brill; Eerdmans, 1999., 202-204; "Astrology and the Worship of the Stars in the Bible," *ZAW* 103 (1991): 86-99.

responsible for all or some aspects of existence. Prayers were addressed to them, offerings were made to them, and their opinions on important matters were sought through divination."[6]

But it was not merely the pagans who made this connection of heavenly physical bodies with heavenly spiritual powers. The Old Testament itself equates the sun, moon, and stars with the angelic "sons of God" who surround God's throne, calling them both the "host of heaven" (Deut. 4:19; 32:8-9).[7] Jewish commentator Jeffrey Tigay writes, "[These passages] seem to reflect a Biblical view that... as punishment for man's repeated spurning of His authority in primordial times (Gen. 3-11), God deprived mankind at large of true knowledge of Himself and ordained that it should worship idols and subordinate celestial beings."[8]

There is more than just a symbolic connection between the physical heavens and the spiritual heavens in the Bible. In some passages, the stars of heaven are linked *interchangeably* with angelic heavenly beings, also referred to as "holy ones" or "sons of God" (Psa. 89:5-7; Job 1:6)[9]. Consider the following passages that equate the host of heaven with both astronomical bodies and angelic spirits *simultaneously*:

> Job 38:4-7
> "Where were you when I laid the foundation of the earth?...when the morning stars sang together and all the sons of God shouted for joy?"
>
> Neh. 9:6
> "You are the LORD, you alone. You have made heaven, the heaven of heavens, with all their host, the earth and all that is

---

[6] "Astrology", Berenbaum, Michael and Fred Skolnik, eds. 2nd ed. *Encyclopaedia Judaica*. Detroit: Macmillan Reference USA, 2007, p. 8424.
[7] See also Deut. 4:19; Deut. 17:3; 2 Kgs. 23:4-5; 1 Kgs. 22:19; Neh. 9:6.
[8] Tigay, Jeffrey. *JPS Torah Commentary: Deuteronomy*. Philadelphia: The Jewish Publication Society, 1996): 435; as quoted in Heiser, Michael S. "Deuteronomy 32:8 and the Sons of God," *Bibliotheca Sacra* 158 (January-March 2001): 72; Copyright © 2001 Dallas Theological Seminary; online: http://thedivinecouncil.com/
[9] See also Psa. 148:2-3, 1 Kgs. 22:29 & 2 Kgs. 21:5. In Isa. 14:12-14 the king of Babylon is likened to the planet Venus (Morningstar) seeking to reign above the other stars of heaven, which are equivalent to the sons of God who surround God's throne on the "mount of assembly" or "divine council" (see Psa. 89:5-7 and Psa. 82).

on it, the seas and all that is in them; and you preserve all of them; and <u>the host of heaven worships you</u>"

Dan. 8:10-11
"It grew great, even to <u>the host of heaven</u>. And <u>some of the host and some of the stars</u> it threw down to the ground and trampled on them. It became great, even as great as the <u>Prince of the host [Michael]</u>"

In these passages, we see the mythopoeic equivocation of sun, moon, and stars with heavenly angelic powers. But there is another symbolic connection made in the Old Testament of the sun, moon, and stars with earthly human authorities such as kings and rulers. It is as if these earthly principalities are empowered by or representative images of those spiritual beings and principalities.

In the passages below, notice that the destruction of earthly powers is expressed through the figurative language of a collapsing universe: The sky rolling up and the sun, moon, and stars being darkened or falling. Another way to describe this discourse is the language of "decreation."

Kings at war early 13th Century B.C.

Judg. 5:19-20
"The <u>kings came, they fought</u>… From heaven <u>the stars fought</u>, from their courses they fought against Sisera."

The destruction of Babylon in 539 B.C.

Isa. 13:10
"the stars of heaven and their constellations will not flash forth their light; The sun will be dark when it rises, And the moon will not shed its light."

The destruction of Edom in 586 B.C.

Isa. 34:4
"all the host of heaven will wear away, And the sky will be rolled up like a scroll; All their hosts will also wither away."

The destruction of Egypt in 587 B.C.

Ezek. 32:7
"When I blot you out, I will cover the heavens and make their stars dark; I will cover the sun with a cloud, and the moon shall not give its light. All the bright lights of heaven will I make dark over you, and put darkness on your land, declares the Lord GOD."

The destruction of Edom in 586 B.C.

Isa. 34:2-5
"For the LORD is enraged against all the nations, and furious against <u>all their host</u>; He has devoted them to destruction, has given them over for slaughter…All <u>the host of heaven</u> shall rot away, and <u>the skies roll up like a scroll</u>. All <u>their host shall fall</u>, as leaves fall.

During none of these historical events did the sky "literally" roll up or the stars fall or the sun and moon turn dark. These passages correlate the collapsing universe figuratively with the fall of earthly regimes and the spiritual powers behind them. Apologetic historical writing is embedded with mythopoeic imagery.

And this mythopoeic understanding is not a new invention. Eschatology expert Gary DeMar writes, "Before the advent of speculative exegesis, most Bible commentators who studied the whole Bible understood the relationship of collapsing universe language with the destruction of the religious and civil state."[10] Scholar Kenneth L. Gentry adds, "In Scripture, prophets often express *national catastrophes* in terms of *cosmic destruction*. The famed twelfth-century Jewish theologian Maimonides notes that such language 'is a proverbial expression, importing the destruction and utter ruin of a nation.'"[11]

Perhaps some clarity can now be brought to the New Testament usage of the same exact imagery when describing the last days and the destruction of the Temple in Jerusalem.

---

[10] DeMar, Gary. *Last Days Madness: Obsession of the Modern Church.* Powder Springs, GA: American Vision, 1999, p. 144.
[11] Ice, Thomas and Kenneth L. Gentry Jr. *The Great Tribulation Debate: Past or Future?* Grand Rapids, MI: Kregel, 1999, p. 55.

Matt. 24:29

"Immediately after the tribulation of those days the sun will be darkened, and the moon will not give its light, and the stars will fall from heaven, and the powers of the heavens will be shaken."

Rev. 6:12-14

"When he opened the sixth seal, I looked, and behold, there was a great earthquake, and the sun became black as sackcloth, the full moon became like blood, and the stars of the sky fell to the earth as the fig tree sheds its winter fruit when shaken by a gale. The sky vanished like a scroll that is being rolled up, and every mountain and island was removed from its place"

Within the Church, there are several interpretations of when these prophesies are fulfilled, past, present, or future. But that does not concern us here. My main point is that these passages are so often used to look for a series of astronomical or geophysical catastrophes in creation, but now we see that they are actually a figurative expression rooted in Old Testament poetic imagery of the fall of ruling powers.

What I will argue next is that in the New Testament, the usage of these images denotes more than just ruling powers being vanquished, it figuratively depicts the end of the old covenant order itself.

The Last Days

The term "last days" comes from several New Testament passages (Acts 2:17-21; 2 Tim. 3:1; Heb. 1:2; Jas. 5:3; 2 Pet. 3:3), but the one that encapsulates the issues addressed in this chapter is Acts 2:17-21:

> "'And in the last days it shall be, God declares,
> that I will pour out my Spirit on all flesh,
> and your sons and your daughters shall prophesy,
> and your young men shall see visions,
> and your old men shall dream dreams;
> even on my male servants and female servants
> in those days I will pour out my Spirit, and they shall
> prophesy.

> And I will show <u>wonders in the heavens</u> above
> and signs on the earth below,
> blood, and fire, and vapor of smoke;
> the sun shall be turned to darkness
> and the moon to blood,
> before the <u>day of the Lord</u> comes, the great and magnificent day.
> And it shall come to pass that everyone who calls upon the
> name of the Lord shall be saved.'"

This passage seems to have it all: Day of the Lord, last days, wonders in heaven and earth. But let's take a closer look. This is an Old Testament prophecy that the apostle Peter is quoting to a large crowd of Jews and devout believers from all over the known world gathered in Jerusalem for the Day of Pentecost. He is preaching one of the first recorded salvation sermons on the resurrection of Jesus Christ and the need for all men everywhere to repent and be baptized in light of God's coming judgment.

The question arises: Is this "Day of the Lord," or "last days," something yet to occur in the distant future, a part of the end of the space-time universe? Is it the beginning of a series of momentous geophysical catastrophes including astronomical phenomena like a blood red moon and an eclipsed or darkened sun? As indicated earlier, most New Testament imagery is rooted in Old Testament concepts, so let's take a look at the Old Testament background for this concept of "the last days" in order to understand what the New Testament writers intended with their words.

First off, in the Old Testament, the "Day of the Lord" never meant the end of history or the destruction of the physical heavens and earth. It was used in varying contexts to proclaim God's judgment upon a specific city or nation. It was like saying "your day is coming when God will punish you."

Obadiah prophesied the destruction of Edom as *the day of the Lord* (Obad. 15), judgment on Judah and Jerusalem in the time of Zephaniah was called *the day of the Lord* (Zeph. 1:7, 14), Amos called the Assyrian destruction of the northern tribes *the day of the Lord* (Amos 5:18-20), Isaiah called the fall of Babylon to the Medes *the day of the Lord* (Isa. 13:6, 9). So when we read of "the Day of the Lord" in the New Testament, we must be careful not to expand it into an end of the universe scenario as we might think, but to understand it in context as coming earthly judgment upon a nation or people.[12]

The Old Testament precedent for "last days" is translated in some English Bibles as "latter days." In some instances it simply meant events that would happen years later from when the subject was addressed (Num. 24:14; Job 8:7). But with the prophets it became an eschatological reference about the children of Israel some day returning from exile and renewing the Kingdom of David, the archetype of Messiah, whose kingdom would be eternal after crushing the four previous kingdoms of Nebuchadnezzar's dream statue (Dan. 2:28; 10:14; Hos. 3:5).

The "stone cut from a mountain by no human hand" (Dan. 2:35) that would crush the other successive kingdoms has been long known to be the "cornerstone" of God's Kingdom: Messiah, Jesus Christ (Isa. 28:16; Acts 4:11). That cornerstone that toppled the kingdoms of man came during the Roman Empire, the kingdom of iron mixed with clay in the First Century (Dan. 2:40-45). Daniel then says that, "the stone that struck the image became a great mountain and filled the whole earth" (2:35).

So now the question is, when does this mountain begin filling the earth? The prophets Isaiah and Micah further explain that "in the last days, the mountain of the house of the Lord shall be established as the highest of the mountains and many nations shall come, and say: "Come, let us go up to the mountain of the LORD, to the house of the God of Jacob" (Isa. 2:2-3; Mic. 4:1-2).

When do the nations begin coming to the mountain of the Lord? Are these last days at the Second Coming of Christ at the end of time or is this a figurative reference to the spread of the Gospel after the first coming of Christ? In their book *The Early Church and the End of the World*, scholars Gary DeMar and Francis Gumerlock list early church scholars such as Justin Martyr, Irenaeus, Tertullian, and others who understood Isaiah 2/Micah 4 and other Old Testament prophecies to be about the first coming of Christ rather than the second coming.[13] But don't

---

[12] In 2 Thes. 2:2, Paul exhorts the Thessalonians not to believe anyone who says that the Day of the Lord has come. But he doesn't make the obvious rebuttal of saying "because it would be the end of the universe, duh." Instead he gives them other events that will happen first, thus proving that the Day of the Lord was a localized event not a universal or global one. If it was universal or global, they could not possibly be deceived into missing it. See Isa. 34:8, 35:4 in conjunction with Luke 21:22ff and Matt. 21:33-43. In these passages, the destruction of Jerusalem in A.D. 70 was the "days of vengeance" of God upon Israel for rejecting Messiah. "Days of vengeance" is a synonym for "Day of the Lord."

[13] DeMar, Gary and Francis Gumerlock. *The Early Church and the End of the World*. Powder Springs, GA: American Vision, 2006, pp. xi-xiii. Among other important scholars who held

take early church scholars' word for it. The New Testament apostles clearly claimed that they were in fact living in "the last days."

If we return to Peter's sermon in Acts 2, and read it in context we see from the very start that Peter claims that the mysterious tongues speaking that the crowd was hearing was in fact the fulfillment of the Joel prophecy about God pouring out His Spirit *in the last days* (Acts 2:16). This Pentecost event, with its explicit proclamation of the Kingdom of God in the various tongues of the nations, marked the beginning of that drawing in of the nations to the Mountain of God, Messiah and the New Covenant (Heb. 12:22-24).

But Peter did not stop with the prophesying, dreams, and visions. He also included — in that current day fulfillment — the astronomical catastrophic phenomena of the sun, moon and stars which we now know are references to falling principalities and powers both earthly and heavenly. Peter claims that those prophecies were being fulfilled *in their very day,* not in some distant end of the universe. And Peter reiterates his belief of being in "these last times" (1 Pet. 1:10) when he claims in his letters that "the end of all things is at hand" (1 Pet. 4:7), not in some distant future.

But Peter was not the only one who explicitly proclaimed their era as the "last days." Both Peter and Paul referred to the scoffers and depraved people *of their own time* to be a sign that they were in the last days in the first century (2 Pet. 3:1-4; 2 Tim. 3:1-9). Paul wrote to the Corinthian church that they were the generation "on whom the end of the ages has come" (1 Cor. 10:11), the same generation that Jesus said would see the destruction of the Temple that occurred in A.D. 70 (Matt. 23:36; 24:34). The writer of Hebrews said conclusively that "Long ago, at many times and in many ways, God spoke to our fathers by the prophets, but in <u>these last days</u> He has spoken to us by His Son" (Heb. 1:1-2).

So if the New Testament writers believed they were living in the last days, then what could that concept mean if not the last days of the space-time universe? As I will explain in the next section, I think the cosmic language of the Bible indicates that they believed they were living in the last days of the Old Covenant and the beginning days of the New Covenant. And in a further

---

this preterist interpretation of the last days or "end of the world" (especially of Matt. 24) were St. John Chrysostom, Bede, Eusebius, Augustine, Origen, Hugo Grotius, John Lightfoot, Milton Terry, Moses Stuart, John Calvin, Philip Dodderidge, Thomas Newton, John Gill, Adam Clarke, and F.W. Farrar.

concluding section I will explain why this interpretation does not necessarily deny a Second Coming of Christ. You'll have to bear with me.

Shaking the Heavens and Earth

In chapter 2, "Biblical Creation and Storytelling," I argued that the establishment of covenants by God is spoken of in the Bible in figurative terms of the creation of the heavens and earth. After all, the Jews' entire existence and reality was interpreted through their covenant with God, so it makes perfect ancient Near Eastern sense to speak of it in the big picture terms of heaven and earth.

God describes the creation of His covenant with Moses as the creation of the heavens and the earth (Isa. 51:14-16). The creation of Israel through deliverance and Promised Land was likened to God hovering over the waters and filling the formless and void earth (Deut. 32:10-12), separating the waters from the dry land (Exod. 15:8, 16-17), establishing the sun and moon, and defeating the mythical sea dragon of chaos to create His ordered world (Psa. 74:12-17; 89:6-12; Isa. 51:9-14).

If the creation of a covenant is spoken of as the creation of heavens and earth, and the ruling powers are referred to as sun, moon and stars, then what would the destruction of those powers be but the destruction of the heavens and the earth, including the fall of those astronomical symbolic entities? And what was the embodiment of that covenant but the holy Temple in the holy city of King David?

The first time that Jerusalem and the Temple was destroyed in 586 B.C. by the Babylonians, the prophets used the language of decreation to express the covenantal violation of Israel. The destruction of the Temple and exile of the Jews through God's providence was likened to the destruction of the heavens and earth and a return to a pre-creation chaotic state, a reversal of Genesis 1 language:

> Jer. 4:23-26
> I looked on the earth, and behold, it was <u>without form and void</u>;
> and to the <u>heavens</u>, and they <u>had no light</u>.
> I looked on the <u>mountains</u>, and behold, they <u>were quaking,</u>
> I looked, and behold, there was <u>no man,</u>

> and all the <u>birds</u> of the air <u>had fled</u>.
> I looked, and behold, the fruitful land was a <u>desert</u>...
> For this the earth shall mourn,
> and the heavens above be dark.
>
> Isa. 24:1-23
> Behold, the LORD will empty the earth and make it desolate...
> The <u>earth</u> shall be <u>utterly empty</u> and utterly plundered...
> The <u>earth staggers</u> like a drunken man;
> On that day the LORD <u>will punish</u>
> the <u>host of heaven</u>, in heaven,
> and the <u>kings of the earth</u>, on the earth...
> Then the moon will be confounded
> and the sun ashamed.

In the same way that the first temple destruction was earth shattering in its covenantal impact, so the second destruction of Jerusalem and the holy Temple in A.D. 70 was of equal spiritual significance in God's covenantal relations with Israel. It was the shaking of the heavens and earth with a punishment of the host of heaven, both astronomical and political/spiritual. This is a perfect example of C.S. Lewis' "myth become fact," an apologetic of God's Word being true.

In the year A.D. 66, revolutionary Zealots and other factions had fueled a revolt against their Roman occupiers. The leaders of Israel had rejected Jesus of Nazareth as being the Messiah, but they knew the calculations of Daniel's prophecy (Dan. 9:24-27). The 490 years were up. Messiah would arrive, crush the Roman pagan oppressors and establish the long awaited eternal Kingdom of God (Dan. 2:44-45) on earth.

The Roman emperor Nero sent his general Vespasian to crush the Jewish rebellion and bring peace back to Roman rule. The city of Jerusalem was besieged by Vespasian's son Titus, and by the summer of A.D. 70, was completely destroyed, along with the Jewish Temple. A million or more Jews were killed, a hundred thousand were made slaves and exiled,[14] and the Temple has never since been rebuilt from its ruins.

---

[14] Flavius Josephus. *Wars of the Jews,* 6.9.3 (6:420).

This important piece of history was extensively recorded by a Jewish historian in the Roman court, Flavius Josephus, in his book *The Wars of the Jews*. In this single historical event lies the key to understanding many mysterious metaphors and perplexing poetry of end times apocalyptic. What appears to modern Americans as esoteric Nostradamus-like riddles in Biblical language about the "end of the age," when interpreted through the images and metaphors of the Old Testament, becomes a powerful mythopoeic testimony of the New Covenant.

This all sheds light on Jesus' prophecy about the impending destruction of the Jerusalem Temple when He was asked by His disciples on the Mount of Olives, "Tell us, when will these things happen, and what will be the sign of Your coming, and of the end of the age?" (Matt. 24:3).

The Greek word for "age" is not *cosmos* as in the physical world, but *aion*, as in a time era. Jesus was not describing the end of the space-time universe, He was talking about the end of the Old Covenant era, the last days of the Old Covenant that culminated in the destruction of the sacramental incarnation of that Old Covenant: The Temple in Jerusalem (Matt. 24:1-2).

As scholar N.T. Wright put it,

> "The 'close of the age' for which they longed was not the end of the space-time order, but the end of the present evil age, and the introduction of the (still very much this-worldly) age to come... Matthew 24:3, therefore is most naturally read, in its first-century Jewish context... as a question of Jesus 'coming' or 'arriving' in the sense of his actual enthronement as king, consequent upon the dethronement of the present powers that were occupying the holy city...When will the evil age, symbolized by the present Jerusalem regime, be over?"[15]

The destruction of the Old Covenant order would be likened to the destruction of the heavens and the earth.

In Hebrews 12:18-22, the writer tells us that God shook the heavens and the earth when He established His covenant with Moses on Sinai. But then in verses 23-24 he says that the New Covenant is a heavenly city of God on the Mount Zion of the heavenly Jerusalem, far superior to the Mosaic covenant.

---

[15] Wright, N.T. *Jesus and the Victory of God*. Minneapolis, MN: Fortress Press, 1996, p. 345-346.

Then he concludes that the end of that Old Covenant is near because a new shaking of the heavens and earth is coming, and that shaking is the establishment of the New Covenant.

> Heb. 12:26-28
> At that time His voice shook the earth, but now He has promised, "Yet once more I will shake not only the earth but also the heavens." This phrase, "Yet once more," indicates the removal of things that are shaken — that is, things that have been made — in order that the things that cannot be shaken may remain. Therefore let us be grateful for receiving a kingdom that cannot be shaken.

J. Stuart Russell answers the relevant question, "What then, is the great catastrophe symbolically represented as the shaking of the earth and heavens?"

> "No doubt it is the overthrow and abolition of the Mosaic dispensation, or old covenant; the destruction of the Jewish church and state, together with all the institutions and ordinances connect therewith… the laws, and statutes, and ordinances."[16]

The book of Hebrews was written before A.D. 70, when the Temple was destroyed. So the physical embodiment of the Old Covenant was still on earth even though the New Covenant had been inaugurated by the death and resurrection of Christ. It was not until the Temple was destroyed that the New Covenant was considered fully inaugurated. They were living in a transition period between covenants during the years of AD 30-70.

This is why the writer of Hebrews says, "In speaking of a new covenant, He makes the first one obsolete. And what is <u>becoming</u> obsolete and <u>growing old</u> is <u>ready</u> to vanish away" (Heb. 8:13). Notice how the author says that the Old Covenant was becoming old and obsolete but was not yet replaced. That is because the incarnation of the old heavens and earth, the Jerusalem Temple, was not yet destroyed at the time of his writing. The Old Covenant

---

[16] Russell, J. Stuart. *The Parousia: The New Testament Doctrine of Our Lord's Second Coming.* Grand Rapids, MI: Baker, 1999, p. 289.

was the heavens and earth that was shaken and replaced by the New Covenant, which is the eternal kingdom that will never be replaced or shaken.

The Day of the Lord in 2 Peter

> 2 Pet. 3:10–13
> But the day of the Lord will come like a thief, and then the heavens will pass away with a roar, and the elements will be burned up and dissolved, and the earth and the works that are done on it will be exposed...
>
> Since all these things are thus to be dissolved, what sort of people ought you to be in lives of holiness and godliness, waiting for and hastening the coming of the day of God, because of which the heavens will be set on fire and dissolved, and the elements will melt as they burn! But according to His promise we are waiting for new heavens and a new earth in which righteousness dwells.

The interpretation I have presented in this essay is no doubt earth shattering for some eschatological paradigms about the end times. Such radical departures from the futurist's received wisdom always begs plenty of questions about other passages and concepts taken for granted by the futurist interpretation.

One of them is the apparently clear description in 2 Peter about the day of the Lord and the passing away of the heavens and the earth replaced by a new heavens and earth. Isn't that unambiguous language to be taken literally? Well, actually, no. As a matter of fact, orthodox believers have wide ranging interpretations of this passage, so it is a controversial one to begin with.[17]

We must remember our dictum to seek to understand the text within its ancient Jewish setting steeped in Old Testament imagery and symbols. I believe when we do this, we will have to conclude that the decreation of the heavens and earth is covenantal mythopoeia, *not* literal physical scientific observation. Peter writes figuratively about the final ending of the Old Covenant, with God's judgment on Israel for rejecting Messiah, and the final

---

[17] Bauckham, Richard J. Vol. 50, *Word Biblical Commentary: 2 Peter, Jude*. Word Biblical Commentary. Dallas: Word, Incorporated, 2002, p. 315-319.

establishment of His New Covenant as a New World Order, or in their case, a "new heavens and new earth."

In the beginning of chapter 3, Peter compares the scoffers of his day and their impending judgment with the scoffers of Noah's day before their judgment. So the judgment is near, and what's more, these scoffers are in the "last days" which we have already seen were considered the last days of the Old Covenant that the New Testament writers were living within. Those last days would be climaxed by judgment. But what kind of judgment?

Peter references creation of the heavens and earth (red flag about covenants!) and then the destruction of that previous world by water. Scholars have indicated how the flood of Noah is described using terms similar to Genesis 1, as if God is "decreating" the earth because of sin, in order to start over with a new Noahic covenant.[18] The ark floated over the chaotic "face of the waters" (Gen. 7:17) like God's spirit hovered over the chaotic face of the waters before creation (Gen. 1:2). The dry land recedes from the waters (8:3) just as it was separated in creation (1:9). God makes the same command to Noah to be fruitful and multiply and fill the earth (9:1) that He gave to Adam and Eve (1:28). So the covenantal connections are loud and clear.

As already noted, the Day of the Lord is always used in the Bible for a localized judgment upon a people, which by way of reminder, Jesus had already prophesied was coming upon Jerusalem to the very generation He spoke to (Matt. 23:36-24:2). But what makes some interpreters think this is the final judgment of the universe is the very bad translation of the Greek word *stoicheion* as "elements" in some English texts. This makes modern readers think of the periodic table of elements as being the most foundational building blocks of the universe. They conclude that the Bible must be talking about the very elements of helium, hydrogen, deuterium and others being burned up and melted!

But this is not what the Greek word means. Though some Greek thinkers believed in the existence of atoms, the common understanding was that there were four basic elements — earth, water, wind, and fire.[19] Though someone may conjecture that these could still be considered physical elements that could be destroyed, a simple look at the usage of *stoicheion* throughout the

---

[18] Wenham, Gordon J. Vol. 1, *Word Biblical Commentary: Genesis 1-15*. Word Biblical Commentary. Dallas: Word, Incorporated, 2002, p. 207.
[19] Schreiner, Thomas R. Vol. 37, *1, 2 Peter, Jude*. electronic ed. Logos Library System; The New American Commentary. Nashville: Broadman & Holman Publishers, 2007, p. 384.

New Testament shows that the Hebrew usage had nothing to do with Greek primitive scientific notions.

In every place that *stoicheion* shows up in the New Testament it means elementary principle rudiments of a worldview, sometimes a godless worldview (Col. 2:8), but more often the elementary principles of the Old Covenant law described as a "cosmos" (Gal. .4:3; 9; Col. 2:20; Heb. 5:12).[20]

Remember how the cosmic language of creating heavens and earth was used to describe the cosmic significance of God establishing a covenant? And remember how in the Old Testament, the destruction of covenants, nations, and peoples was described in *decreation* terms as the collapsing of the universe?

That is the case in these passages as well, with the term "cosmos" being used metaphorically for the "universe" of God's covenantal order as embodied in the Old Covenant laws of Jewish separation: Circumcision, dietary restrictions and sabbaths. Paul is telling his readers that the *stoicheion* of the Old Covenant *cosmos* are no longer over them because the people of God are under new *stoicheion*, the elementary principles of faith (Gal. 4:1-11).

Peter means the same thing. When he says that the heavens will pass away and the *stoicheion* will be burned up, he is claiming that when the Temple in Jerusalem is destroyed, it will be the final passing away of the Old Covenant cosmos, along with all the elementary principles tied to that physical sacramental structure, the laws that once separated Jew and Gentile. The new cosmos is one in which both Jew and Gentile "by God's power are being guarded through faith for a salvation ready to be revealed in the last time" (1 Pet. 1:5).

As Gary DeMar concludes, "The New Covenant replaces the Old Covenant with new leaders, a new priesthood, new sacraments, a new sacrifice, a new tabernacle (John 1:14), and a new temple (John 2:19; 1 Cor. 3:16; Eph. 2:21). In essence, a new heaven and earth."[21] Eminent Greek scholar John Lightfoot agrees, "The destruction of Jerusalem and the whole Jewish state is described as if the whole frame of this world were to be dissolved."[22]

---

[20] Leithart, Peter J. *The Promise of His Appearing: An Exposition of Second Peter*. Moscow, ID: Canon Press, 2004, p.101. Bauckham argues that "The heavenly bodies (sun, moon and stars) is the interpretation favored by most commentators," for *stoicheion*. But then we are right back to the sun, moon, and stars as figurative language of covenantal elements. Bauckham, *2 Peter, Jude*, 316. But I doubt this interpretation because the clear words for "heavenly bodies" are not *stoicheion*, but *epouranios soma* (1 Cor. 15:40-41).
[21] Gary DeMar, *Last Days Madness,* p. 192.
[22] Lightfoot, John. *Commentary on the New Testament from the Talmud and Hebraica: Matthew – 1 Corinthians*, 4 vols. Peabody, MA: Hendrickson, 1859, 1989, 3:454.

The new heavens and new earth in which righteousness dwells that Peter was waiting for was the New Covenant cosmos of righteousness by faith inaugurated by Christ's death and resurrection. That New Covenant inauguration and implementation was not merely an abstract claim of contractual change, it was physically verified with the destruction of the Old Covenant emblem, the Temple, that finalized the dissolution of the Old Covenant itself.

> Matt. 23:36-38
> "O Jerusalem, Jerusalem, the city that kills the prophets and stones those who are sent to it! How often would I have gathered your children together as a hen gathers her brood under her wings, and you would not! See, your house [Temple] is left to you desolate.
>
> Truly, I say to you, all these things will come upon this generation.

Coming on the Clouds

Jesus' Olivet Discourse in Matthew 24 is the classic reference used by futurists to point to the future second coming of Christ. I have been exegeting the decreation language about the sun, moon, and stars as referring to the end of the Old Covenant. Yet, right after those verses that speak of the collapsing universe, Jesus speaks of His "coming on the clouds":

> Matt. 24:29-30
> "Immediately after the tribulation of those days the sun will be darkened, and the moon will not give its light, and the stars will fall from heaven, and the powers of the heavens will be shaken. Then will appear in heaven the sign of the Son of Man, and then all the tribes of the land will mourn, and they will see the Son of Man coming on the clouds of heaven with power and great glory."

I want to focus on the phrase, "coming on the clouds of heaven" to prove that it is not the physical return of Christ, but rather a metaphor for God's judgment upon Jerusalem for rejecting Messiah. I believe Jesus Christ will physically return to this earth, but I do not think that this passage teaches that doctrine. It teaches something else. And I am in good company with orthodox scholars through history who have posited this very interpretation of Matthew 24; Eusebius, John Calvin, John Lightfoot, John Gill, Phillip Schaff, Gary DeMar, Kenneth L. Gentry, R.C. Sproul and many others.[23]

When considering the ancient Near Eastern context of this "cloud" image, I have previously written that the notion of deity coming on clouds or riding clouds like a chariot was already a powerful metaphor used of the god Baal in Canaan when Israel arrived there. Baal, the storm god, was called the great "Cloud-Rider"[24] who would dispense his judgments through thunder and lightning in his hand.[25] To ride the clouds was a sign of deity and judgment to the Canaanites. So it makes sense that the Biblical writers who were dispossessing Baal and his worshippers from the land would use the same epithets of Yahweh in a subversive way of saying Yahweh is God, not Baal.

In light of this connection of cloud-riding with deity and judgment, Jesus' statement becomes an implicit reference to His own deity and Messiahship rejected by the first century Jews which resulted in God's judgment upon Jerusalem (Matt. 21:33-45). Jesus is coming in judgment to vindicate His claims (Matt. 26:64), and He is going to do so by using the Roman armies of Titus to do His bidding.

---

[23] DeMar, Gary. *End Times Fiction: A Biblical Consideration of the Left Behind Theology.* Nashville, TN: Thomas Nelson, 2001, 111-115. For more, see "Preterist Scholarship" on the Preterist Archive: http://www.preteristarchive.com/Preterism/index.html.

[24] KTU 1.2:4.8–9; 1.3:3.38–41. All these Ugaritic texts can be found in N. Wyatt, *Religious Texts from Ugarit*, 2nd ed., The Biblical Seminar, vol. 53 (London: Sheffield Academic Press, 2002).

[25] Baal sits…
in the midst of his divine mountain, Saphon,
in the midst of the mountain of victory.
Seven lightning-flashes,
eight bundles of thunder,
a tree-of-lightning in his right hand.
His head is magnificent,
His brow is dew-drenched.
his feet are eloquent in wrath.
(KTU 1.101:1–6)
The season of his rains may Baal indeed appoint,
the season of his storm-chariot.
And the sound of his voice from the clouds,
his hurling to the earth of lightning-flashes
(KTU 1.4:5.5–9)

Look at these Old Testament passages that use the concept of coming on the clouds as a metaphor for God coming in judgment upon cities or nations:[26]

God's judgment on Egypt

Isa. 19:1
Behold, the LORD is <u>riding on a swift cloud</u>, and is about to come to Egypt.

Ezek. 30:3
For the day is near, the day of the LORD is near; it will be a <u>day of clouds</u>, a <u>time of doom</u> for the nations.

God's judgment on Ninevah

Nah. 1:3
In whirlwind and storm is His way, And clouds are the dust beneath His feet.

God's judgment on Israel

Joel 2:2
Surely it is near, A day of darkness and gloom, A day of <u>clouds and thick darkness</u>.

Messiah as deity and kingly judge

Dan. 7:13-14
"I kept looking in the night visions, And behold, <u>with the clouds of heaven</u> One like a Son of Man was coming, And He <u>came up</u> to the Ancient of Days And was presented before Him. And to Him was given dominion, Glory and a kingdom."

Did God literally or physically come riding on a cumulus nimbus in these passages? The answer is obvious: No. The notion of coming on the clouds with storm and lightning was an ancient Near Eastern motif of deity coming in judgment upon a city or nation. Egypt was plundered by the Assyrians (Isa.

---

[26] See also Psa. 18:9-10; 68:32-33; 104:3; 2 Sam. 22:10; Zeph. 1:15; Isa. 30:30-31 cf 31:15; Deut. 33:26.

9:23-25). Ninevah was destroyed by the hand of Nebuchadnezzar of Babylon (Ezek. 30:10). But God is described as the one who was using these pagan forces as His own means of judging those cities. This is how God "came on the clouds."

So Matthew 24 is God's description of judging Israel for rejecting Messiah by using the Roman armies to destroy the Temple and Jerusalem. Jesus didn't physically come riding on a cumulus nimbus, He "came on the clouds" in judgment by using the Roman armies to vindicate His claims of Messiahship. This was not a physical Second Coming, but a spiritual coming.

Once it is realized that creation and decreation language regarding the heavens and the earth is covenantal in its reference, and not scientific, the natural question arises, does this deny the second coming of Christ altogether? Is this a heterodox view that leads us on the slippery slope into heresy? My answer is again, "no."

Context is everything. Just because *some* passages are shown to be fulfilled in the past, does not mean that *all* passages are fulfilled in the past. For example, many preterists maintain that 1 Corinthians 15 affirms that there will be a future physical return of Christ followed by a physical resurrection of humanity.

> 1 Cor. 15:20-26
> But in fact Christ has been raised from the dead, the firstfruits of those who have fallen asleep. For as by a man came death, by a man has come also the resurrection of the dead. For as in Adam all die, so also in Christ shall all be made alive. But each in his own order: Christ the firstfruits, then at His coming those who belong to Christ. Then comes the end, when He delivers the kingdom to God the Father after destroying every rule and every authority and power. For He must reign until He has put all His enemies under His feet. The last enemy to be destroyed is death.

Other preterists make the argument that the "new creation" and "new heavens and earth" of the New Covenant may have been inaugurated in the first century, but it will not be consummated until this physical return of Christ. At that time, what was a spiritual truth of new creation will become a physical reality. Christ reigns now over every authority and power (Eph. 1:20-22). But His overcoming of every authority and power is a process that is not yet completed (Heb. 2:8). This notion of a seed form of beginning with a future completion is referred to as the "Now/Not Yet" of the Kingdom of God. As scholar Ken Gentry writes,

> "Despite initial appearances, Revelation 21-22 does not speak of the consummate new creation order. Rather, it provides an ideal conception of new covenant Christianity, presenting it as the spiritual new creation and the new Jerusalem. Though the ultimate, consummate, eternal new creation is implied in these verses, (via the now/not yet schema of New Testament revelation), John's actual focus is on the current, unfolding, redemptive new creation principle in Christ."[27]

This now/not yet, inauguration/consummation paints a picture of a New Covenant that is already here with a new creation of a new heavens and earth that will one day be fully consummated at the physical return of Christ and the resurrection of the dead. At that time, Death will be swallowed up in victory, even though we can now speak of it having already lost its sting. This is present reality based on future promise.

> 1 Cor. 15:54-57
> When the perishable puts on the imperishable, and the mortal puts on immortality, then shall come to pass the saying that is written:
> "Death is swallowed up in victory."
> "O death, where is your victory?
> O death, where is your sting?"
> The sting of death is sin, and the power of sin is the law. But thanks be to God, who gives us the victory through our Lord Jesus Christ.

---

[27] Gentry, Kenneth L. Jr. *Navigating the Book of Revelation: Special Studies on Important Issues*. Fountain Inn: SC, Goodbirth Ministries, 2009, p. 167.

Chapter 7
An Apologetic of Biblical Horror[1]

When one thinks of horror movies, the usual images conjured up in the mind are of nubile coeds being lured to isolated locations for the purpose of having sex and then being murdered and carved up in ever innovative and disgusting new ways by a grotesque chimera or phantasm. Likewise, for thriller movies, images that stalk the mind are of innocent men or women being hunted by maniacal serial murderers as a relentless feast of fear and gore for the audience.

Though these repulsive clichés have become the norm for many Hollywood horror and thriller films, they are not the only approach to the genres. In fact, in today's postmodern society so saturated with relative morality, horror and thriller stories have the ability to be an effective apologetic for the Christian worldview.

Some well-meaning cultural crusaders make claims that horror is an intrinsically evil genre that is not appropriate for Christians to create or enjoy. They believe horror is an unbiblical genre of storytelling. One writer argues, "Horror is an example of a genre which was conceived in rebellion. It is based on a fascination with ungodly fear. It should not be imitated, propagated, or encouraged. It cannot be redeemed because it is presuppositionally at war with God."[2] Evidently, God disagrees with such religious critics because God Himself told horror stories thousands of years before Stephen King or Wes Craven were even born.

The prophet Daniel wrote horror literature, based on images and drama cinematically displayed by God Himself in Babylon. Not only did God turn the blaspheming king Nebuchadnezzar into an insane wolfman to humble his idolatrous pride (Dan. 4), but He storyboarded horror epics for kings Belshazzar and Darius as allegories of the historical battle between good and evil to come. Huge hybrid carnivorous monsters come out of the sea like Godzilla, one of them

---

[1] This chapter has been adapted from the article, "An Apologetic of Horror" in the *Christian Research Journal* Vol. 32 / No. 04 (2009).

[2] Doug Phillips, Doug's Blog, November 1, 2006, "The Horror Genre," http://www.visionforum.com/hottopics/blogs/dwp/2006/11/1878.asp.

with large fangs and ravishing claws to devour, crush, and trample over the earth (7:1–8) until it is slain and its flesh roasted in fire (7:11); there are blasphemous sacrileges causing horror (8:13), including an abomination of desolation (9:26–27), angels and demons engaging in warfare (10:13), rivers of fire (7:10), deep impact comets and meteors colliding with the earth, *Armageddon* style (8:10), wars, desolation, and complete destruction (9:26-27). The book of Daniel reads like God's own horror film festival.

It is not merely the human being Daniel who crafted this work of epic horror allegory, it is *God Himself* who rolled the camera and directed the action. God Himself enjoys the horror genre. That's God-breathed inerrancy. The author of this faith didn't grow out of it after the Old Testament. In fact, He may have received an even harsher movie rating in His later production, the New Testament.

The book of Revelation is an epic horror fantasy sequel to Daniel, complete with science fiction special effects, and spectacles of horror darker than anything in a David Cronenberg Grand Guignol theater of blood. In this apocalyptic prophecy we read of a huge demonic spectacle of genetically mutated monsters chasing and tormenting screaming people (9:1–11), armies of bizarre beasts wreaking death and destruction on the masses (9:13–18), a demonic dragon chasing a woman with the intent to eat her child (12:3–4), a seven-headed amphibious Hydra with horns that blasphemes God and draws pagan idol worship from everyone on earth (13:1–10), massive famines (6:8), gross outbreaks of rotting sores covering people's bodies (16:2), plagues of demonic insects torturing populations (9:1–11), fire-breathing Griffon-like creatures (9:17), supernatural warfare of angels and demons (12:7), the dragging of rotting corpses through the streets while people party over them (11:7–13), rivers and seas of blood (14:20; 16:3), a blaspheming harlot doing the deed with kings and merchants (17:1-5) who then turn on her, strip her naked, burn her with fire, and cannibalize her (17:16), more famines, pestilence and plagues (18:8), and when the good guys win, there is a mighty feast of vultures scavenging the flesh of kings and commanders in victory (19:17–18). And I might add, this all gives glory to God in the highest.

The prophetic and apocalyptic genres that were used by the prophets and apostles of God relied heavily on images of horror to solicit holy fear of sin and its consequences in their audience and point them to God. Horror and thriller movies (and by extension, other forms of horror storytelling or image-making) can accomplish this same "prophetic" redemptive task several ways.

Original Sin Crouching at the Door

First, horror can be redemptive by reinforcing the doctrine of man's sinful nature. Gothic storytelling prides itself on exploiting man's fear of his dark side through vampires, werewolves, and other half-man/half-monsters. These freaks of nature or supernature personify the cultured, educated man by day and the unbridled beast by night. They represent the gospel truth that our evil nature avoids the light, lest its deeds be exposed (John 3:20), and that true evil is done by otherwise "normal" people who suppress the truth about themselves in unrighteousness (Rom. 1:18–21). We are Jekylls and Hydes, all.

The Victorian era provided western culture with a rich and lasting heritage of Christian metaphors for the depraved side of human nature that requires restraint. Those metaphors have been resurrected in some modern films with equal moral vision. *Dracula* symbolized the struggle of the repressed dark side and its eternal hunger and need for redemption, which is explored with modern fervor in *Interview with the Vampire* and *Dracula 2000*.[3] Dr. Jekyll fought to suppress the increasing inhumanity of his depraved alter ego, Mr. Hyde, just like Jack has to defeat his destructive inner self, Tyler Durden in *Fight Club*. Victor Frankenstein's scientific hubris leads to a vengeful monster in the same way that the conceit of scientists without moral restraint leads to the takeover of Jurassic Park by unpredictable dinosaurs. The corrupted conscience of H.G. Wells' Invisible Man getting away with crime is revisited in the more recent *Hollow Man*.

One movie, *The Addiction,* uses the vampire genre as a metaphor for the addictive sinful nature of humanity. The vampires spout human philosophy as they kill their victims, attempting to prove there is no moral authority to condemn what they do. One of them even concedes R.C. Sproul's theological point, that, "we're not sinners because we sin, we sin because we are sinners." One victim is shocked at being bitten by her friend. She anxiously blurts out, "How could you do this? Doesn't it affect you? How can you do this to me?"

---

[3] The unique twist in *Dracula 2000* is in its depiction of Dracula's origins. Dracula is revealed to be the undead soul of Judas Iscariot prowling the earth in vengeance against his own perdition. This story contains strong Christian metaphors: Dracula/Judas's insatiable lust for blood is a symbol of the eternal need for Christ's blood of forgiveness; the silver abhorrence, a reflection of the thirty pieces Judas betrayed Christ for, and of course, crosses and wooden stakes through the heart, elements of the power of the cross of Christ to destroy evil. *Dracula 2000* resurrects Christian elements that have been buried by many contemporary vampire movies.

To which her vampiress friend sardonically replies, "It was your decision. Your friend Feuerbach said that all men counting stars are equivalent in every way to God. My indifference is not the concern here. It's your astonishment that needs study." This reversal is an apologetic argument against unbelief, par excellence. If God is dead, as the modern secular mindset proposes, and man is his own deity, creating his own morality, then no one should be surprised when people create their own morality by feasting on the blood of others. Ideas have consequences. Without God, there is no such thing as "evil." In the end, the vampiress, believe it or not, has a Catholic conversion! This film embodies the argument for God's existence through the existence of evil.[4]

Your Sin Will Find You Out

Another way in which horror and thriller movies can communicate truth about human nature is in showing the logical consequences of sin. In the same way, the Bible plays out some sexually disgusting scenarios and gruesome violence in order to communicate the seriousness of sin and its negative impact upon our relationship with God.

In Ezekiel 16 and 23, God describes Israel's spiritual condition figuratively as a harlot "spreading her legs" to every Egyptian, Assyrian and Chaldean who passes by, as well as donkeys (bestiality) and idols as sexual devices. The book of Judges depicts the horrors of a society where "every man does what is right in his own eyes," such as gang rapes and dismemberment (19:22-29), burning victims alive (9:49), cutting off thumbs (1:6-7), and disemboweling (3:21-22) among other monstrous atrocities that illustrate their need for repentance.

Hide and Seek is a story in the vein of Dr. Jekyll and Mr. Hyde about a man named David whose daughter is in danger from some kind of scary imaginary man who is stalking her. Like Nathan's parable to King David, this David learns that "he is that man," his dissociated split identity a symptom of his suppressed past sins.

The Machinist and *The Number 23* are both macabre Poe-like tales that illustrate the effect of suppressing sin and guilt, as well as the redemptive power of confession. *The Machinist* is about an industrial worker whose body and mind wastes away from insomnia because of his running away from a past crime. The movie is a literalization of Psalms 32:3–5: "When I kept silent about my sin, my

---

[4] Another vampire film that warns of the subtle and seductive nature of sin is *Let the Right One In*, a story of a young boy befriending a young girl who happens to be a vampire.

body wasted away through my groaning all day long... I said, 'I will confess my transgressions to the LORD'; and Thou didst forgive the guilt of my sin."

The Number 23 is a thriller about a guy whose discovery of a novel that mysteriously reflects his own life leads him to an obsession with the number twenty-three, which ultimately leads him into mental disorder that endangers others. It's not until he faces the fact that all the mysterious coincidences in his life are the bubbling up of suppressed sin and guilt that he can repent and find redemption. Not coincidentally, the filmmaker put a Bible verse at the end of the film to express this very theme: "Be sure your sin will find you out" (Num. 32:23).

Ghost stories have been a staple of humanity's storytelling diet since the beginning. From the Bible's witch of Endor, to Shakespeare's Hamlet, to modern campfire yarns, people love to tell ghost stories to scare the Beetlejuice out of each other. Christians sometimes condemn ghost stories because they seem to imply a purgatory that is not in the Bible, or because they appear to violate the Scriptural prohibition against calling up the dead. But the purpose of some ghost stories has nothing to do with "reality." They are often metaphors depicting morally "unfinished business" or the demand for justice against unsolved crime, very much in the Biblical spirit of the voice of Abel's murdered blood crying to God for justice from the ground (Gen. 4:10).

A Stir of Echoes, *The Haunting*, *Gothika*, and *The Haunting in Connecticut* are all movies where ghosts are not haunting people because they are evil, but because they are victims of unsolved murders who can't rest until the murderer pays for his crimes. These are parables communicating that there is no spiritual statute of limitations on the guilt of sin. They are fables about the telltale heart of moral conscience.

Some sincere Christians will often find Bible passages that in their eyes appear to discredit the narrative depiction of sin and its guilty consequences. One such common passage is Philippians 4:8:

> "Finally, brethren, whatever is true, whatever is honorable, whatever is right, whatever is pure, whatever is lovely, whatever is of good repute, if there is any excellence and if anything worthy of praise, dwell on these things."

Contrary to some interpretations, this passage does not depict Christianity as an episode of *Veggie Tales* or *Little House on the Prairie*. It is not only true, honorable and right to show the glorious blessings of the gospel. It is also true, honorable and right to show the intestines of Judas, the betrayer of that gospel, bursting out after hanging himself (Acts 1:18–19). It is not only pure, lovely and of good repute that Noah was depicted in the Bible as a righteous man, but it is also pure, lovely and of good repute that all the other inhabitants of the earth around him were depicted as entirely wicked and worthy of destruction (Gen. 6:5). It is not only excellent and worthy of praise that Lot was revealed as a righteous man, but it is also excellent and worthy of praise that the destroyed inhabitants of Sodom were revealed as unrighteous men "who indulge the flesh in its corrupt desires" (2 Pet. 2:10).

The portrayal of good *and* evil, as well as their consequences, are two sides of God's one honorable, pure, lovely, excellent, and praiseworthy truth. According to the Bible, pointing out wrong is part of dwelling on what is right, exposing lies is part of dwelling on the truth, revealing cowardice is part of dwelling on the honorable, and uncovering corruption is part of dwelling on the pure.

Monsters of Modernity: Hubris

Horror and thriller stories can also be redemptive when they illustrate the consequences of modern man's hubris. In his book, *Monsters from the Id*, Michael E. Jones writes about the origins of modern horror as a reaction to the Enlightenment worldview. Jones points out that the Enlightenment rejection of the supernatural, the exaltation of man's primary urges, and scientific hubris created Frankenstein, Dracula, Jekyll and Hyde, and others.[5] He argues that the evils of horror are the result of suppressing morality, which backfires on us in the form of the monsters it breeds.

Jones explains the origins of Frankenstein as author Mary Wollstonecraft Shelley's personal attempt to make sense out of the conflict between the Enlightenment's naturalism and sexual libertinism and the classical Christian moral order. Mary Wollstonecraft had been initiated into the inner circle of libertine poets Percy Shelley and Lord Byron. By the time Mary wrote her novel, she had married Shelley and experienced an avalanche of the consequences of living out Enlightenment sexual and political "liberation" with her husband: familial alienation, jealousy and betrayal, promiscuity, adultery, incest, psychosis, suicides, and drug abuse. These men espoused "nature" in place of morality and therefore behaved as animals. In the novel, Dr. Frankenstein is the symbol of enlightened man. He is the "hero" or high priest

---

[5] Michael E. Jones, Monsters from the Id: The Rise of Horror in Fiction and Film (Dallas: Spence Publishing, 2000).

of the religion of science, the belief that man is ultimately a machine, reducible to chemistry and physics. His creation of the monster is his ultimate act of hubris in playing God. The monster's pursuit of vengeance against the doctor is a playing out of the miserable consequences Shelley herself had experienced in her own life.[6]

A common staple in many horror films is the calmly deliberate, logical-minded scientist who tortures or kills in the name of scientific therapy or advancement. The scientist's often flat affect or calm in the face of others' suffering represents the repression of emotions or humanity that modern science and reason demand. This scientist "monster" is a powerful moral critique of the dangers of science without moral restraint and can be seen in such movies as *The Boys from Brazil*, *Blade Runner*, *The Island of Dr. Moreau*, *Hollow Man*, *The Island*, *Turistas,* and *The Jacket*.

Another example of the Frankenstein monster motif is the serial killer, who becomes the evil yet rational extension of evolutionary survival ethics, as in *Collateral*; or the amoral monster created by a society that rejects the notion of sin, as in *Se7en*; or the beast that is justified by humanistic theories of behaviorism, as in *Primal Fear* and *Silence of the Lambs*. In *From Hell*, an investigating criminologist explains to an inspector that Jack the Ripper was probably an educated man with medical knowledge. The inspector replies with shocked incredulity that no rational or educated man could possibly engage in such barbaric behavior. All these serial killer films make the point that humanistic and Enlightenment beliefs about man's basic goodness blind us to the reality of evil.

Enlightened modern man has another weakness: the inability to deal with real supernatural evil. Because he believes that there is a natural scientific explanation for all spiritual phenomena, he is blinded to the truth of a spiritual dimension to reality. The classic example of this is *The Exorcist*, where a little girl possessed by a demon is analyzed by medical and psychological doctors. All of them seek natural explanations that remain inadequate because their worldview blinds them to the truth. This blindness to the supernatural is updated in the horror films *The Exorcism of Emily Rose*, *The Last Exorcism,* and *Paranormal Activity*.

The Reaping carries that naturalistic ignorance to new heights when a small southern town is being besieged by supernatural phenomena replicating

---

[6] Jones, 66–100.

the ten plagues of Egypt. A Christian apostate professor, who specializes in debunking paranormal phenomena, seeks to give natural scientific explanations for each plague, only to be confronted with true demonic spiritual reality. Her faith is restored in God when she experiences a supernatural arrival of God in judgment on the evil.

Social Commentary

Lastly, the horror and thriller genres can be effective social commentaries on the sins of society. Many Christians claim that we should not tell stories that focus on the evils of sin. They appeal to verses such as Ephesians 5:12: "It is disgraceful even to speak of the things which are done by [the sons of disobedience] in secret." I write about this "hear no evil, see no evil, speak no evil" interpretation in my newly updated and expanded edition of *Hollywood Worldviews: Watching Films with Wisdom and Discernment*. These critics read this Bible verse, and others, to teach that we should not speak of, let alone watch, acts of depravity in movies. But look at the verses before and after this "disgraceful to speak" verse. Ephesians 5:11: "Do not participate in the unfruitful deeds of darkness, but instead *even expose them*." Ephesians 5:13: "But all things become visible *when they are exposed* by the light, for everything that becomes visible is light."

Paul is not telling us to *avoid* revealing deeds of darkness because of their disgracefulness; rather, he is telling us to *expose* them by talking about them. By bringing that which is disgracefully hidden out into the light, we show it for what it really is. This proper Biblical use of shame aids us in the pursuit of godliness.

This is exactly the tactic God uses with His prophets under both Old and New Covenants. God uses horrific explicit images in order to put up a mirror to cultures of social injustice and spiritual defilement. God used gang rape of a harlot and dismemberment of her body as a metaphor of Israel's spiritual apostasy (Ezek. 16, 23), and the resurrection of skeletal remains as a symbol for the restoration of His people within the covenant (Ezek. 37). Our holy, loving, kind, and good God also used the following horror images to visually depict cultural decay and social injustice: skinning bodies and cannibalism (Mic. 3:1–3), Frankenstein replacement of necrotic body parts (Ezek. 11:19), cannibalism (Ezek. 36:13–14; Psa. 27:2; Prov. 30:14; Jer. 19:9; Zech. 11:9), vampirism (2 Sam. 23:17; Rev. 16:6), cannibals and vampires together (Ezek.

39:18–19), rotting flesh (Lam. 3:4; 4:8; Psa. 31:9–10; 38:2–8; Ezek. 24:3, 33:10; Zech. 14:12), buckets of blood across the land (Ezek. 9:9, 22:2–4), man-eating beasts devouring people and flesh (Ezek. 19:1-8; 22:25, 27; 29:3; Dan. 7:5; Jer. 50:17), crushing and trampling bodies and grinding faces (Amos 4:1; 8:4; Isa. 3:15), and bloody murdering hands (Isa. 1:15, 59:3; Mic. 7:2–3). Horror is a strongly Biblical medium for God's social commentary.

Invasion of the Body Snatchers is a story that has had many movie remakes, with all of them reflecting the current cultural fears of each era. The basic template is a story about an epidemic of alien life forms coming to Earth and replacing human bodies with people who look the same but are part of a conspiracy to take over the planet. The original (1956) was a political analogy of the Red Scare of communist infiltration of the United States in the 1950s. The 1978 remake, starring Donald Sutherland, was a parallel to the 1970s conformity to the herd mentality of the New Age "me decade." *Body Snatchers* was the 1993 version that analogized the doppelganger takeover to a monolithic conformism to U.S. "military industrial complex," with a touch of AIDS paranoia thrown in. In 2007, *The Invasion*, with Nicole Kidman, became a parable of cultural imperialism and the postmodern "other."

Strong social criticism has been leveled by horror movies at various relevant issues in our culture. In *Underworld*, racism is paralleled and condemned through an "inter-species" romance between a werewolf and a vampire; *The Wicker Man*, damns neo-pagan Gaia religion in its murderous matriarchal colony of goddess-worshipping, man-abusing feminists. In one segment entitled "Dumplings" in the movie *Three Extremes*, abortion is likened to the sci-fi quest for eternal youth through cannibalizing our offspring.

One common theme in some horror movies is the degeneration of society into a selfish survival of the fittest ethic that animalizes us, versus a Christian ethic of self-sacrifice that humanizes us. In a sense it becomes a cinematic dialectic of the evolutionary worldview versus the Christian worldview.

28 Days Later is about Jack, who awakens in a hospital bed to discover all of London is empty of people — except for roaming zombies seeking human flesh. The zombies are the result of a viral contagion that sends people into a murderous rage. When Jack stumbles upon a fortress of military survivors besieged by the zombies, this isolated human society degenerates into its own animalistic survival. It is a parable of how untamed male aggression can become an evil culture of "zombies within."

In the sequel, *28 Weeks Later,* a father struggles with the moral guilt of saving himself at the expense of his wife's life when escaping from the zombies. He finds it hard to face his own surviving children later. The entire movie is an incarnation of the ethic of survival versus the ethic of sacrifice, the first making us no different than a zombie, the other making us human. Those in the movie who try to save themselves tend to end up stricken; those who try to rescue others at risk to themselves demonstrate the potential nobility of the human race.

This is not unlike God's own metaphor usage of zombie flesh eating to depict the depravity to which Israel's leaders had sunk in rejecting Yahweh's law:

> Mic. 3:1-3
> And I said, "Hear now, heads of Jacob And rulers of the house of Israel. Is it not for you to know justice? "You who hate good and love evil, Who tear off their skin from them And their flesh from their bones, And who eat the flesh of my people, Strip off their skin from them, Break their bones, And chop them up as for the pot And as meat in a kettle."

I Am Legend is a parable of a lone survivor, Neville, maintaining his humanity in the face of wild flesh-eating zombies. It becomes a Christ parable as Neville's blood contains the antibody to the viral contagion that caused the zombies in the first place. As a Christ figure, Neville must sacrifice himself to save others, but only after struggling with his doubts about God's goodness in light of all the evil. A fellow survivor's unwavering faith that "God has a plan" wraps up this movie that wrestles with God's sovereignty and evil, the primal instinct for survival, and the values of religion, sacrifice, and atonement.

30 Days of Night portrays vampires as metaphors for an atheistic evolutionary survival of the fittest ethic. When one victim whispers a prayer to God for help, the head vampire stops, repeats the word, "God," looks all around the heavens to see if He will answer, and then replies very simply, "No God" before devouring her.

It is important to remember that in a story, the worldview that the villain holds is the worldview that the storyteller is criticizing. So the fact that the vampires in this movie are atheistic, inhuman predators without mercy is a metaphor for the consequences of evolutionary ethics not a support of it. In contrast with this ethic, the people who do battle with them can only win by being more human, which is through altruistic sacrifice of themselves for others. Much like Christ taking on sin, the hero in this movie deliberately allows himself to be bitten and become a vampire in order to defeat the monsters before dying.

Discerning Good From Evil in Good and Evil

Horror and thriller movies are two powerful apologetic means of arguing against the moral relativism of our postmodern society. Not only can they reinforce the Biblical doctrine of the basic evil nature in humanity, but they can personify profound arguments of the kind of destructive evil that results when society affirms the Enlightenment worldview of scientism and sexual and political liberation. Of course, this is not to suggest that *all* horror movies are morally acceptable. In fact, I would argue that many of them have degenerated into immoral exaltation of sex, violence, and death. But abuse of a genre does not negate the proper use of that genre.

It would be vain to try to justify the unhealthy obsession that some people have with the dark side, especially in their movie viewing habits. Too much focus on the bad news will dilute the power that the Good News has on an individual. Too much fascination with the nature and effects of sin can impede one's growth in salvation. So, the defense of horror and thriller movies in principle should not be misconstrued to be a justification for *all* horror and thriller movies in practice. It is the mature Christian who, because of practice, has his senses trained to discern good and evil in a fallen world (Heb. 5:14). It is the mature Christian who, like the apostle Paul, can explore and study his pagan culture and draw out the good from the bad in order to interact redemptively with that culture.

If you liked this book, then please help me out by writing an honest review of it on Amazon. It's usually pretty easy. That is one of the best ways to say thank you to me as an author. It really does help my exposure and status as an author. Thanks! — *Brian Godawa*

• • • • •

More Books by Brian Godawa

See https://godawa.com/ for more information on other books by Brian Godawa. Check out his other series below:

Chronicles of the Nephilim

Chronicles of the Nephilim is a saga that charts the rise and fall of the Nephilim giants of Genesis 6 and their place in the evil plans of the fallen angelic Sons of God called, "The Watchers." The story starts in the days of Enoch and continues on through the Bible until the arrival of the Messiah: Jesus. The prequel to Chronicles of the Apocalypse.
ChroniclesOfTheNephilim.com

Chronicles of the Apocalypse

Chronicles of the Apocalypse is an origin story of the most controversial book of the Bible: Revelation. An historical conspiracy thriller trilogy in first century Rome set against the backdrop of explosive spiritual warfare of Satan and his demonic Watchers. ChroniclesOfTheApocalypse.com

Chronicles of the Watchers

Chronicles of the Watchers is a series that charts the influence of spiritual principalities and powers over the course of human history. The kingdoms of man in service to the gods of the nations at war. Completely based on ancient biblical, historical and mythological research.
ChroniclesOfTheWatchers.com

Great Offers By Brian Godawa

Get More Biblical Imagination

Sign up Online For The Godawa Chronicles

https://godawa.com

Special Updates on the novels of Brian Godawa
Special Discounts, Free Articles,
Cool Artwork and Videos!

About the Author

Brian Godawa is the screenwriter for the award-winning feature film, *To End All Wars,* starring Kiefer Sutherland. It was awarded the Commander in Chief Medal of Service, Honor and Pride by the Veterans of Foreign Wars, won the first Heartland Film Festival by storm, and showcased the Cannes Film Festival Cinema for Peace.

He also co-wrote *Alleged*, starring Brian Dennehy as Clarence Darrow and Fred Thompson as William Jennings Bryan. He previously adapted to film the best-selling supernatural thriller novel *The Visitation* by author Frank Peretti for Ralph Winter (*X-Men, Wolverine*), and wrote and directed *Wall of Separation,* a PBS documentary, and *Lines That Divide*, a documentary on stem cell research.

Mr. Godawa's scripts have won multiple awards in respected screenplay competitions, and his articles on movies and philosophy have been published around the world. He has traveled around the United States teaching on movies, worldviews, and culture to colleges, churches and community groups.

His popular book, *Hollywood Worldviews: Watching Films with Wisdom and Discernment* (InterVarsity Press) is used as a textbook in schools around the country. His novel series, the saga *Chronicles of the Nephilim* is in the Top 10 of Biblical Fiction on Amazon and is an imaginative retelling of the primeval history of Genesis, the secret plan of the fallen Watchers, and the War of the Seed of the Serpent with the Seed of Eve. The sequel series, *Chronicles of the Apocalypse* tells the story of the Apostle John's book of Revelation, and *Chronicles of the Watchers* recounts true history through the Watcher paradigm.

Find out more about his other books, lecture tapes and dvds for sale at his website https://godawa.com/.

BLANK PAGE

BLANK PAGE

BLANK PAGE

BLANK PAGE

BLANK PAGE

BLANK PAGE

Made in the USA
Las Vegas, NV
14 August 2023